On Armor

Recent Titles in The Military Profession
Bruce Gudmundsson, Series Editor

On Air Defense
James D. Crabtree

Steel Wind: Colonel Georg Bruchmüller and the Birth of Modern Artillery
David T. Zabecki

On Infantry (Revised Edition)
John A. English and Bruce I. Gudmundsson

On Armor

Bruce I. Gudmundsson

The Military Profession

Westport, Connecticut
London

Library of Congress Cataloging-in-Publication Data

Gudmundsson, Bruce I.
 On armor / Bruce I. Gudmundsson.
  p. cm.—(The Military profession, ISSN 1074–2964)
 Includes bibliographical references and index.
 ISBN 0–275–95019–0 (alk. paper)—ISBN 0–275–95020–4 (pbk. : alk. paper)
 1. Tank warfare. 2. Tanks (Military science) 3. Armored vehicles, Military.
I. Title. II. Series.
UE159.G84 2004
358'.18—dc22   2004052151

British Library Cataloguing in Publication Data is available.

Copyright © 2004 by Bruce I. Gudmundsson

All rights reserved. No portion of this book may be reproduced, by any process or technique, without the express written consent of the publisher.

Library of Congress Catalog Card Number: 2004052151
ISBN: 0–275–95019–0
       0–275–95020–4
ISSN: 1074–2964

First published in 2004

Praeger Publishers, 88 Post Road West, Westport, CT 06881
An imprint of Greenwood Publishing Group, Inc.
www.praeger.com

Printed in the United States of America

The paper used in this book complies with the Permanent Paper Standard issued by the National Information Standards Organization (Z39.48–1984).

10 9 8 7 6 5 4 3 2 1

Contents

Preface		vii
1	Diverging Paths	1
2	Open Flanks	19
3	Broken Ground	35
4	Iron Steed	53
5	The Third Way	65
6	Beyond Theory	83
7	Mixing It Up	95
8	The Armored Guerilla	113
9	A Family Resemblance	133
10	Breakthrough	145
11	Gunslinger	157
12	The Future of Armor	173
Notes		181
Bibliographical Note		219
Index		223

Preface

In the past half-century, the number of books published on the subject of armored fighting vehicles has easily exceeded the combined total of those published on all the other arms and services of modern land armies. A query of the catalog of the Library of Congress, for example, reveals 249 post-1945 entries filed under the subject heading of "tanks." In the same period, only 132 books dealing with artillery (field, fortress, and air defense) and a mere 75 on the subject of infantry were catalogued. Thus, the publication of the first three books of this series, *On Infantry*, *On Air Defense*, and *On Artillery*, could be defended on the simple grounds that they shed some light on dark corners. The writing of yet another book on armor, however, requires some other justification. At the very least, it ought to present a perspective that is substantially different from that contained in the scores of tank books still readily available on the shelves of libraries and bookstores.

The cornerstone of my apologia for this work is its actual subject. *On Armor* is not just another book about tanks. Rather, it is an attempt to make sense of nearly a hundred years of interplay between the two definitive characteristics of armored fighting vehicles—tactical utility and operational mobility. (The former is the ability to fight. The latter is the ability to rapidly travel over long distances in the absence of significant enemy forces.) To this end, *On Armor* pays a great deal of attention to those armored vehicles that often get short shrift in books about tanks—armored cars, armored personnel carriers, armored engineer vehicles, tank destroyers, and assault guns. Put another way, rather than viewing other types of armored vehicles as poor relations of the main battle tank, *On Armor* treats these weapons with the respect that they deserve.

Because the full panoply of twentieth-century armored fighting vehicles is so large and complex, *On Armor* requires a simple overarching theme. This is provided by the aforementioned interplay between tactical utility and operational mobility. At the start of the twentieth century, these characteristics were mutually exclusive. A vehicle that possessed operational mobility—an armored car or truck—could carry very little in the way of armored plate or offensive armament. A vehicle that was well armed and well protected was both slow and tethered to its *tankodrome,* the base that provided it with fuel and maintenance. In the era of the *Blitzkrieg,* improvements in engines, transmissions, and suspensions did much to reduce the distinction between battle tanks and armored cars. While the former were still more powerful and the latter retained their "longer legs," the battle tank had become an important element of formations designed for operational maneuver. It is thus not surprising that the first armies to recognize this—those of Germany and the Soviet Union—were those that possessed the strongest traditions of operational art.

This approach is not without cost, the most obvious of which is a detailed discussion of equipment. Such a wealth of hoplophile information on the subject of armored fighting vehicles is available to the English-speaking reader, however, that I have been able to omit all but the most necessary technical details with a spotless conscience. Books about the various models of tanks and how they compare to one another are as numerous as the proverbial lilies of the field. Serious books about the context of such weapons are, by comparison, remarkably rare.

The other great lacuna in *On Armor* is the superficial treatment given to some of the better-known aspects of the history of armor, particularly the evolution of British tanks during World War I, British armored theory in the interwar period, and the fighting that took place in North Africa during World War II. This material is missing, not because of any lack of interest on my part, but because it is so well described in so many other places. In other words, as this work is an attempt to complement, rather than replicate, the existing body of English-language literature on armored warfare, I see no need to try to go over ground so thoroughly covered by Paul Harris, David Fletcher, Harold Winton, and Robert Larson. Indeed, whatever insights I have gleaned concerning the British experience with armored fighting vehicles is largely a result of the high quality and considerable accessibility of the work of these scholars. (A similar richness of secondary literature in English has also caused me to skip over much of the history of the rise of the German *Panzerwaffe* in the 1930s. That is to say, rather than repeating the work of such scholars as Mary Habeck, Robert Citino, James Corum, and Richard DiNardo, I focus on those aspects of the development of the German armored force that are less familiar to readers in the English-speaking world.

On Armor would not have been possible without the generous assistance of the Institute for Tactical Education in Quantico, Virginia, and its president, Lieutenant Colonel John J. Sayen, Jr, USMCR. The Institute provided me with an office, full access to its library and files, and permission to use material originally published in its journal, *Tactical Notebook*. In addition, Lieutenant Colonel Sayen took pains to complete his own research on French, American, and Italian armor so that I could make use of it in writing this book. Colonel Eric Walters, USMC, helped a great deal with the chapters on armored warfare after 1945, providing insights and sources that I could not have otherwise obtained. Colonel Nicholas Reynolds, USMCR, the author of an important work on the life of Ludwig Beck, did much to shape my thinking on the role that this officer played in the genesis of the German armored force. Lieutenant Colonel John English, CD (Ret.), generously provided documents that I otherwise would have missed.

Dan Eades was, in this as in the three other books I have done with Praeger, the ever-forbearing godfather of this work. Heather Ruland Staines, who inherited the project from Dan, was a model of patience during the many troubles that delayed the completion of this project for several years. Robin Cookson, of the U.S. National Archives, was a wise and cheerful guide to the German and American records held therein. Mary Porter, Pat Selkirk, Dolores Knight, and Ralph Lowenthal of the Marine Corps Research Center in Quantico were likewise indispensable collaborators. The staff of the Social Science Reading Room at the Library of Congress was always helpful, even when my appetite for old military journals caused them to deliver bound volumes to my desk by means of shopping cart. William S. Lind, my partner in the television program *Modern War*, and our mutual friend John Patrick, took great pains to find paying work for me during a critical period in the writing of this book. Robert Citino, an eminent student of both armor and the interwar German Army, did a superb job of reviewing the manuscript. All errors of fact and interpretation are, needless to say, entirely my own.

1

DIVERGING PATHS

The honor of having invented the armored fighting vehicle is claimed for many nations. Argentines, Australians, Austrians, Englishmen, Frenchmen, Italians, and Russians can all point to century-old drawings, patent applications, models, and, in some cases, full-scale prototypes of armed and armored motor vehicles. Indeed, the sheer volume of this evidence suggests that it would have taken the assassination of every backyard tinker, writer of fantastic fiction, and would-be da Vinci to prevent the creation of some sort of armored fighting vehicle in the first two decades of the twentieth century.

The invention of tanks and armored cars was made easy by the fact that all of the necessary components were widely available. A wide variety of motor vehicles—ranging from tiny motorbikes to huge tractors with caterpillar treads—had found work in the civilian economy. The manufacture of armor plate for use on naval vessels, land fortifications, and gun shields was being developed to a high art by the large armament concerns. These same "merchants of death" also offered a range of light yet powerful weapons, particularly rifle-caliber machine guns and small-caliber cannon that were originally intended for use in fortresses, on warships, and on the frontiers of various empires.[1]

Projects for various types of armed and armored cars started to fill the in-boxes of the world's war ministries in the late 1890s. Touring cars and trucks armed with light cannon or machine guns were improvised for use in the Second Anglo-Boer War in 1901 and the continuing French effort to pacify Morocco in 1902. The first purpose-built armored vehicle was produced in

1904 by the Austrian automotive engineer Paul Daimler. This vehicle had many features that would come to characterize armored cars for the next hundred years—all-wheel drive and a fully rotating turret.[2] In that same year, the Russians used a handful of improvised armored cars against the Japanese in Manchuria. By 1908, a number of arms manufacturers, to include Vickers in Great Britain, Schneider in France, and Ehrhardt in Germany, were offering a variety of armored cars for sale.

By 1914, the concept of the armored car was so well established that, without any sort of central direction, enterprising individuals all over the world built several hundred of them the weeks immediately following the outbreak of what we now know as World War I. As might be imagined, the variety of these weapons was considerable, with a dozen or so different types of machine guns and light cannon mounted on scores of models of trucks and touring cars. Armor protection ranged from decent—in the case of the small number of improvisers with access to proper armored plate—to non-existent. Crews were provided in much the same way as the other components of these armored cars, with naval personnel, recently uniformed civilians, and colorful characters of all sorts very much in evidence.

The widespread appeal of the armored car concept (not to mention the ease with which such weapons could be created) is perhaps best illustrated by the tale of Lieutenant (*Lieutenant de Vaisseau*) M. F. E. Destremau of the French Navy. The outbreak of war found Destremau in command of the *La Zelée*, a wooden coast defense vessel protecting the French coaling station at Papete on Tahiti. News of the possible approach of a pair of German cruisers—the famous *Scharnhorst* and *Gneisenau*—convinced Destremau that his ship would not stand long between the German ships and the 7,000 tons of naval-grade coal he was honor-bound to protect. He therefore took six obsolescent 37mm cannon off his ship and mounted them on six Ford trucks. (These guns, of a model approved in 1885, still fired shells filled with black powder.) Crewed by sailors, Marines, and a hastily inducted Polynesian volunteer, these provided a reaction force capable of dealing with the sort of landing parties the German cruisers might send ashore, at least until the 160 or so Marines and sailors under his command could join the fray.

As Lieutenant Destremau had feared, the *Scharnhorst* and *Gneisenau* did, in fact, find their way to Tahiti. Firing at a range of 6,000 meters, they shelled the fort and harbor at Papete, sinking *La Zelée*. The French responded with fire from the 65mm guns Lieutenant Destremau had taken off his ship and installed on shore. These, however, were less of a deterrent to the well-armored German cruisers than the prospect of mines. And so, without putting the six improvised *autos-canons* to the test, the *Scharnhorst* and *Gneisenau* continued their cruise, moving about the Pacific without the aid of Lieutenant Destremau's coal.[3]

While the *autos-canons* of Tahiti were able to fulfill their mission without fighting, the same cannot be said for most of the armed cars and trucks that were assembled in France, Belgium, and Great Britain during the first three months of World War I. These tended to find their way to the front within days—and sometimes hours—of being put together, with the same people who did the cutting, fitting, welding, and riveting often ending up as part of the crew. This was particularly true in Belgium, where the German march through the southeastern part of the country had created, for a time, a broad expanse of disputed territory between the North Sea and the relatively slow advance of the German second-line troops charged with finishing the conquest of Belgium.

In the English-speaking world, the most famous of the quasi-guerillas who took part in this war-within-a-war was Charles Rumney Samson, an Englishman who might well be described as the most inadvertent (as well as least known) of the pioneers of modern armored warfare. In the late summer of 1914, Commander Samson was in command of a squadron of the Royal Naval Air Service that had attached itself to the French garrison of Dunkirk. With far too few aircraft to do what he thought the situation demanded, Samson took to roaming around the French and Belgian countryside in the privately owned touring cars that some of his officers had, in the grand British tradition of amateur officership, taken to war.[4]

Samson's first patrol had consisted of nine men, two touring cars, and one machine gun.[5] Within a month, most of the touring cars associated with Samson's squadron had been armed and some, according to the design of Samson's younger brother, had been armored. These were soon joined by additional touring cars that, prior to leaving Britain, had been hastily armored. Most of this work seems to have been done at Royal Navy workshops. In at least one case, however, the job of armoring a civilian motorcar destined to join Samson's force had been done by a Peer of the Realm in his local garage. To round out the force, a handful of trucks were converted into rudimentary "infantry fighting vehicles" by the addition of armor. So that the Marines carried in these trucks might be able to fire their rifles without exposing themselves, the armor was provided with loopholes.

The vehicles modified in Great Britain for Samson were provided with hardened steel plates. The vehicles that had started the campaign with Samson's squadron, however, were armored in Dunkirk by a local shipbuilding concern. Because armored plate was not available there, the French shipwrights had used boilerplate to protect the area where the driver sat. (The machine gunner, it seems, had to do without any sort of protection at all.) The car modified in the local garage was in even worse shape—the pieces of soft iron that had been attached to its chassis displayed an unfortunate tendency to fall off whenever the car was in motion.[6]

These teething problems notwithstanding, Samson's private army proved successful. At a time when the Germans lacked a clear sense of what was going on in the region between Dunkirk and Antwerp, aggressive patrolling by Samson's armored cars did much to prevent the German cavalry divisions from clarifying the situation. With Belgian postal employees using the still intact telephone network to report on German movements, Samson was able to drive deeply into German-held territory. The effect this had on the peace of mind of German commanders, who were already nervous about their position as guardians of the long, overextended right flank of the German army in the west, can only be imagined.

Closer to the base at Dunkirk, Samson's armored vehicles assisted French, British, and Belgian detachments in contact with the Germans. In these comparatively small affairs, rarely involving more than 1,000 combatants on either side, the action of a few armored cars often tipped the scales in favor of the Allies. This sometimes took the form of "stiffening" the muscle-powered units. (As the Allied troops involved in these combats—to include most of the Marines under Samson's command—tended to be reservists who had been deemed too old or poorly trained to fight on other fronts, stiffening was not a mission to be scoffed at.) At other times, the armored cars made full use of their mobility and machine guns to exploit open flanks, cover retreats, or race the Germans to a piece of important terrain.

Commander Sampson's unit of improvised armored cars, trucks, and small-caliber naval guns had many counterparts in the French forces. Operating mostly as groups of two, three, or four (but sometimes in units that contained as many as thirteen vehicles), the French *autos-canons* and *autos-mitrailleuses* (as vehicles carrying machine guns were called) were most active in support of French cavalry formations. Though already provided with a small number of 75mm field pieces and machine guns carried in horse-drawn carriages, the French cavalry, like its German counterpart, was very much aware of its relative lack of firepower. (Once men had been detailed to hold horses, it took four cavalry divisions of 1914 to put into action as many rifles, machineguns, and field pieces as a contemporary infantry division.) It is thus not surprising that, in addition to welcoming such armored cars that came their way, French cavalry commanders managed to build a few of their own.[7]

Considerable as it was, the enthusiasm of the commanding generals of French cavalry corps and divisions for armored cars paled in comparison to that of the Military Governor of Paris, Gen. Joseph Simon Gallieni. Brought back from retirement to serve in what had originally been seen as a rear-area command, Gallieni found, in the first week of September 1914, that the fortunes of war had brought the front to his neighborhood. His most famous reaction to this unexpected event was the requisitioning of Paris taxicabs to move troops and supplies to the battlefields of the Battle of the Marne. Less well known is his program to build more than one hundred *autos-mitrailleuses* and *autos-canons*, initially to equip the raiding parties he was in the habit of sending into the disputed territory northeast of Paris and then for the French army as a whole. Making the most of the fact that he was located in the seat of government, Gallieni convinced the French naval authorities to provide a 37mm naval cannon and the Ministry of War to provide one hundred machine guns for his vehicles.[8]

Some of the first armored cars to be produced by Gallieni's program were used to equip the Belgian *Bataillon des Autos-Canons Mitrailleuses*. This unit, with ten armored combat vehicles, nine trucks and cars providing various logistical services, one hundred bicycles, and twelve motorcycles, was the first regularly consisted military unit to be both substantially more mobile than contemporary infantry and free of any dependence whatsoever on horses.[9] This unit, which spent part of its short tour of active service in the west cooperating with Belgian armored trains, was soon joined at the front by *Groupes d'Autos-Canons* of twelve gun-carrying vehicles and four unarmed "tenders." As might be expected from the use of naval terminology for the logistical vehicles, these units were commanded—and to a large extent crewed—by naval officers.[10]

Before Gallieni's newly minted *autos-canons* and *autos-mitrailleuses* could see much action, the conditions that had permitted the employment of armored cars ceased to exist. By the middle of October 1914, the great open areas in northern France and western Belgium had filled with troops. The great stalemate that was the western front for most of the next four years had begun. Commander Sampson's organization returned to England, where it formed the core of an impressive, but short lived, Royal Navy Armoured Car Division.[11] The Belgian and French *autos-canons* and *autos-mitrailleuses* were pulled back behind the lines, there to prepare to exploit the resumption of the war of grand maneuvers that most military leaders of the time expected no later than the following spring.

Motivated by the promise of the imminent return of open warfare, the French authorities lost little time in turning their improvised force of improvised fighting vehicles into a regular part of the French armed forces. The first step toward this goal was the replacement of all unarmored vehicles with ones protected by at least 5mm of armored plate. The second step was to rationalize the various ad hoc units. Most of the surviving automotive adventurers in the autumn of 1914 found themselves formed into seventeen "mixed groups of motorized machineguns and canons" *(Groupes Mixte d'Autos-Mitrailleuses Autos-Canons)* of six cars armed with 37mm cannon, four cars armed with machine guns, two unarmed liaison cars, and two cargo trucks (See Figure 1.2). The small number of *autos-canoniers* who had gone to war in trucks armed with the heavier 47mm naval gun was formed into two *Groupes d'Autos-Canons de 47* (See Figure 1.1). With their four 47mm *autos-canons* and four *autos-mitrailleuses*, these latter units actually had a higher proportion of machine-gun vehicles than the *Groupes Mixtes* did.[12]

In keeping with most military units and formations of the era, the internal organization of each of the French armored car units of the winter of 1914–1915 was square. Each *groupe*, which corresponded to a company (and not, like French artillery *groupes* of the time, to a battalion), was commanded by a lieutenant (*lieutenant de vaisseau*) of the French Navy. It was divided into two platoons, each commanded by an ensign or lieutenant junior grade. Each platoon, in turn, had five or six vehicles (two or three armed with canon and two with machineguns). As the *autos-canons* had pride of place and the *autos-mitrailleuses* were still very much in a supporting role, the platoon commander delegated direct command of the machine-gun-armed armored cars to his second-in-command, who was either an ensign or senior naval cadet (*aspirant*).[13]

Given the urgency of the situation in the early autumn of 1914, the use of naval personnel to man the newly formed armored car units made a great deal of sense. Like other major European navies of the time, the institution of reserve systems like those of contemporary armies had provided the French navy with far more officers and men than could immediately be put

Figure 1.1
Groupe d'Autos-Canons de 47

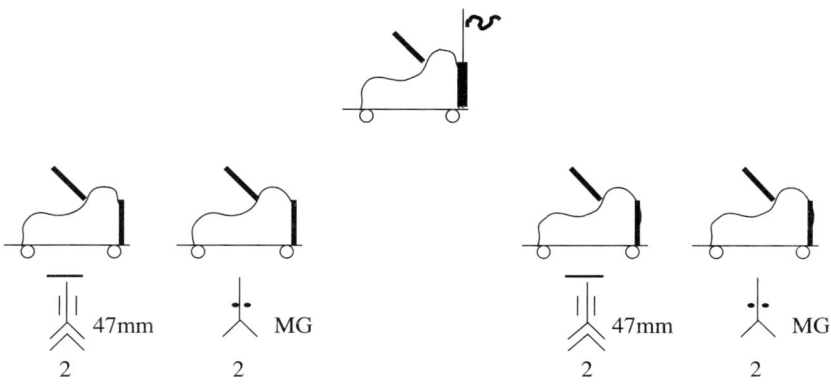

Figure 1.2
Groupe Mixte d'Autos-Mitrailleuses Autos-Canons

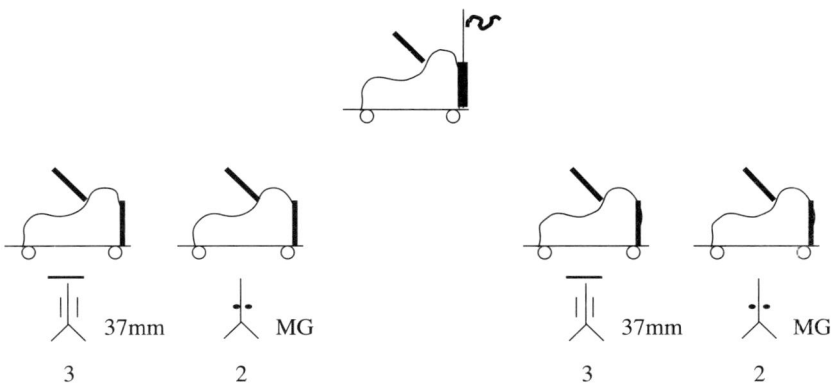

to use at sea. A good number of French sailors thus found themselves—like many of their British and German counterparts—fighting as ground troops in the first few months of the war. With the stabilization of the front, however, came the question of the proper source of manpower for armored car units. The mechanical nature of the armored car suggested that naval personnel, who had been dealing with fuel-burning machines for three generations, were best suited for this work. The work that armored cars were called to do in position warfare, which usually consisted of long-range fire in support of infantry, suggested that the French armored car units, like their Belgian equivalents of the *Groupe des Autos-Canons Auto-Mitrailleuses*, should belong to the artillery. (This work may have preserved the French armored cars from the fate of some of those in the Belgian and British forces, which was to be sent to Russia as part of an aid package for the hard-pressed army of the Tsar.)[14] The experience of 1914, in which armored cars had cooperated closely with cavalry formations, indicated an affiliation with that arm.

A decision of sorts was forced upon the French army in February of 1916, when the French Navy asked the army for the return of its officers and sailors. The War Ministry reacted by asking the field artillery to take responsibility for manning the armored car units. Thus, for a short time, the French armored car units were attached to the (inauspiciously numbered) 13th Regiment of Artillery. The fact that the field artillery had no men to spare at this time soon led to the abandonment of this idea. In May of 1916, the armored car units became part of the cavalry, which was perhaps the only branch of the French army of the time that was not suffering from an acute manpower shortage.[15]

It was as part of the French cavalry that the French armored cars of World War I achieved their greatest success in the filling of some of the more critical gaps torn in British and French lines by the German spring offensives of 1918. Making use of the excellent French road network, the armored cars were often the first reinforcements to arrive in a threatened area. As such, they blocked the progress of the most advanced of the German attackers and bought time for the rest of the French reinforcements—the railroad-riding infantry divisions that made it impossible for the Germans to effectively exploit their breakthrough. This work, more than any other, earned for the armored car units a permanent place in the French army of the twentieth century.[16]

The same enthusiasm for armored cars displayed by General Gallieni and the French Navy had a worthy equivalent on the other side of the English Channel. Encouraged by Commander Sampson's exploits, in the spring of 1915 the Royal Navy formed eighteen armored car squadrons. (Each of these, like their French counterparts, consisted of twelve armored cars plus a variety of support vehicles.) By the time these units were ready for action, however, there was little demand for their services on the western front. The majority of the new units were, therefore, disbanded. Those few armored car squadrons that survived were transferred to the other fronts. Some ended up chasing German guerillas in East Africa. Two took part in the suppression of a tribal revolt in Italian-held Libya. One, like the Belgian armored car battalion, found its way to Russia. As a result, three years would pass in which the only armored cars in the British Empire forces serving in France and Flanders were not British but Canadian.[17]

Like the other armored cars of the Western Allies, the Canadian armored car units formed in the late summer and fall of 1914 were the handiwork of enthusiastic amateurs, successful men who used their own wealth, connections, and energy to do what bureaucracies could not. In Ottawa, Toronto, and Montreal, energetic businessmen recruited men, bought machine guns, and engaged automobile makers to design and build a variety of armored cars and trucks. The godfather of this activity was Minister of Militia Sam Hughes, a brash politician with a rather romantic view of what the Canadian way of war ought to be. Though this view was never consigned to a manifesto, its chief feature was the mounted rifleman, a citizen-soldier who need only know how to shoot and ride.[18] Although armored cars were not an essential part of this vision, they fit neatly into it, as a complementary arm that could both keep pace with the mounted rifleman and provide them with a sort of mobile artillery.

Two categories of units resulted from this confluence of ideas and capabilities. The first category consisted of the independent "motor machine gun batteries." As both funding for armored cars and an operational concept for these units were lacking, they soon took on the character of the British motor machinegun batteries, in which machine guns and their crews were mounted on motorcycles, rather than armored cars or trucks. Like their British counterparts, the Canadian motor machine-gun batteries soon found themselves in the role of "spare machine gun units," used to plug holes in the line or bolster weak spots.[19] The second category consisted of the Motor Machine Gun Brigade, a uniquely Canadian type of unit that had been formed by Raymond Brutinel, a former French officer who had immigrated to British Columbia some years before.[20]

During the period of trench warfare, the Motor Machine Gun Brigade left its armored cars and motorcycles in the rear and served as a conventional machine-gun battalion. As such, it played a major role in the development of the machine-gun barrages and other techniques suitable to position warfare.[21] Nonetheless, the men of the Motor Machine Gun Brigade never forgot their original raison d'etre. This proved useful when, on 23 March 1918, the unit was asked to join in the work of dealing with the huge gap that the Germans had just created in the sector of the British Fifth Army. It therefore brought its remaining armored cars and motorcycles out of storage, mounted its machine guns (by twos) on specially modified trucks, and reconfigured itself for mobile warfare.

The situation faced by the Motor Machine Gun Brigade in late March and April of 1918 was similar to the one being dealt with by the French armored cars coming up from the south. German units were advancing. British units were retreating. French reinforcements were arriving by rail. Knowledge of what unit was where and which side possessed a given bit of terrain was in short supply. Open flanks abounded, along with unprecedented opportunity for rapid movement and skillful maneuver. The task of the Canadian motorized combat troops, however, was somewhat different from that of their French counterparts. The French armored cars served as advanced guards for the French infantry divisions coming into the area to fill the great gap created by the German attack. The Motor Machine Gun Brigade, on the other hand, ended up providing a means of making contact with, and aiding the withdrawal of, isolated British units. The reasons for this were painfully simple. Because the Motor Machine Gun Brigade was the only reserve available to the Fifth Army, there were, for quite a few days, no follow-on forces in need of an advanced guard. The experience was, nonetheless, a harbinger of things to come, as well as the first employment as a mobile unit of an organization that had been waging a very different sort of war for nearly three years.[22]

Encouraged by the success of the Motor Machine Gun Brigade, and taking advantage of elements made available by the dissolution of the 5th Canadian Infantry Division, Brutinel organized, in June of 1918, the 2nd Motor Machine Gun Brigade. Although he was by now a Brigadier General and commanding officer of the Canadian Machine Gun Corps, Brutinel could not provide the new unit with armored cars. Most of the Canadian-built armored cars that had accompanied the original Motor Machine Gun Brigade on its trip across the Atlantic had, during the long years of trench warfare, been transferred to internal security forces in India and Ireland. What Brutinel could do was provide a few more motorcycle scouts and provide two machine-gun firing mounts for each of the machinegun-carrying trucks. He also instituted a training program to develop the skills that the Canadian "motor machine gunners" would need to wage the new type of semimobile warfare that had emerged on the western front. Techniques practiced included the forming of defensive flanks, the use of armored cars as an advanced guard, the use of armored cars as a mobile reserve, the holding of ground, and the overcoming of strong points by means of flanking actions.

In addition to working with each other, the two motor machine gun brigades practiced these techniques in the company of the bicycle troopers of the Canadian Corps Cyclist Battalion, the horse cavalrymen of the Canadian Light Horse, and the gunners of trench mortar batteries.[23]

On 8 August 1918, Brutinel's motor machine gunners, now united under his command in the aptly named Canadian Independent Force, got an opportunity to put some of their new skills to practical use. On that day, they took part in one of the most ambitious Allied offensives attempted that year on the western front. In company with eleven British tank battalions, eleven infantry divisions (four Canadian, four Australian, and three British) would attempt to break through the recently erected German defensive positions east of Amiens. The Canadian Independent Force would be on the extreme right edge of the this array, advancing down the Amiens-Roye road. (This was the section of national highway that connected Amiens with the locally important railroad center of Roye, some thirty kilometers to the south and east.) In the course of making this advance, the Canadian Independent Force was to control that road, protect the long, open flank of the attacking force, and provide information about what was going on in the German rear area. It was also to cooperate with the British and Canadian cavalry brigades that would be attempting to exploit the planned rupture of the German main line of resistance.

The action of the Canadian Independent Force, like that of the cavalry, took place within the framework of the methodical advance of the attacking infantry divisions. On the first day of the offensive, the attack was to move forward in a series of bounds, each of which was three to five kilometers deep and corresponded to a zone in the German defensive scheme. The first two bounds were the exclusive province of the infantry divisions, heavy tank battalions, and reinforcing artillery. Their purpose was to capture the German outpost zone and the main defensive position. (The former was a thinly held line of observation posts and squad positions. The latter was a thick belt of strongpoints where almost all of the German heavy machine guns, two-thirds of the German infantry, and a good portion of the German field guns were located. Once the main line of resistance had been overrun, the British and Canadian cavalry brigades, supported by the recently introduced "Whippet" tanks, would pass through the infantry lines and begin the exploitation phase of the attack. While the first bound was to be conducted in accordance with the well-established techniques of trench warfare, and the second by methods that were only somewhat less methodical, the exploitation was to be a free-form affair. The fresh infantry units that were to provided support for this third phrase of the attack were not to go forward of the "blue line"—a series of low ridges some ten to fourteen kilometers east of the line of departure. The mobile elements—the Canadian Independent Force, the Anglo-Canadian horse cavalry brigades, and the one British armored car battalion in the Australian sector—were given no such limit. They were to advance as far as the situation permitted.[24]

The role of the Canadian Independent Force in this mad dash into the German rear areas was a multifaceted one. On the most prosaic level, it was to control the Amiens-Roye highway, stopping any German counterattacks that may have come up from the south. In doing this, it also protected the French attacks that, in support of the British offensive, were scheduled to take place in that area. Additional missions that could not be so rigidly tied to a line on a map included cooperating with the cavalry, providing information on German activities (particularly the arrival of counter-attack forces), and maintaining contact with forward elements of the French First Army.[25] (The fact that Brutinel had been born and educated in France made him particularly well suited to fulfill this task.)

To accomplish its mission, the Canadian Independent Force, reinforced by the Canadian Corps Cyclist Battalion and a pair of truck-mounted 6-inch (152mm) trench mortars, was task organized into a headquarters, two armored car detachments (one forward and one rear), and the two motor machinegun brigades (See Figure 1.3). While the trench mortars were kept together as a section and placed at the rear of the column, each of the other elements was provided with ten to twenty motorcycle riders and somewhere between one and four platoons of bicycle troops. The latter added greatly to the rifle strength of the force, augmenting its ability to both deal with resistance and hold ground, particularly in wooded areas where machine guns would have limited fields of fire. The motorcycle riders, on the other hand, were to be employed primarily as scouts and messengers, serving both to keep the various elements of the Canadian Independent Force working together and to make contact with the many French, British, or Canadian (and perhaps even Australian) units they might encounter (See Figure 1.4).[26]

As an aid to fulfilling that part of its mission that involved gathering information on activities in the German rear area, the Canadian Independent Force received a special radio set, a special frequency, and special permission to transmit its reports in the clear. The radio set was a Mark III Continuous Wave Set, a powerful set with the (then impressive) range of twenty kilometers or more.

Figure 1.3
Canadian Independent Force August 1918

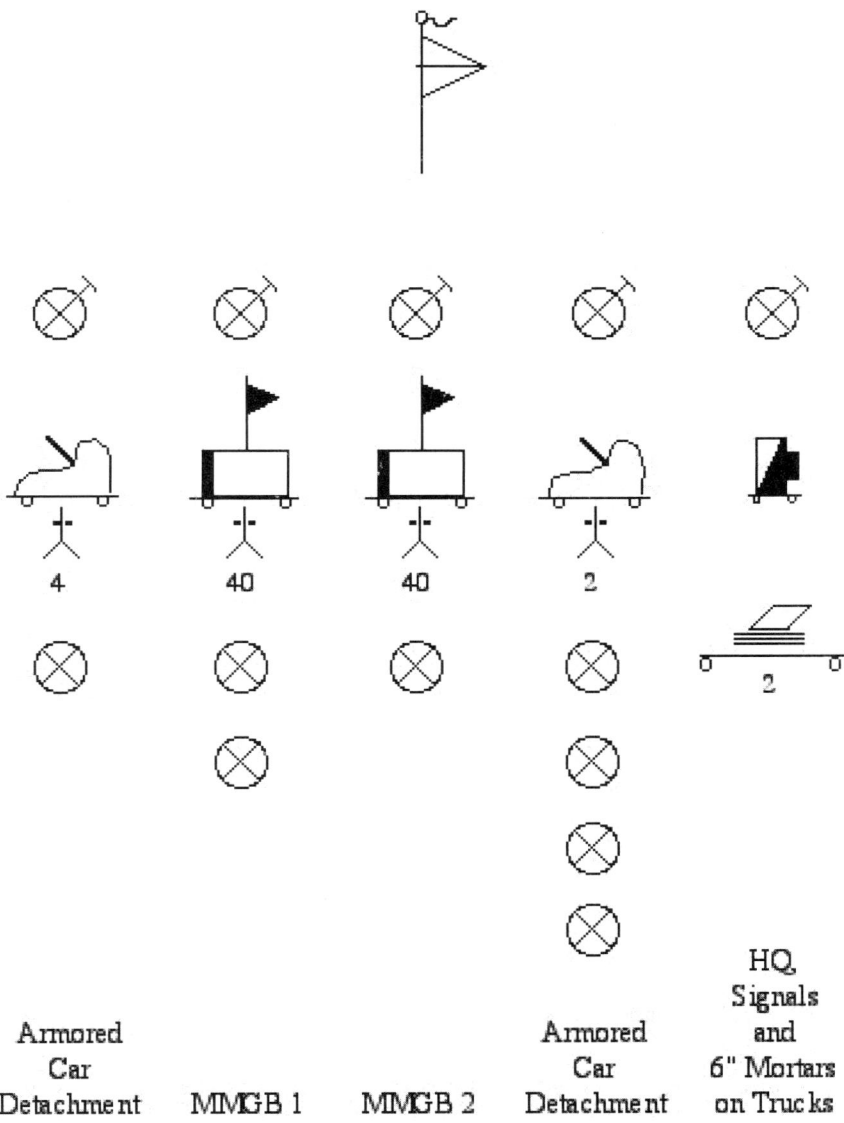

Figure 1.4
Orientation Map Canadian Independent Force 8 August 1918

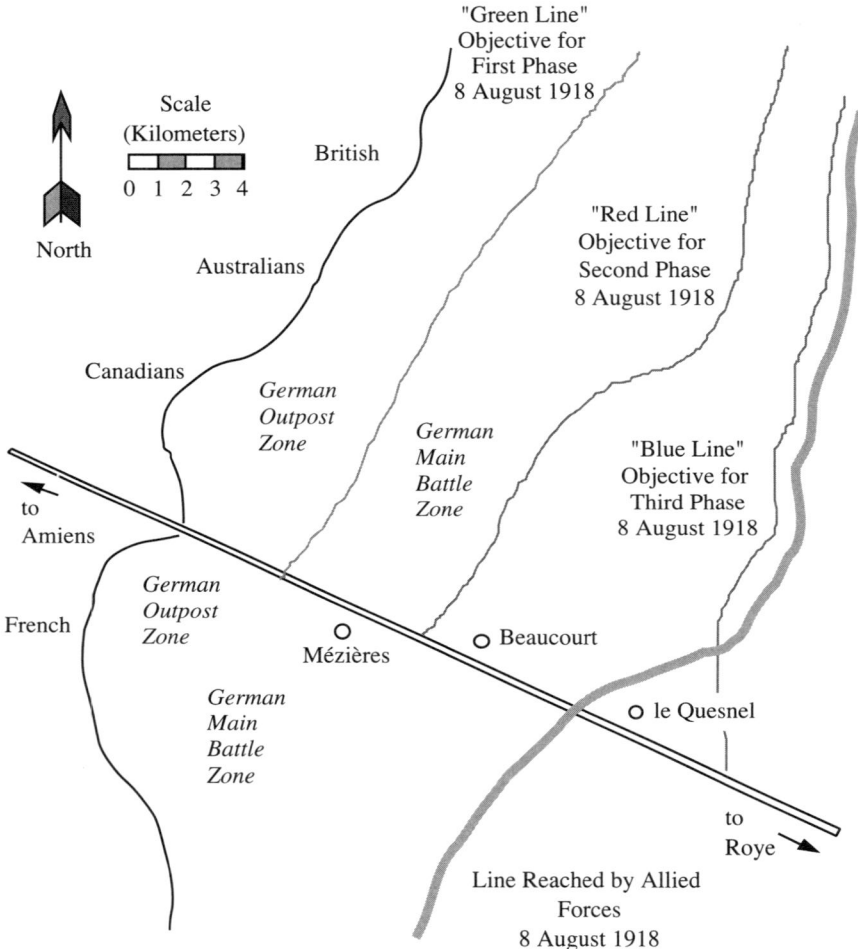

(The transmitting power of this set was enhanced by the fact that the Amiens-Roye highway was located on ground that was slightly higher than most of the surrounding country.) Because of its rarity, the Mark III set was normally given only to division headquarters and the counter-battery organization of the corps artillery. The special wavelength (1,450 meters) was provided because it was one that the Germans had had difficulty jamming in the past. The permission to send messages without recourse to encryption was a function of the nature of the intelligence-gathering mission. Since the Germans would presumably already know what was going on in their own rear area, there was no sense in delaying the transmission, receipt, or dissemination of timely information in order to keep them in the dark.[27]

The initial attack of the Canadian 3rd Infantry Division—the one that, among other things, was to pave the way for the release of the Canadian Independent Force onto the Amiens-Roye highway—took a little more than five hours. It started at zero hour (4:20 A.M.) and lasted until 9:30 A.M., two hours after the division was supposed have taken the first objective. The four German infantry battalions in the area—with less than one hundred riflemen each but a full complement of machine guns and trench mortars—had proven a tougher nut to crack than the battle plans had anticipated. The Canadians remained, nonetheless, on schedule, as the sacrifice of four German battalions had, at least where time was concerned, cost them only the two-hour "breather" that had been inserted between the first and second phases of the attack.[28]

It was at the beginning of this second phase of the attack, as fresh Canadian infantry and additional British tanks leapfrogged over the victors of the early morning battle for the German outpost zone, that Brutinel sent the Canadian Independent Force into action. The first elements to go forward were the six armored cars, which were told to maintain contact with the Germans, and a platoon of bicycle troops. The bulk of this force—four armored cars and most of the cyclists—raced four kilometers down the road. There, near the village of le Quesnel, they ran into considerable German resistance. The rest—two armored cars and a section of cyclists—turned off the road a bit to the village of Mézières, where they captured a heavy field howitzer (150mm) and thirty German soldiers.[29] Behind the armored cars, the machine gunners of the two motor machine gun brigades set up defensive positions along the length of the Amiens-Roye highway while motorcycle scouts drove off in nearly every possible direction.

Though they did not know it at the time, the force of armored cars and cyclists that had been stopped near le Quesnel had run into the forward edge of one of the two German counter-attack divisions in the area.[30] The armored cars pulled back a kilometer or two, covered the advance of three machine-gun batteries that were moving into position, and, when the cavalry started to arrive, got involved in a fight with another portion of the German counter-attack reserve—three infantry battalions in the woods north of Beaucourt.[31] This second engagement was costlier than the first, with three of the four armored cars being put out of action by German fire and the fourth, as a result, pulled back to an area that was securely under the control of one of the motor machinegun brigades.

While its units were engaged between Mézières, Beaucourt, and le Quesnel, the headquarters of the Canadian Independent Force set up both its headquarters and radio set at a house called Maison Blanche, just north of place where the road from Mézières joined the Amiens-Roye highway. As it possessed the only transmitter of any significance for several miles around, this headquarters become a focal point for all sorts of information about the progress of the various Allied contingents and the activity of German units. Intended only as a means of keeping the headquarters of the Canadian Corps apprised of the situation on its right flank, the service provided by Brutinel's radio transmissions was instantly appreciated by radio operators at all of the division and corps headquarters involved in the battle. This became apparent when, on the afternoon of the first day of the offensive, the Canadian Independent Forces made an unannounced change of the radio frequency upon which it transmitted its messages. Within minutes, the switchboard at the headquarters of the Canadian Corps lit up with calls from all over the British front, each of which demanded to know why the station had been shut down.[32]

The German counter-attack division near le Quesnel did not, as might be expected from its name, conduct any significant counterattacks on 8 August. It did, however, prevent both the Canadian Independent Force and the 3rd Canadian Infantry Division from reaching its objectives that day. Elsewhere, the battle was going extremely well for the Allies. The Canadian, Australian, and British infantry divisions all succeeded in breaking through the German outpost zone and main defensive positions. Most reached their objectives for the day. The British and Canadian cavalry brigades had outrun their Whippet tanks (but not the British armored cars working in the Australian sector) and begun to run amok in the German rear areas.[33] To the south of the Amiens-Roye highway, the attacks of the French First Army were also making good progress. A little after noon, the three motor machine gun batteries near the village of Mézières fired in support of a French infantry regiment coming up from the south. Later that evening, at 9:30 P.M. or so, French troops that had just overcome stiff German resistance just south of the Amiens-Roye highway linked up with the forward Canadian troops in front of le Quesnel.[34]

In the course of the night that connected 8 August with the following day, the Germans reinforced their division in le Quesnel, whereas the French and Canadian forces planned deliberate attacks. The next day was one in which the rapid advance of 8 August was replaced by slow progress through the woods and villages on both sides of the Amiens-Roye highway. In this fighting, some elements of the Canadian Independent Force supported Allied infantry with machine-gun fire while others stood watch over open flanks, maintained contact with the French, or made wide detours around le Quesnel in order to discover what was going on in the villages that lay behind it. Le Quesnel itself fell on the morning of 10 August, to a task force made up two motor machine gun batteries and a battalion of Canadian infantry.[35]

In a month-long string of similar battles that followed the Allied victory at Amiens, the Canadian Independent Force was formed and disbanded several times, changing its name twice and receiving, at times, attachments of horse cavalry, heavy armored cars, and additional bicyclists.[36] Despite these changes, the core of the unit—machine gunners on trucks, armored cars, bicyclists, and heavy trench mortars—remained the same as that of 8 August. The services that the Canadian Independent Force performed were likewise similar to the ones it provided at Amiens. Using roads of the same type as the Amiens-Roye highway, it pushed through gaps made by the infantry in order to establish a line of machine guns in the German rear area. In doing this, the Canadian Independent Force enjoyed considerably more success in defending stretches of road than in using them as routes of advance. This was sometimes due to the destruction wreaked upon roads by heavy artillery and sometimes a function of the inability of cavalry and bicyclists to work their way around the flanks of German units blocking the road. (This, in turn, happened whenever the ground was open enough for a handful of German machine guns, often sited at leisure in the weeks before the battle, to control it.)[37]

By the middle of September 1918, the nature of German resistance began to change. The defense of prepared positions was giving way to what the Germans would soon christen *delaying resistance* (*hinhaltende Widerstand*), a combination of long-range fire, temporary occupation of key terrain, and deception followed by rapid withdrawal.[38] Dealing with such a matador's cloak—particularly the threadbare one wielded by the German army of the last months of 1918—greatly increased the opportunities for exploiting the particular virtues of the Canadian Independent Force. It had the firepower to call the bluff of small delaying forces, the ability to outflank roadblocks (at least in places where houses or woods provided sufficient cover for the bicyclists), and the mobility to chase units attempting to escape to the next delay position. With its motorcyclists and radio, moreover, the Canadian Independent Force had the means to keep other elements of the Canadian Corps well informed about situations that changed with every passing hour. Indeed, while Brutinel had been previously obliged to work hard to keep his brigade in the exploitation business, his great administrative challenge during the last few weeks of the war was to keep the Canadian Independent Force from being broken up. After seeing what Brutinel's brigade could do, each division commander in the Canadian Corps wanted a mobile force of his own.[39]

Hard-pressed as the Canadian Corps was for units that could keep up with the retreating Germans, it was in a much better position than the rest of the British Empire forces in France and Flanders. The twelve other British Empire corps engaged in the pursuit were thus forced to make do with horse cavalry, their corps cyclist battalions, and the possibility of benefiting from the services of the single British armored car unit then in service on the western front. This was the 17th Armoured Car Battalion of the Tank Corps, the same armored car unit that had proved so helpful to the British cavalry operating in front of the Australian Corps sector at the Battle of Amiens.[40] The French, with their twenty *groupes mixtes d'autos-mitrailleuses autos-canons* were even more fortunate than the Canadians were when it came to mobile elements capable of keeping contact with an increasingly elusive enemy. Even though the terrain in which the French formations were operating was rarely as open or as well-provided with roads as the country where British Empire troops were advancing, the French armored car units spent much of the last few weeks of the war well ahead of their muscle-powered counterparts.

2
OPEN FLANKS

The story of the armored fighting vehicle in World War I is, in many respects, a baby story. It tells of the joys of conception, the tedium of pregnancy, the pain of labor, and many sleepless nights dealing with the military-technical parallels to teething, colic, and wet diapers. In much the same way, the story of the next phase in the life of the armored fighting vehicle—that of the period between the two world wars—is a tale of childhood. As might be imagined, it is filled to the brim with visions of unlimited potential, outbursts of childish enthusiasm, and the inevitable limits imposed by adults. Like many childhood stories, the history of armored warfare in the 1920s and 1930s is one in which a good number of the grown-ups were more encouraging than limiting, more avuncular than dour. One of these, the horse cavalry, was almost as old as warfare itself. Others, including the motor transport and bicycle units formed in the years just before World War I, were only slightly older than both armored cars and tanks, and thus played the role of helpful older siblings to the new arms.

The military organizations that would prove so helpful to the progress of both tanks and armored cars in the interwar period had not found much scope for action on the Western Front. (The great exception was the huge park of trucks and cars assembled behind the Western Front by the French. While these were important to the outcome of the war, they were not concerned with operational maneuver per se.) Mounted military units had, however, enjoyed considerable triumphs on other fronts, where a much lower ratio of military units to space greatly increased the odds of finding a gap to exploit or an open flank to strike. The stage upon which German horse cavalry, bicycle units, and motor transport played their most memorable operational roles was the great expanse of land belonging to the Russian Empire and its local allies, Serbia and Romania. The place where British mobile formations came into their own was the Middle East, particularly that portion of the Fertile Crescent currently occupied by Israel, Jordan, and Syria.

As might be expected, all of the mobile divisions that fought in World War I were horse cavalry formations. In 1914, most cavalry divisions in the world had consisted of somewhere between six and nine cavalry regiments (each of 500 or so horsemen) and three batteries of horse artillery (each of four to six field guns.) In countries large enough to raise more than one cavalry division, two or three cavalry divisions were sometimes assembled to form a cavalry corps. In the French and German armies, cavalry formations were provided with additional units that greatly increased their capacity for dismounted combat. A typical German cavalry division of the first year of World War I, for example, had four companies of *Jäger* (elite light infantry) carried in trucks, two machine gun companies, and a company of bicycle troops. (The Jäger companies, the bicycle company, and one of the machine gun companies were part of a Jäger battalion.) A French cavalry division of the same period had a small battalion (450 men) of *Chasseurs* (also elite light infantry) mounted on bicycles and three independent machine gun platoons (of two machine guns each.) A French cavalry corps—only one of which was formed in 1914—was also provided with three or four battalions of infantry carried in requisitioned Paris omnibuses.[1]

While the onset of trench warfare interrupted the development of French cavalry formations, the German cavalry formations that served on the Eastern Front continued to evolve in the direction of increased reliance on nontraditional elements. That is to say, while the role of horsemen and horse artillery diminished, the role of infantry mounted on motor vehicles and bicycles grew more important. By the summer of 1916, the German army on the Eastern Front was at a point where it could deploy mobile elements—a task-force mounted in trucks and a complete infantry brigade on bicycles—in which the part played by horse cavalry was either secondary or nonexistent. These mobile elements played a key role in one of the most successful campaigns conducted by the German army in World War I.

Like most of the German victories on the Eastern Front in World War I, the German conquest of Romania in the second half of 1916 was an improvised affair. Surprised by Romania's opportunistic entry into the war, the Germans cobbled together two polyglot invasion forces and, within three weeks of the onset of the crisis, unleashed two armies upon their new enemies. From the north, the German Ninth Army, made up of German and Austro-Hungarian forces, attacked through the Carpathian Mountains. From the south, Army Group Mackensen (made up of Bulgarian, Austro-Hungarian, and Turkish elements) attacked along the Black Sea Coast. As was both customary and necessary, the Germans provided this army group with its commander (Field Marshal August Mackensen), general staff officers, technical services, and "corset-stays"—German combat units intended to stiffen the mediocre fabric of the overall force.

Like other armies that fought on the continent of Europe at the time, the German armies invading Romania were supplied almost entirely by railroad. This presented problems for the Ninth Army, which, having fought its way through the Carpathians, now found those mountains between itself and its logistical lifeline. While this was not a critical problem, it was a major irritant that required more and more resources be devoted to carting supplies through narrow mountain passes. These resources could be diverted to other purposes if the Germans could find a means of reopening the railroad between Budapest and Bucharest. (The former was a major supply and transport center for the Central Powers. The latter was the capital of Romania, a city that was about to be caught between the hammer of the Ninth Army and the anvil of Army Group Mackensen.) The chief obstacle preventing the Central Powers from using this railroad was Romanian control of a geographical feature known as the Iron Gate, the place where both the railroad and the Danube River entered the Romanian heartland.[2]

The Romanians were well aware of the importance of the Iron Gate and had taken steps to keep it out of enemy hands. Fortifications of the coastal variety, with heavy guns permanently pointed towards the Danube, protected the Iron Gate from both the Bulgarians on the south bank of Danube and from gunboats attempting to use the river as a highway. An infantry division, though under-equipped by the standards of the day, proved strong enough to prevent Austro-Hungarian forces from taking the Iron Gate from the northwest. There were few defenses, however, against an attack coming from the east, the direction of Bucharest and the yet to be defeated main body of the Romanian army.

To exploit this vulnerability, one of the component divisions of the German Ninth Army organized a highly unusual force.[3] The core of this force was an ordinary infantry battalion mounted on cargo trucks borrowed from the divisional supply column. The artillery consisted of two truck-mounted field guns from an anti-aircraft battery. Organic reconnaissance took the form of a handful of horsemen from the divisional cavalry regiment. (This was the only nonmotorized element of the force.) A few linemen and radio operators from the divisional signal unit provided the capability to tap into the Romanian telegraph system and maintain contact with the rest of the Ninth Army. Because it was led by a certain Captain Picht, this task force was given the somewhat grandiloquent title of *Sturmgruppe Picht.*

Making use of the road that ran beside the railroad track and profiting from the painfully slow decision cycle of the Romanian leaders in the area, Sturmgruppe Picht required less than two days to reach the eastern defenses of the Iron Gate. Once there, the task force lost no time in capturing a coastal defense fort from its undefended landward side. Having done this, the Germans set up an ambush for the Romanian reaction force. (It had been previously established by the German task force's organic wiretapping service that this reaction force was on the way.)

When the Romanians failed to show up in strength, Captain Picht decided to push forward to Turnu Severin, a town of 24,000 inhabitants. There, after taking hostages to ensure the good behavior of local civilians, he set up his defenses. The next morning, four Romanian battalions attacked. On the second day, the better part of a Romanian division attacked. While both attempts failed and the bodies of dead Romanians littered the outskirts of the town, the strain on Sturmgruppe Picht was enormous. Ammunition was running low, machine guns were worn out beyond repair, and one of the two field guns had been knocked out.

Had it been acting on its own, Sturmgruppe Picht would have been in a very bad position. As it turned out, at the point when the little task force was on its last legs, help came from both ends of the Iron Gate. From the east, the German bicycle brigade of Baron von Quadt, which had been dispatched from the Ninth Army upon receipt of one of Captain Picht's requests for help, was the first to arrive. From the west, an Austro-Hungarian brigade exploited the fact that nearly all the Romanian units had been concentrated against Turnu Severin, and managed to march over an obstacle that had proved impossible to force only a few days earlier. With powerful enemies on both sides, the Romanian division fled towards Bucharest, leaving the Iron Gate, and thus the new supply route of the Ninth Army, firmly in the hands of the Central Powers.

Sturmgruppe Picht was a temporary organization that did not long survive the mission that gave it birth. Within weeks of the capture of the

Iron Gate, the infantry battalion returned to its parent regiment, the trucks went back to hauling supplies, and Captain Picht faded into to obscurity. As no new motorized combat units were formed, and as the handful of armored cars in the German inventory were both too few and too heavy to serve with advantage in a fast-moving unit, the place left vacant was taken up by the bicycle brigade that had helped to rescue Sturmgruppe Picht at Turnu Severin.

In October of 1917, Bicycle Infantry Brigade von Quadt was included in the landing force assembled to capture the Baltic Islands of Oesel and Moon (See Figure 2.1). Why the bicycle brigade, rather than a horse cavalry formation, was chosen to provide the mobile element for the landing force seems to have been largely a matter of logistics. The bicycle brigade, with more than 3,500 riflemen and 32 machine guns (See Figure 2.2), had about twice the foxhole strength and firepower of an entire division of horse cavalry. By the same token, the bicycle brigade required far less space aboard ship, was far easier to keep supplied and, because it is far easier to patch a bicycle tire than shoe a horse or prevent an epidemic of mange, required far less maintenance than a cavalry division.[4] Similar considerations prevented the use of motor vehicles to form a larger version of Sturmgruppe Picht. Putting 3,500 riflemen and 32 machine gun crews on motor vehicles would have required about 220 cargo trucks. As it was, the embarkation officers in charge of shoehorning the landing force into the motley collection of tramp steamers available for the operation had a difficult enough time finding space for the fifty or so trucks belonging to supply and communications units.[5]

The strategic importance of Oesel and Moon derived from their position in the mouth of the Gulf of Riga. Taken together, the two islands filled nearly all 125 kilometers of that mouth, leaving only two narrow channels to connect the inland waters with the larger Baltic. Because these channels could easily be dominated by coastal artillery emplaced on the southwestern side of Oesel and the easternmost extremities of Moon, the side that controlled the two islands effectively controlled the Gulf of Riga. Late in 1917, this was important because the Gulf of Riga served as a haven for the Russian Baltic Fleet and as a base for British submarines. Russian control of the Gulf of Riga also inhibited German military operations on the Baltic Coast, particularly the march to St. Petersburg that loomed so large in the German contingency planning of the time.[6]

The Russian defenses on Oesel and Moon included both fixed and mobile elements. Batteries of up-to-date coastal artillery protected by con-

Figure 2.1
Baltic Islands 1971

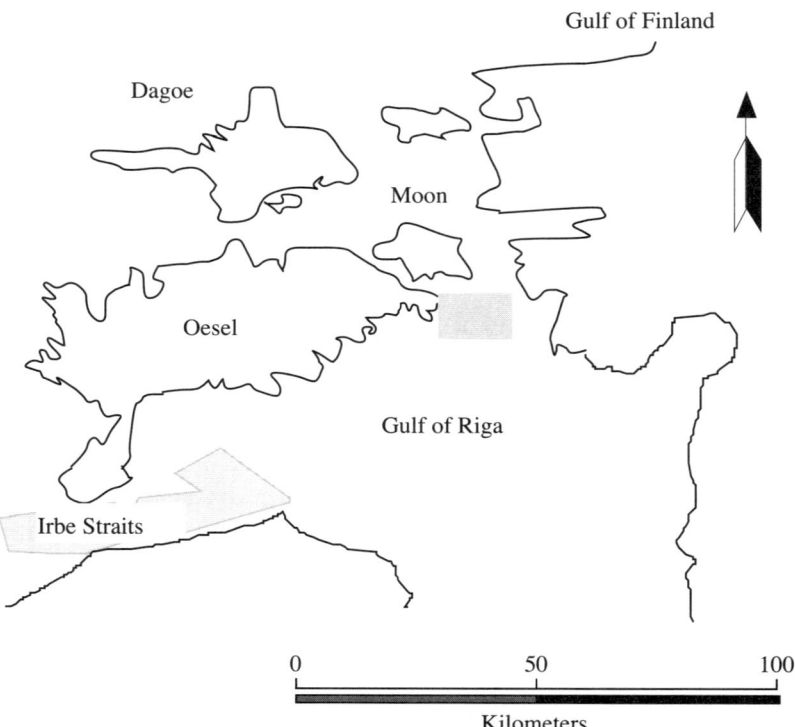

Figure 2.2
Bicycle Brigade von Quadt October 1917

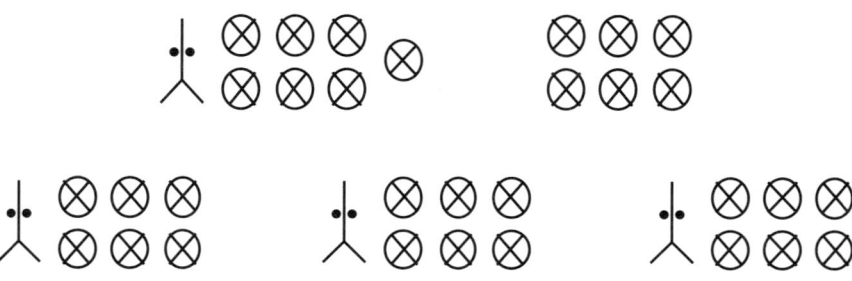

Figure 2.3

crete emplacements, antiaircraft guns, and small guard units faced towards the sea. The strongest concentrations of these guns, which ranged in caliber from 120mm (4.7 inch) to 300mm (11.8 inch), were at the two entrances to Gulf of Riga, on the Sworbe Peninsula (on the southwest corner of Oesel) and the eastern shore of Moon. Three smaller batteries, with 120mm or 150mm (5.9 inch) guns were distributed along the north coast of the larger island of Oesel. A division of infantry was divided among three garrisons on the western half of Oesel. With a little hard marching, this division could concentrate against any point on the western half of Oesel in a day or so, and any point on Eastern Oesel in less than two days.

A strong force of Russian cruisers, monitors, and torpedo boats stationed in the channel between Moon and the mainland, as well as shallow waters that were extremely hard to navigate, made it unlikely that the Germans would attempt a landing on Moon. In case of need, however, the Russian infantry could march over the stone causeway that connected the two islands. At the same time, this causeway was the easiest means by which German troops could get onto Moon, capture the coastal artillery battery, and, if particularly enterprising, turn the big guns on the Russian flotilla lying off of the east coast of the island.

Before they could do this, the Germans had to deal with the Russian forces on the main island of Oesel. Their plan to do this was based on making two surprise landings on the north coast of Oesel. Among the first to get ashore in these landings would be four of Baron von Quadt's five bicycle infantry battalions.

Two of these battalions would land at Pamerort, an overland march of about sixty-five kilometers from the causeway. The other two would land further west at Tagga Bay. This, which was also the landing point for the twelve infantry battalions and fourteen artillery batteries of the landing force, was about eighty kilometers west the causeway and seventy kilometers north of the Sworbe Peninsula.

In general terms, the mission of the bicycle battalions was to create favorable conditions for the deployment of the rest of the German landing force. It also fell to von Quadt's cyclists to seize the one feature of the islands that was both critical to the success of the German attack and far away from the landing site. This feature was the area around the village of

Orissar, which overlooked the stone causeway that connected Oesel to Moon. If they controlled this causeway, the Germans would not only be able to cut the Russian defense in two, but would also be able to avoid having to land on Moon Island, an undertaking made very difficult by the lack of suitable landing sites.

The German plan to take the islands called for a two-phase operation, with the taking of Moon following the defeat of the Russian forces on Oesel. Luckily for the Germans, the former was facilitated by the failure of the Russians to properly defend the one site suitable to the landing of the main body of the German landing force. This was Tagga Bay, thirty kilometers from Arensburg, the only significant town on the islands and the location of most of the Russian defenders. At Tagga Bay, the Germans had a natural beachhead, with many routes into the interior, terrain that was easy to defend, and, what was most important in an area characterized by excessively shallow waters, a natural harbor where all sorts of naval and cargo vessels could come close to shore.

The one great disadvantage of Tagga Bay was its distance—sixty kilometers as the crow flies and many more by road—from the causeway at Orissar. To compensate for this, the Germans planned a subsidiary landing at Pamerort, less than forty kilometers east of Tagga Bay and thus a little more than twenty kilometers closer to the causeway. The waters leading to Pamerort were too shallow for most German vessels and purpose-built landing craft had yet to be invented. The landing force was therefore limited to what could be carried in shallow-draft torpedo boats—two battalions from von Quadt's bicycle brigade and, to facilitate their landing, an infantry assault company. The other three battalions of the bicycle brigade, along with the artillery, the horse cavalry, the support troops, the supplies, and the bulk of the infantry, had to land at Tagga Bay.

Russian resistance to both landings turned out to be negligible. As a result, the bicycle battalions were able to move out as soon as they were landed. One of the two bicycle battalions landed at Pamerort rushed strait for the causeway at Orissar. The other moved south, with the mission of blocking any Russian force moving against Orissar from that direction. The three bicycle battalions landed at Tagga Bay also pushed towards Orissar. In the course of doing this, they also covered the landing and deployment of the main body of the landing force.

Well aware the importance of the causeway at Orissar, the Russians reacted to news of the landing by attempting to bolster their forces in that area. The result was a curious encounter battle in which a Russian infantry regiment found itself sandwiched between the two German bicycle battalions that had landed at Pamerort and the three that had been landed at Tagga Bay. After some hard fighting, the result of this maneuver was the destruction of a Russian regiment and German control of the causeway. Elsewhere on the island, the main body of the landing force enjoyed victories of its own. These took a form that was typical of German action on the Eastern Front, with German infantry units annihilating opponents that were similarly armed, but not nearly as well led. These were followed by naval action that resulted in the expulsion of the Russian fleet from the Gulf of Riga and the capture of the attached island of Moon and the nearby, but separate, island of Dagoe.

Compared to the German forces that took the Iron Gate and the Baltic Islands, the cavalry formations that helped Sir Edmund Allenby conquer Palestine and Syria in the course of two campaigning seasons in 1917 and 1918 were somewhat old-fashioned. For that reason, those in the English-speaking world of the 1920s and 1930s who argued for the retention of significant forces of horse cavalry often used Allenby's campaigns as an example of the continued utility of large numbers of fighting horsemen. It would be a mistake, however, to see the British, Australian, and New Zealand horse cavalry formations that fought in the Middle East as complete anachronisms. While it is true that their most famous exploit was not the sort of thing that could be repeated with any chance of success, their manner of fighting was as much a harbinger of things to come as that of Bicycle Brigade von Quadt. That is to say, while the means of transport would change, the century to come would provide much employment for soldiers who rode into battle, but fought on foot.

The event that captured the imagination of horse cavalry advocates of the interwar period—and of military history enthusiasts ever after—was the capture of Beersheba on 31 October 1917 by 18,000 horsemen of the Desert Mounted Corps. This action began with a night march to a secret rendezvous in the wilderness southeast of the ancient town. After three days of rest, a second night march of thirty miles brought the ten brigades of British, Australian, and New Zealand horsemen to the high ground east of the Turkish-held town. While a British infantry division took the Turkish positions south and west of Beersheba, the mounted troops attacked from the northwest. The action ended with the famous charge of the 4th Australian Light Horse Brigade, in which the Australian mounted riflemen used their long-bladed bayonets in lieu of sabers.[7]

Those English-speakers who believed that the era of horse cavalry had ended took a very different view of these same events.[8] Where the operational movement of cavalry formations was concerned, they pointed out that the same desert that provided the Desert Mounted Corps with the freedom to maneuver could only support large numbers of horses in exceptional circumstances. In particular, they pointed to the extensive infrastructure that British engineers had to build before the Desert Mounted Corps could be assembled for its march through the desert.[9] One part of this infrastructure shared with the rest of the British force in the Sinai—a force of 358,000 men and 150,000 horses, camels, mules, and donkeys. It featured a new port on the Suez Canal, a double-tracked railroad for the transport of fodder and other supplies, and a system of water delivery and storage with a capacity of 600,000 gallons per day. The other part of the infrastructure was set aside for the particular use of the Desert Mounted Corps. This included a branch line of the main railroad and vast water storage system of ancient cisterns and canvas tanks, fed by a combination of newly sunk wells and water bags carried across the desert on the backs of camels and donkeys.[10]

Those skeptical about the future of horse cavalry were also eager to point out that the spectacular saber charges at Beersheba were also favored by exceptional conditions. The Turkish riflemen, machine gunners, and artillerymen in a position to do so much damage were unable to do so because the sights on their otherwise murderous weapons had not been properly set. For example, an officer examining captured Turkish rifles after the battle at Beersheba found that 75% of them were sighted at ranges in excess of 800 yards.[11] This allowed the charging horsemen to benefit from the *Solferino effect*—the closer they got to the firing Turks, the more likely they were to pass underneath the flying bullets and the less likely they were to be hit.

The aspect of the employment of cavalry in Palestine and Syria that both advocate and opponent of horse cavalry missed was the relatively close cooperation between elements of the Desert Mounted Corps and nearby infantry formations. The pattern of this cooperation was as simple as it was innovative. As an infantry formation (usually a single division) moved along a major highway in order to attack (or at least pin down) the enemy from the front, a cavalry force would work its way around an open flank in order to strike the Turks from another direction. While this attack sometimes took the form of a mounted charge, it was usually conducted by troopers on foot. There was even one case in November of 1917 where a British cavalry division advancing along a particularly difficult track sent most of its horses to the rear and continued to march on foot of several days.[12]

This latter form of cooperation was novel in two respects. The first was its departure from the notion that bodies of cavalry smaller than a division were chiefly concerned with local reconnaissance. The second was the up-to-date way in which the troopers were organized and equipped for dismounted combat. The basic tactical unit, a troop of eighteen to forty men, compared favorably to the elite German *Stosstrupps* then serving on the western front.[13] Common characteristics included a high ratio of leaders to soldiers (with designated leaders for groups as small as three or four men), the availability of light machine guns (one or two per troop), and the liberal use of hand grenades. In both cases, the men were volunteers with a high standard of intelligence, self-reliance, and physical fitness. Both types of unit also tended to be relatively fresh when they went into combat.[14] Indeed, the chief difference between the two sorts of forces was the fact that the British Empire cavalry lacked the mortars, flamethrowers, and light infantry guns that played such an important role in the tactics of the Stosstrupps.[15]

An example of the new technique of cooperation between infantry and cavalry can be seen in the British attack against the town of Amman, some twenty-five miles east of the Jordan River, in April of 1918. Now the capital of the Kingdom of Jordan, Amman was, at that time, a relatively small town dominated by Hill 3039, a piece of high ground to the immediate south-southeast. To control this hill, the Turks built two field fortifications that the British, borrowing a term from the North West Frontier of India, called *sangars*. While elements of the 60th Infantry Division approached Amman from the west and halted before the low-lying defenses of the town, the New Zealand Mounted Brigade approached from the southwest in order to take Hill 3039 in the flank. Making use of a night march to avoid the Turkish defenses on the forward (western) slope of the hill, they took one of the two Turkish sangars on the summit. As dawn broke, the New Zealanders found themselves looking down upon both the rear of the Turkish troops on the hill and the eastern edge of Amman. In the opinion of the German officer commanding the Turkish defenders of Amman, there was nothing to prevent the New Zealanders from walking into Amman and attacking the Turkish defenders of the town from the rear. Instead of doing this, however, the New Zealanders fell prey to the temptation to fight the Turks located in the sangars that they had bypassed the night before. As a result, an easy victory was turned into a three-day contest of endurance; a replay, in miniature, of the very sort of position warfare that mobile troops were supposed to avoid.[16]

The enduring influence of Allenby's campaigns on British military thinking can be seen in the maneuvers conducted by the British army in the 1920s. In September of 1925, for example, the southwest of England was the scene for a mock struggle between the fictitious nations of "Mercia" and "Wesex." The former had a relatively conventional force. (The core of this consisted of three muscle-powered infantry divisions and one brigade of horse cavalry.) The latter had a much higher proportion of mobile troops—two brigades of horse-cavalry, one armored car company, and an infantry brigade mounted in commercial-type trucks as well as one infantry division. Each side also had a proportion of support units (field artillery, engineers, signal, and logistics) as well as a small air force and a battalion of tanks. Many of these support units were fully motorized, with a higher proportion of petroleum-powered units assigned the more mobile Wesex forces.

As might be expected, the Wesex forces planned maneuvers of the sort that had made Allenby so famous. These included a wide movement in which a Wesex cavalry brigade attempted to avoid Mercian combat units in order to attack Mercian lines of communication as well as a "spirited tour" by a portion of the Wesex armored car company. What was less predictable was the response of the Mercian commander, who used two of his foot-mobile infantry divisions to fix the Mercian force while he attempted a turning movement with his third infantry division, cavalry brigade, motorized artillery, and tanks. This, in turn, led to a counter-response by the Wesex troops, which included the deployment of its two cavalry brigades to threaten the exposed flank of the Mercian turning movement.[17]

While exploits of the Desert Mounted Corps captured the imagination of horse cavalry advocates in the English-speaking world, Central Europeans did not have to search so far afield for arguments in favor of retaining horse cavalry. The wars that took place on the vast plains of Poland and Russia in the immediate aftermath of World War I—the Russian Civil War of 1917–22 and the Russo-Polish War of 1920–21—provided many examples of the effective use of large bodies of horse cavalry for operational purposes. It is thus not surprising that the Polish and Soviet armies that emerged from these conflicts included large numbers of horse cavalry units in their orders of battle. In 1922, for example, the recently demobilized Polish army could muster forty cavalry regiments.[18] Given that Poland had a population of twenty-seven million people and an army of ninety infantry regiments, this number compares favorably to the 102 cavalry regiments of the peacetime German army of 1914. (In 1914, the population of Germany had been sixty-three million and its peacetime army had consisted of 211 infantry regiments.)[19]

Just to the west of Poland, the 100,000-man army allowed to Germany by the Treaty of Versailles also had an extraordinarily high proportion of horse cavalry (See Table 2.1). This proportion was not only high in relation to the armies of Germany's neighbors, but also in terms of the German army of the immediate past. One reason for this high proportion of cavalry to other arms was the apparent desire of the authors of the Versailles Treaty to give Germany an old-fashioned army that was strong enough to deal with internal difficulties but not strong enough to threaten its neighbors. What the victors of World War I failed to realize, however, was that the German cavalry was as rich a nursery for innovation as the technical branches aviation and heavy artillery) that Germany was forbidden to possess.

Table 2.1
Relationship of Cavalry to Infantry in the German Army[20]

	1899	1911	1920–33
Cavalry Divisions	7	8	3
Infantry Divisions	51	51	7
Ratio	14:100	15:100	42:100
Cavalry Regiments	96	102	18
Infantry Regiments	208	211	21
Ratio of Cavalry Regiments to Infantry Regiments	46:100	48:100	85:100
"Sabers" - Cavalrymen	57,600	61,200	12,600
"Rifles" - Infantrymen	624,000	633,000	63,000
Ratio of "Sabers" to "Rifles"	9:100	10:100	20:100

In many respects, the German cavalry of the 1920s bore a close resemblance to the one that served General Allenby so well in 1917 and 1918. Like Allenby's cavalry, its favorite combat technique was an attack against the flank of an enemy who had been fixed to the front by the action of other friendly troops. There was, however, to be no large-scale charges like that of the Australian Light Horse at Beersheba. When the German cavalry attacked all but the most disorganized of opponents, it was trained to attack in the manner of contemporary infantry. "Riding and shooting must be the lifeblood of the cavalry," wrote Major Albert Benary in a privately published manual for the horse soldiers of the *Reichswehr*. "It rides in order to shoot, and shoots in order to ride. The horse brings the rider towards the enemy. Carbines and heavy weapons beat the enemy down."[21] A few years later, a young captain (and future *Panzer* general) by the name of Hasso von Manteufel expressed a similar thought in even stronger terms. "In dismounted combat the cavalry must use of the means at its disposal to have the same effect as infantry, that is to say, dismounted troopers fight on foot in exactly the same manner as the infantry."[22]

In keeping with the idea of dismounted troopers serving as infantrymen, German cavalry units acquired, over the course of the 1920s, an increasing number of various heavy weapons. Officially, these consisted of the four heavy machine guns of the regimental machine-gun platoon and the light machine guns given to each squadron. Unofficially, Germany's thinly veiled rearmament program called for cavalry regiments that were provided with twelve heavy machine guns (twice as many as had been provided to a German cavalry *division* in 1914) and two "cavalry guns." (These would turn out to be the same 75mm "infantry guns" then being developed for infantry regiments.)[23] The same program provided each cavalry division, which officially consisted of six cavalry regiments and a single horse artillery battalion, with several additional combat units. These included a bicycle battalion, machine-gun battalion, infantry battalion (to be carried in trucks), additional field artillery, and a unit of six to twelve armored cars. These additional units added several dozen heavy machine guns to the arsenal of the cavalry division, as well as a variety of light mortars, field guns, and antitank guns.[24] The result was a unit that had about one-third of the artillery (including mortars and anti-tank guns), a little more than half of the "foxhole strength;" and roughly the same number of heavy machine guns of a standard German infantry division of the time.

Whereas French and German cavalry divisions were remarkably similar where equipment was concerned, the contemporary French conception of cavalry was as different from the German as it could be. The same sort of weapons, therefore, ended up being used for very different purposes. While the Germans viewed cavalry as an arm that would allow them to keep a more powerful opponent at bay by keeping the operational situation as fluid as possible, the French saw cavalry formations as a tool for minimizing the fluidity of the battlefield. In particular, they thought in terms of the rapid creation of a wide screen of combat outposts that, together with the early occupation of key terrain features, would protect the mobilization of the rest of the army. Once the infantry formations were in place, the cavalry would serve as a "reserve of firepower" to plug gaps in the line. Put another way, just as the German cavalry was trained to attack in the manner of contemporary German infantry, the French cavalry was expected to defend in the manner of the French infantry of the time. To that end, squadrons were as well provided with automatic rifles as infantry companies and cavalry regiments with as many heavy machine guns as infantry battalions. As was the case with the Germans, the French planned to use a bicycle battalion (*groupe cycliste*) to both bolster the "foxhole strength" of each cavalry division and to provide it with additional heavy weapons. (Both the French and the German bicycle battalions were armed with twelve heavy machine guns and two to three trench mortars.)

The French cavalry division lacked the spare infantry battalion that the Germans planned to give to each of their cavalry divisions in wartime. It also lacked the cut-down field pieces ("cavalry guns" and "infantry guns") that were so much a part of German small unit tactics. These gaps were, however, more than filled by the practice of pairing-up cavalry divisions to form cavalry corps, each of which was provided with a complete infantry division mounted in trucks and six fully motorized field artillery battalions. The French cavalry formations were, however, richly provided with armored cars. These would, in the twenty years that passed between the two world wars, be the proverbial "nose of the camel" in the tent of the horse cavalry.

3
BROKEN GROUND

The great deficiency of the armored car was its need for a flat, smooth, and stable surface to move over. As such surfaces were increasingly hard to find on the battlefields of World War I, the same people who had turned wheeled automobiles into weapons of war might well have done the same to the fully tracked "caterpillar" tractors available since 1908. While not nearly as common as touring cars or cargo trucks, they were available to anyone who could get to the United States to buy them. Indeed, had the Allied purchasing commissions in North America been as keen to buy caterpillars as they were to buy artillery shells, agricultural products, and horses, the British and French armies of the middle of 1915 might well have possessed a force of armored tractors as large as their fleet of armored cars.

This second great act of improvisation did not, however, take place. Instead, nearly two years would pass between the onset of the position warfare on the Western Front and the debut of a proper cross-country armored fighting vehicle. As with so many other aspects of the history of the armored fighting vehicle, the reason this took so long was less a matter of technology than of imagination. Though well established in agricultural circles in the United States, caterpillar tractors were not nearly as familiar to people in France and Britain. A small number were at work in Western Europe in 1914. A few had even been pressed into military service, either as a means of hauling cargo or a device for pulling very large artillery pieces.[1] Nonetheless, far fewer people were struck by the idea of arming caterpillar tractors than had been inspired to turn wheeled vehicles into war wagons. In the winter of 1914–1915, moreover, most of those who were inclined to think about armored fighting vehicles had become engrossed with the other features of the war. Lieutenant Colonel Swinton of the Royal Engineers, for example, was an officer who had already made a name for himself as a writer of imaginative fiction. The press of his duties on behalf of the Committee of Imperial Defense, however, led him to let more than two months pass between forming the idea of an armored caterpillar and beginning his campaign to turn that conception into reality.[2]

Once Swinton's campaign began in earnest, the simple conversion of caterpillar tractors into tracked armored cars ran into a second complication. The people who took up the idea, most of whom were naval officers or officials of the Admiralty, could not leave it alone. Instead, they let their own imaginations soar. In February of 1915, the senior civilian at the Admiralty, a promising young politician by the name of Winston Churchill, wrote up a proposal for the building of 300-ton "landships." Armed with six 100mm (4-inch) naval guns, these behemoths were to be fourteen meters (forty-four feet) tall and thirty-three meters (107 feet) long, and. The "Landships Committee" formed to realize this dream quickly cut Churchill's juggernaut down to a more manageable size. Even so, the contracts placed with manufacturers a few weeks later called for vehicles that were four meters (thirteen feet) high and eleven meters (thirty-five feet) long. Six of these—aptly known "Big Wheels"—were to be propelled by gigantic wheels. The other twelve were to use "pedrails"—somewhat smaller wheels with flexible feet mounted all around the rim. While these monstrosities were being built, the Landships Committee entertained a more modest proposal for vehicles mounted on specially made caterpillar treads. At a time when most caterpillar tractors were about two meters (six feet) long, this vehicle was to have a length of eight meters (twenty-six feet).[3]

Explaining Churchill's vision is easy. He was a man with a well-documented fondness for "thinking big." Making sense of the large size of subsequent landships, however, requires a little more sympathy for the perspective of the designers. Most were either naval officers or naval engineers. Many were both. All had grown up in a world where it was easier to build a large machine than a small one, where the steam engines that propelled ships had been slowly evolving for a century but the internal combustion engine was still a relative novelty. Few, if any, had any experience of mass production. It was thus natural for such men to think in terms of custom-building a small number of wonder weapons rather than creating an army's worth of a trench-crossing equivalent of the Ford Model T.

As might be expected, the thirty-five-foot vehicles turned out to be extremely unwieldy, and, by the end of June, 1915, the Landships Committee began to focus its attention on the twenty-six-foot, twenty-two-ton design. The switch from a huge machine to one that was merely large also represented a shift in concept for employment. The thirty-five-foot landships had been seen primarily as a means of carrying a "storming party" of fifty men and three Maxim guns across "no man's land" and into a hostile trench. Any weapons mounted on the landship, whether a trench-cutting device, a device for removing barbed-wire obstacles, grenade throwers, or even a howitzer, took second place to the task of carrying infantry. The twenty-six-foot landship was, on the other hand, designed from the very start to be a gun carrier. Ideally, the committee agreed, the shorter model should mount a 75mm field gun. Failing that, another sort of weapon—perhaps a 47mm automatic anti-aircraft gun, the 2-pounder "pom-pom"—would be carried.[4] (In the end, the British tanks descended from the twenty-six-foot prototype ended up carrying various mixtures of machine guns and 57mm, 6-pounder naval guns, with the latter being chosen for no other reason than their immediate availability.)

The demise of the thirty-five-foot landship in the summer of 1915 presented the Landships Committee with a first-class opportunity to try a less risky approach to the problem of creating an armored cross-country vehicle. That is to say, they could have imported large numbers of Holt tractors, fitted armored car bodies to them, and sent them off to war. In 1915, however, the country that British strategists (particularly those of the Royal Navy) wanted to cross was not country of an ordinary sort. Rather, the terrain that interested them was that of the Belgian province of Flanders.

In 1915, as today, much of Flanders was low, flat, and wet. Hills were rare and the water table was very high. The rest of the ground, which ran in a wide "maritime belt" along the North Sea coast, was lower, flatter, and wetter. This was terrain that, in its natural state, could only be described as a marsh. Over the course of centuries, the people of Flanders had turned much of this marsh into farmland. In the process of doing so, they had created a dense network of dikes, locks, canals, and drainage ditches. In fact, a landship moving off-road in the "maritime belt" might face fifty or so obstacles of this sort for every mile traveled.[5]

It was thus that the twenty-six-foot landship became the direct ancestor of the first series of British tanks—the rhomboid Marks I through VIII that, in the last year of the war, would achieve fame at Cambrai and Amiens. As it turned out, vehicles of this series never spent much time in the "maritime belt" of Flanders. They thus rarely made use of their ability to cross dikes and drainage ditches. Indeed, by the time that the ability to cross wide ditches became an immediate problem for British tanks, it was solved in a way that was unrelated to the length of the tank. (A proportion of the tanks taking part in the Cambrai attack of 20 November 1917, carried *fascines*, bundles of wood bound with chains. When they approached a ditch, these dropped the fascines into it, thereby creating a crude bridge that tanks could cross.)

On 25 August 1914, one of the most creative military minds in the French army declared, "victory in this war will belong to the belligerent which is the first to put a canon on a vehicle capable of moving over all kinds of terrain."[6] On 1 December 1915, a few weeks after he had become aware of the British tank program, this officer, Colonel Jean Baptiste Estienne,[7] wrote a letter to the French General Headquarters proposing that the French army undertake a similar effort. In particular, he advocated the creation of a force of all-terrain armored vehicles; one large enough to assist 20,000 infantrymen in breaking through the full depth of a German defensive position. Armed with light artillery pieces, these vehicles would also serve to transport men, equipment and supplies across the forty kilometers or so that separated French assembly areas from the open terrain on the other side of German defensive positions.[8]

In sharp contrast to the documents setting up the "Landships Committee," Colonel Estienne's letter stressed the importance of building the fleet of all-terrain armored vehicles as soon as possible. This sense of urgency carried over into the building program that was begun, early in 1916, in response to Estienne's letter. One sure sign of the emphasis on speed of procurement was the decision to base the first two types of French tank on the chassis of the Holt tractor. Another was the absence of the bureaucratic hurdles usually placed in the way of new items of equipment for the French army. As a result, prototypes of the first French tank—the sixteen-ton Schneider—were ready for testing by early February of 1916.

The concept of employment for the Schneider tank was very much in keeping with the one presented in Estienne's letter of 1 December 1915. It was to serve as a means of transporting infantry units across no man's land as well as provide short-range artillery and machine-gun fire in support of those units. Unfortunately, the weight and bulk of the new tank's weapons (a short 75mm gun and two machine guns) were such that there was little room in the interior of the vehicle for passengers. Instead, both men and materiel were to travel behind the tanks, towed in purpose-built armored sleds. Even then, the Schneider was too big for either its chassis or its engine. It was thus much less nimble than it might otherwise have been.

While the tank program initiated and later run by Colonel Estienne was underway, another branch of the French army—the same "Automobile Service" that was in charge of French armored cars—was building a tank of its own. Though also based on the Holt chassis, this tank (the twenty-four-ton Saint Chamond) was larger (and thus even less maneuverable) than the Schneider. It was also armed with a more powerful weapon (a 75mm field gun of the type used by the French field artillery of the day).[9] It was thus closer to the weapon that Estienne imagined in August of 1914, rather than the one he described in December of the following year.

The French decision to overbuild the first two series of tanks had little to do with the ability to cross ditches. In fact, the combination of a large body and relatively small tracks made the St. Chamond tank extremely prone to becoming stuck in the very trenches it was designed to cross. Rather, the French desire to overload their Holt chassis was a function of their fascination with the 75mm field gun. More specifically, the fitting of a 75mm field gun, which was the largest piece of ordnance anyone would fit into a tank for more than two decades, reflected an idea that had been current in the French army in the years before the outbreak of World War I. This was the idea of "assault artillery."

Between 1908 and 1912, the Inspector of Artillery for the French army was a general by the name of Alexandre Percin. While in office, Percin worked hard to resist the trend towards the exclusive use of indirect fire techniques by the French field artillery. A portion of 75mm guns, Percin argued, should be used as "assault artillery" ("*artillerie d'assaut*"). Operating as single guns, pairs, and four-gun batteries, 75mm guns of the assault artillery would move forward with, or just behind, the infantry. While other field artillery units fired at more distant targets, the guns of the assault artillery would use direct fire to eliminate whatever hostile elements might stand in the way of the immediate progress of the men on foot. In other words, Percin wanted a portion of the French field artillery to perform the kind of service for the French infantry that 76mm trench mortars and infantry guns would later provide to the German infantry.

Unfortunately for Percin's concept, the onset of trench warfare toward the end of 1914 resulted in complete victory for the school of thought within the French army that wanted to devote all field guns within a division to the task of providing long-range fire from positions in defilade. One reason for this was an overall shortage of modern field guns. At a time when battle losses and the formation of new divisions were reducing the number of available field guns, the demand for long-range fire was growing by leaps and bounds. Another reason for the death of the assault artillery concept was the difficulty of moving the M1897 75mm field gun—which was the heaviest field gun of its class—over the kind of ground encountered in trench warfare. As a result, the few field guns employed as short-range, direct-fire weapons by the French army of World War I were obsolescent pieces that lacked modern recoil mechanisms. These latter field guns, moreover, were used exclusively as defensive weapons (a means of firing canister at attacking German troops who had crested a hill or turned a corner).[10]

At the very moment that Percin's concept of "assault artillery" seemed doomed to the dustbin of history, the mounting of 75mm field guns on the chassis of Holt tractors gave the idea a new lease on life. The same development also gave the French tank fleet one of its collective names: tank units were "units of assault chariots" (*unités de chars d'assaut*)" whereas the tank force as a whole was either the "special artillery" ("l'Artillerie Speciale") or the "assault artillery" (*l'Artillerie d'Assaut*). Unfortunately, the Holt tractor was not nearly powerful enough to reliably carry itself and twenty-odd tons of gun, armor, and crew across the shell-torn battlefield. Indeed, the Holt tractor was hard pressed to carry the much lighter superstructure of the Schneider tank. This was made painfully obvious to the French leadership when, on 16 April 1917, the Schneider tanks went into action for the first time against the enemy.

The location for the baptism of fire for the Schneider was the vicinity Berry-au-Bac, a town on the east bank of Aisne River, just south of the great ridge known as the Chemin des Dames. The ground was chosen for the tank attack because, unlike the terrain to the north, it was relatively flat. That is to say, French forces attacking against German positions on the Chemin des Dames would have to attack up steep hills. French forces fighting in the vicinity of Berry-au-Bac, however, had only to deal with a smoothly rising slope.

Some 120 Schneider tanks participated in the French attack of 16 April 1917. The lion's share took part in the attack of the army corps designated to make the main breakthrough that day. These eighty tanks were from five groups ("*groupes*") that had been temporarily organized into a task force ("*Groupement I de l'Artillerie Speciale*"). (A full-strength group was usually commanded by a captain and consisted of four batteries of four tanks each.) The other forty tanks formed a separate task force ("*Groupement II de l'Artillerie Speciale*") of two standard groups (of sixteen tanks each) and one understrength group (of only eight tanks.) This second *groupement* attacked in concert with an army corps making a supporting attack closer to the high ground of the Chemin des Dames.[11]

Following in the wake of a successful infantry assault against the German outpost line, the first *groupement* advanced slowly up a long gentle slope. Had it not been for the fierce preparatory bombardment by the French heavy artillery, the advance would have been an easy one. As it was, the French heavy howitzers had converted the forward edge of the first German defensive position—a belt more than 100 meters deep—into a chaotic jumble of shell holes, uprooted trees, and half-collapsed trenches. Many of the Schneiders became stuck in this self-inflicted tank trap. Those that avoided this fate were rarely able to move at their rated speed of six kilometers an hour.

The same bombardment that had done so much to hinder the forward movement of the tanks had done little to damage the German field artillery (both the guns themselves and the observation posts that controlled the fire). The first achievement of the German guns was to separate the French tanks from the infantrymen told to help guide them across the first German defensive position. These, provided at a rate of two platoons of infantry for each group of tanks, were so often driven to ground by German artillery fire that they soon lost contact with the tanks they were supposed to assist. The second achievement of the German guns was the systematic destruction of the immobile Schneiders. If there was any saving grace attributable to this process, it was its relatively leisurely pace. The German artillery pieces most in evidence in the destruction of the French tanks were the relatively slow-firing heavy howitzers (150mm and 210mm pieces firing very large—40 kilogram and 120 kilogram—shells).[12]

Forty-four tanks of the first *groupement* (more than half of the total) fell prey to the German artillery fire. Thirty-one of these caught fire and burned. The second *groupement* fared much worse. Thirty-three of its forty tanks were destroyed in the course of the attack of 16 April 1917. In human terms, the fact that most of the French tank crews left their vehicles before they started to burn meant that the butcher's bill was less than what might be expected from the catastrophic loss of sixty-four tanks. Even so, a full quarter of the effectives of the French tank force sent into battle on 16 April 1917—180 out of a total of 720 officers, non-commissioned officers and men—were either killed, seriously wounded, or reported missing in action that day.[13]

After the disaster of 16 April 1917, the French tanks stayed out of battle for six months. During this time, new tank units were formed, existing tank units were brought up to strength, and the St. Chamond tank took its place alongside the Schneider. This period also saw a major change in French strategy. Rather than attempting a decisive breakthrough (one that would lead to a resumption of mobile warfare) the French would limit their offensive ambitions to the taking of discrete pieces of terrain. They hoped this would allow them to accumulate tangible victories while rebuilding an army shattered by tactical failure, heavy losses, and widespread mutiny. The first of these offensives "with limited objectives," the offensive of 20 August, took place north of Verdun and resulted in the recapture of ground lost to the Germans in 1916. The second, the offensive of 23 October at Malmaison, was even more successful. In addition to attaining its stated goal—the reduction of a salient near the Chemin des Dames—the Malmaison offensive convinced the Germans to evacuate the Chemin des Dames itself.

It was at Malmaison that the French tanks made their second debut. This time, however, additional measures were taken to suppress the German field artillery. In particular, the density of the French artillery deployed in support of the attack at Malmaison (one artillery piece for every six meters of frontage) was nearly twice that of the offensive of 16 April (one artillery piece for every ten meters of frontage.) In addition to this, the French artillery at Malmaison contained a much higher percentage of modern weapons—particularly quick-firing heavy pieces—and was well supplied with poison gas (phosgene) shells. The latter were particularly well suited to the task of keeping the German gunners from bringing effective fire upon the attackers. Thanks to the success of this counter-battery effort, the second French employment of tanks was a complete success. Seventy-six tanks went into battle on the morning of 23 October 1917. By the end of the day, seventy-one of these tanks were still in the fight.[14]

The attack at Malmaison resulted in one of the most impressive French victories of the entire war. Not only did the French attackers take their objectives with minimum casualties, but they also managed to convince the Germans to evacuate the entire Chemin des Dames ridge. The writing was on the wall. Tanks were as dependent upon large numbers of guns and howitzers as the infantry of the day was. In the course of the last year of World War I, this not only involved the use of large amounts of poison gas to neutralize the German field artillery, but also the extensive use of smoke, high explosives, and shrapnel. On 15 August 1918, for example, each attacking infantry division in the French Tenth Army set aside a field artillery group of twelve 75mm field guns for the exclusive task of protecting tanks from anti-tank guns. As an aid in finding these antitank guns, each of these groups was provided with the services of an observation aircraft. In addition to this, the fire plans for the attack included the creation of heavy smoke screens in front of likely German observation posts.[15]

During the last four months of World War I, from 15 July to 11 August 1918, the French, British, and American armies conducted scores of operations on the model of the successful attack at Malmaison. At first, these American operations took place under French tutelage, with a great deal of assistance from French tanks and artillery. Later, as American soldiers graduated from the French school of methodical battle, they introduced some peculiarities of their own. One of the most important of these was the use of infantry accompanying guns (two-gun sections of horse-drawn 75mm field pieces attached to advancing infantry battalions) as a partial replacement for tanks.[16] Although their 18-pounder field guns were harder to move over broken terrain, many British commanders also got into the habit of attaching two-piece field gun sections to infantry battalions.[17]

In both the British and the American armies, the introduction of infantry accompanying batteries was a direct imitation of the contemporary German practice. It was also a result of one of the many paradoxes of the last few months of World War I—the precipitous drop in the number of tanks available to the British and American armies. In the British case, where tank production had failed to keep up with tank losses (both mechanical and combat), the drop in the number of tanks was absolute.[18] In the American case, the tank shortage was a relative one. Many American tank units were formed in 1918. However, the fact that American tank production had yet to begin made these units dependent upon French and British machines. This, in turn, ensured that the growth of the new American armored branch would fail to keep up with the explosive growth of the American Expeditionary Force as a whole. The French army also experienced an unmitigated shortage of medium tanks in 1918, but was preserved from sharing the fate of its American and British allies by the timely arrival of large numbers of a new type of armored fighting vehicle: the seven-ton Renault.[19]

How the new light tank fit in with the French art of battle is well illustrated by the Battle of Montdidier, a series of attacks that began on 8 August

1918. From the point of view of the field army that carried it out (the First Army of General Debeney), the French attack at Montdidier was part of an asymmetrical double envelopment; a larger maneuver designed to lever, rather than merely push, the Germans out of their position. This maneuver resembled a lopsided crab, with the larger claw being formed by the attacks of British Empire forces east of Amiens and the smaller provided by the French First Army. Below the level of the field army, however, the Montdidier attack consisted of a series of shallow, largely frontal attacks by whole army corps. Similarly, while a number of interesting measures, to include feints designed to induce the German artillery to unmask, had been ordered by the army commander, the attacks of subordinate echelons were somewhat predictable terrain-oriented attacks on the model of the previous year's attack at Malmaison.[20]

After a long and heavy artillery bombardment designed to tear holes in the German barbed wire and destroy the shelters that protected the German infantry, each attack would begin with a thick wall of artillery fire, creeping forward in accord with a centrally established timetable. Protected by this curtain of exploding shells and, when close to the enemy, by the assault fire of the three or four automatic rifles in each platoon, the infantry would advance at a walk in long, sparsely populated skirmish lines. When faced with determined resistance, which usually translated into a machine gun nest, infantry squads, half-platoons, and platoons would attempt local maneuvers. Fire from the automatic rifles and grenade launchers would pin the machine guns down, while men with hand grenades closed in for the kill.[21]

The role of the new light tanks at Montdidier was to bolster the firepower, close combat capability, and, most importantly, the morale of the infantry. When the infantry walked forward, a platoon of five Renaults would be mixed in with the three rifle companies of each attacking infantry battalion.[22] When the attack broke down into small-scale engagements, those tanks that were on the spot took part, either adding to the fire of the automatic rifles or attempting to run down the offending machine gunners. French tanks were thus less of a complementary arm that cooperated with the French infantry than a supplement that reinforced the actions of the men on foot. Thus, they were often and quite appropriately referred to as "accompanying tanks" (*chars d'accompagnement*).

Strangely enough, while the French expressed interest in the ability of tanks to help the infantry deal with machine guns, they paid little attention to what the infantry could do to protect tanks from attacks at close quarters. Though the means for carrying out such attacks—hand grenades bundled to form ball charges, explosives tied to the end of poles, crude antitank mines, flamethrowers, machine guns firing armor-piercing ammunition, and the antitank rifle—were all plentiful by 1918, the French focused on the threat posed by antitank guns. Moreover, the preferred means of dealing with these latter weapons was not infantry but artillery.[23] This, in turn, limited the depth of any tank attack (or, more precisely, any infantry and tank attack) to the reach of the available field artillery. In other words, even without significant enemy resistance, an attack by French infantry and tanks was limited to a depth of about five kilometers.[24]

In the years following the end of World War I, the Battle of Montdidier that captured the official imagination of the French army.[25] Writers of textbooks and professors at the *École Supérieure de Guerre* ignored maneuvers such as the trap sprung by the Fourth Army at Reims (15 July 1918) and the surprise attack at Soissons (18 July 1918).[26] Instead, they composed detailed paeans to the virtues of *la bataille conduite*, a methodical series of limited objective attacks. This vision of battle was very much in keeping with the material on hand in the 1920s and early 1930s. France finished World War I with a fleet of some 3,300 tanks, by far the largest in the world. Less than 10% of this arsenal consisted of first generation vehicles, such as the Schneider and St. Chamond tanks. The remainder of the fleet was composed of Renaults. As the larger vehicles were, for the most part, worn out, these little machines, barely capable of exceeding the pace of a man on foot, represented the lion's share of the tanks actually deployed by the French army in the 1920s.[27] In 1925 and 1926, Renaults were also the only French tanks to see combat (against the Berber partisans of Abd el-Krim in Morocco) during this period.[28]

Because of the intimate relationship between the Renault and the *poilu*, French tank units were, in the reorganization that followed World War I, assigned to the infantry. The immediate result of this reform was the transfer of cavalry and artillery officers, of whom many had been with tank units since 1916, back to their arms of origin. This contributed to the most important result of the subordination of tanks to the infantry, which was a decade in which the employment of tanks was hobbled by an extremely narrow view of their role on the battlefield.

That the development of French tanks escaped complete stagnation was largely resultant of the fact that responsibility for the design of tanks was assigned to an agency that was completely independent of the infantry.

Heavily influenced by General Estienne throughout the 1920s, this organization, the *Section Technique de Chars*, focused on what might be called "breakthrough tanks." These were relatively heavy vehicles, weighing twenty-five to fifty metric tons, capable of both breaking into the depths of the enemy's defensive system and of doing considerable damage once there.

Estienne's early conceptions for the employment of these breakthrough tanks, committed to paper as early as May of 1919, had little in common with the dominant French view of the tank as the fellow-traveler of the infantry. He envisaged a mechanized army of some 100,000 men, carried in 12,000 motor vehicles, and 4,000 of which would be tanks. The breakthrough tanks, which he allowed to weigh as much as one hundred metric tons, would advance,

> disdainful of detours, under the cover of night or perhaps a thick natural or artificial fog, wiping out all obstacles, tearing open houses. The armored infantry and the accompanying artillery follow, making full use of the road cut for them. The forward lines of the enemy are soon broken, and, voila, the rapid exploitation tanks leap forward, as cavalry once did, to achieve victory.[29]

Though Estienne failed to create this fully mechanized army, his vision of the breakthrough tank was partially realized in the form of the *Char B1*. Appearing in prototype in 1929 and as production models in 1934, the Char B1 was the most heavily armored tank to appear during the interwar period. Weighing between twenty-eight and thirty-one metric tons (the later version, the *Char B1 bis*, was heavier than the original version.), the Char B was proof against the antitank guns of its day. Its armament, consisting of a turret mounting both a 47mm antitank gun and a machine gun, and, in the bow of the tank, a 75mm low-velocity gun, was intended to give it the ability to deal with the full range of targets, both human and materiel, that it might encounter.[30]

The only area in which the Char B failed to conform to Estienne's vision was that of operational mobility. Estienne had wanted his mechanized army to be able to move to and from the battlefield as well as through it. He even argued that the force he imagined might be able to move as many as eighty kilometers in a single night. The Char B, unfortunately, had a voracious appetite for fuel. This meant that, at the end of a road march of fifty or so kilometers, a unit of such tanks would have to stop, rendezvous with refueling trucks, and refill their fuel tanks.[31]

From the point of view of the 1920s, when French doctrine assumed that tanks would travel to the battlefield on flatbed railroad cars and, once in action, make frequent stops while waiting for the artillery to catch up, the poor operational mobility of the Char B was of no concern. By the time the Char B was in serial production and French tank units were using the new tanks to replace the aging Renaults, the official French view of tanks had changed. The notion that tanks were the handmaiden of the infantry remained the central tenet of French tank doctrine, but the way in which tanks were to work with the infantry changed. That is to say, in addition to the traditional accompanying tanks there was to be a class of "tanks that maneuvered together" (*chars de manoeuvre ensemble*).

The definitive quality of tanks that maneuvered together was speed. This would allow units composed entirely of such tanks to range ahead of the infantry and strike the enemy where he was "weak, surprised, or disorganized." These tanks could also operate on an axis separate from that used by the infantry, to strike an exposed flank or divert attention from the main attack. In some situations, they would even play the role of Estienne's "rupture tanks," penetrating into the depths of an enemy position in order to complete a victory begun by the infantry and its slow-moving escorts.[32]

Despite some obvious borrowings from the "father of French armor," the concept of *chars de manoeuvre ensemble* was a far cry from Estienne's conception of a fully mechanized armored formation. Though there was some talk of forming ad hoc groups of two or three battalions, these tanks that would maneuver together would generally operate as battalions. Units of tanks that maneuvered together would, moreover, be subordinated to infantry divisions or army corps. This meant that their maneuver was purely tactical, aimed at solving the local problems faced by a division or corps rather than creating problems for the enemy army as a whole.[33]

While it might be argued that the major armies most influenced by French doctrine during the 1920s were those of the United States, Italy, and Argentina, only one country undertook the task of copying the French tank force of that era. That country was the Soviet Union, which began its "sincerest form of flattery" by trying to build its own version of the Renault light tank. Though that attempt failed, the idea that the Soviet infantry should be supported "in the French manner" persisted. This, in turn, led to the creation of two very different types of tank unit and programs to produce two very different types of tank.

To fulfill the role of light accompanying tanks—what Soviet tank theorists called "close support tanks"—the Soviet arms industry built copies of two British light tanks. The first of these, designated the T-26, was based on the Vickers "6-Ton A" light tank—(similar to the French Renault of World War I in all respects except speed). (The 6-Ton A could make up to twenty miles in an hour on a good road.) The second of the Soviet close support tanks, the T-27, was a facsimile of the three-ton Carden-Lloyd tankette. (This latter vehicle, with its very light armor and open-topped crew compartment, was also the direct ancestor of the German *Panzer I*.)

The Soviet versions of the French *chars de manoeuvre ensemble* were called "further support tanks." They were to strike out ahead of the main body of an attacking formation, with the aim of knocking out machine guns, infantry guns, and antitank guns located in the rear of the enemy's most forward trenches. To this end, the further support tank battalions were equipped with particularly well-armed vehicles. These could be up-gunned T-26 light tanks (with high-velocity 37mm or 45mm guns rather than twin machine guns), T-28 medium tanks (with 76.2mm guns) or even the monstrous five-turret, 54-ton T-35 heavy tanks. If there was any difference between the Soviet "further support tank" concept and the French idea of the *chars de manoeuvre ensemble* it was that the former focused their attention on a particular enemy capability while the latter were intended to take particular terrain objectives.[34]

Soviet tank theorists departed from the French model when, in the early 1930s, they created a third category of tanks—that of "distant action tanks." These had the mission of attacking targets in the rear of the enemy defensive array such as artillery batteries that had escaped Soviet counter-battery fire, headquarters, and supply depots. As these targets were both relatively soft and most distant from the starting point of an attack, the tanks detailed to attack them need not have been very well armed, but had to have both speed and a fair radius of action. It is thus not surprising that the tanks most closely associated with the concept of distant action tanks were those of the BT series. This was a sequence of tank models based upon the American Christie tanks.[35]

The tanks designed by J. Walter Christie in the late 1920s and early 1930s, were, by far, the fastest tanks of the interwar period. In an age when the average road speed of postwar models was in the vicinity of twenty miles per hour, various Christies were two or three times as fast. Their cross-country speed—less than ten miles an hour for the most up-to-date competitors and less than five miles an hour for the mechanical veterans of World War I—was over twenty-five miles per hour. This was far more speed than many contemporary observers thought a tank could make good use of. To many Soviet tank theorists, however, the Christie provided a golden opportunity.

How the three types of Soviet tank unit might cooperate in action was demonstrated in the large-scale maneuvers held at Minsk in 1936—the first Soviet maneuvers observed by large numbers of foreign dignitaries. The "Blue" side in these maneuvers comprised three infantry divisions, two cavalry divisions, five "distant action" mechanized brigades (BT tanks) and one "further support" tank brigade (T-28 medium tanks). The Red side also had three infantry divisions and two cavalry divisions (See Figure 3.1). The organization of Red forces, however, was slightly different, as was the allocation of mechanized brigades to Red formations. Two of the Red infantry divisions were each provided with an attached mechanized brigade. Two additional

Figure 3.1
Forces in Soviet Maneuvers of 1936

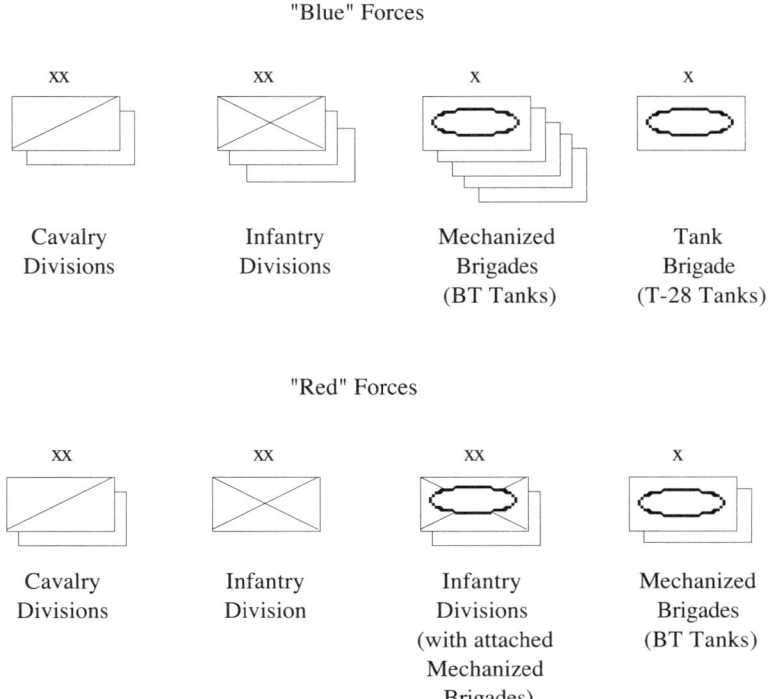

mechanized brigades, subordinated directly to the overall Red commander, and thus playing the role of army-level troops, were also included in the Red array. (The Red side thus had four "distant action" mechanized brigades but no "further support" tank brigade.)[36]

The "further support" tank brigade used in the 1936 Soviet maneuvers consisted entirely of four battalions of T-28 medium tanks. It was thus an all-tank unit, with no combat elements expected to go into battle in any vehicle other than a tank. The "distant action" mechanized brigades, on the other hand, were mixed units. Most consisted of three tank battalions (with BT tanks armed with 37mm guns), one light-tank battalion (with light tanks of an unspecified type), and a truck-borne machine-gun battalion. One of the mechanized brigades was a "motor mechanized brigade." It had only two tank battalions (also with BT tanks), one light-tank battalion, and two battalions of truck-borne machine gunners. Additional infantry, in the form of a small (430-man) infantry battalion, was at times provided to some of mechanized brigades. The men of these attached infantry battalions rode into battle on the outside of the tanks, with as many as seven men riding on a single vehicle.[37]

The actions of armored forces observed in the Soviet maneuvers of 1936 were very much in harmony with a remarkable document published that year. This manual was *PU-36*, a manual that replaced the previous edition of the Soviet field service regulations. Closely associated with the names of Mikhail Tukhachevsky, Viktor Triandafillov, and G. Isserson, *PU-36* promulgated a vision of battle in which the forces that destroyed enemy formations near the front were aided by smaller but more mobile forces that attacked the infrastructure far behind those formations.[38]

> The resources of modern defense technology enable one to deliver simultaneous strikes on the enemy tactical layout over the entire depth of his dispositions. There are now enhanced possibilities of rapid regrouping, of sudden turning movements, and of seizing the enemy's rear areas and thus getting astride his axis of withdrawal. In an attack, the enemy should be surrounded and completely destroyed.[39]

On the surface, this notion had much in common with the venerable German *Kesselschlacht*, the type of battle maneuver in which an enemy was simultaneously enveloped on both flanks and thus surrounded. A key difference between the German and Soviet ideas of surrounding and annihilating the enemy, however, lay in the domain of scale. As a rule, the Soviets tended to imagine operations that involved broader fronts, deeper penetrations, and more troops. For this reason, they had a greater need for the mobile forces that would exploit the breaches and close the ring. This, in turn, may have been the reason that they saw no contradiction between the employment of independent tank forces and independent cavalry formations that, while they contained tanks of their own, consisted largely of men who moved on horseback and fought on foot.[40]

In keeping with the theme of "having your cake and eating it too," Tukhachevsky and his colleagues made no attempt to limit the ways that Soviet commanders could employ their independent tank and cavalry formations. The phrasing of *PU-36* hints that independent cavalry formations would be a little less independent than independent armored formations. Nonetheless, both were judged capable of striking out for objectives far beyond the bulk of the enemy combat force as well as close cooperation with the main attack. Thus, the great dilemma faced by every leader of a successful German breakthrough of World War I was solved. The Soviet commander did not to decide whether to press forward for the chance of a greater reward or turn in to make a lesser victory more certain. Rather, he could simultaneously tighten the ring around the enemy and send his mobile forces on a *chevauchée* through the transportation, communications, and supply facilities so necessary to an army of that era.

The Soviet ability to field an armored force that could simultaneously support the traditional arms and conduct deep operations was made possible by the rapid pace at which the Soviet Union of the 1920s and 1930s converted itself into an industrial superpower. The cost of this transformation was horrendous. Millions of people lost their lives—as slave laborers, victims of engineered famines, and casualties of the collectivization of agriculture. The results of this brutal effort were, nonetheless, impressive. By 1940, the Soviet Union had, by a factor of more than five, the largest tank fleet in the world.[41]

4
IRON STEED

In addition to ending World War I with the largest arsenal of tanks in the world, the French army of 1919 also possessed the largest number of armored cars (twenty squadrons of twelve fighting vehicles each).[1] This was enough to provide each of the fifteen or so French horse cavalry brigades serving in Europe with an armored car squadron of its own and still have enough left over to police French territory, possessions and mandates in North Africa and the Levant.[2] The British, with a number of armored car units that hovered around eight for most of the 1920s, had the second-largest armored car force. Focused almost exclusively on internal security duties, British armored cars were often employed with considerable imagination. Nonetheless, no other army did so much to integrate the armored car into its way of war—particularly into the tactics of its cavalry formations—as did the French.[3]

The importance of armored cars to the French army of the 1920s is well illustrated by the fact that armored car units were the only type of units to emerge unscathed from the demobilization of 1919. Trench mortar batteries and many heavy artillery units were eliminated. The infantry, field artillery, and combat engineers were reduced to a fraction of their former strength, in relation to both their wartime organization and that of 1914. The horse cavalry was reduced somewhat. The armored car squadrons, however, suffered only a change in terminology.[4] Their numbers—some 240 combat vehicles—remained the same. Armored car units were also among the few units of the French army of the 1920s to be equipped with something other than hand-me-downs from World War I. The polyglot collection of hastily built machine-gun cars and cannon-armed trucks that had served for most of World War I were, in the immediate aftermath of the war, completely replaced by a purpose-built vehicle armed with both a rifle-caliber machine gun and a 37mm cannon.[5]

As was the case with the rest of the forces that were retained after the demobilization of 1919, the French army had a very clear idea of what it wanted from both its horse cavalry divisions and the armored car units within them. In the initial phase of war, the cavalry divisions would move rapidly to occupy forward positions. (If the enemy was Germany, these would be in the Rhineland, which French forces would occupy until 1930.) Eschewing all but the most local of offensive actions, the cavalry divisions would occupy these positions until relieved by infantry divisions. Once the infantry divisions were securely in place, the cavalry divisions would be pulled out of line and held in readiness to intervene in case of either crisis or opportunity. If the infantry divisions remained on the defensive, the cavalry divisions would serve as a reserve of firepower, ready to fill any gap that might be torn in the front lines. If the infantry divisions attacked, the cavalry divisions would protect their flanks, permitting the infantry and artillery to focus, without interruption, on the methodical destruction of enemy positions.

While the cavalry division was on the march to its forward positions, the armored cars served as an advanced guard for the rest of the formation. When they reached the forward positions, the armored cars organized a line of outposts, holding the ground while other elements moved forward. After the other elements of the cavalry division arrived in the outposts and had settled into proper defensive position, the armored cars pulled back to form a division reserve, holding itself in readiness to fill any gaps that might be torn in the line of outposts by an overly ambitious enemy. In short, French armored car units provided the same sort of service to cavalry formations that the cavalry formations provided to French field armies.

In the course of the 1920s, the relative importance of armored car squadrons within the French army grew considerably. One reason for this was the high quality of their services in the Riff War of 1925 to 1926, where they played a key role in the defeat of Abd el-Krim, a Berber leader who had earlier driven the Spanish out of most of western Morocco. Another was a decline in the size of the French horse cavalry. Between 1923 and 1930, the number of European (that is to say, recruited from Frenchmen and serving in Europe) horse cavalry regiments in the French army was cut by more than one-third, dropping from forty-three to twenty-seven. In 1928, the number of horse cavalry regiments in each French cavalry division was reduced from six to four and, as a consequence, the number of horse cavalry brigades from three to two.[6] A similar change took place in Great Britain. The thirty horse cavalry regiments of the British army of 1920 had been cut to twenty-two in 1922 and twenty in 1928. In that latter year, the number of saber squadrons in each of the surviving regiments was reduced from three to two.[7] This latter reduction made the loss of British horse cavalry units in the 1920s (fifty squadrons) even greater than the loss of French horse cavalry units (forty-eight squadrons) over the same length of time.[8]

One powerful contributor to the reduction in the number of horse cavalry units—as well as a concurrent reduction in horse-drawn artillery, heavy-weapons, engineer, and transport units in European armies in the 1920s—was a growing shortage of suitable horses. This was most evident in Great Britain, where the loss of Ireland, the mechanization of agriculture, and the motorization of urban transport wreaked havoc with the supply of horses of the types most useful to the cavalry and field artillery.[9] By 1934, keeping a modest army of twelve infantry divisions in the field (a fraction of the British army that fought in the last three years of World War I) would have required that the British army import somewhere between 6,500 and 8,000 horses every month from places like South America.[10]

The internal combustion engine also seems to have been the cause of a horse shortage in Germany, where the rapid restoration of the horse population to its prewar levels was followed by an equally impressive drop in the equine birth rate. After 1926, Germany's horses were not only declining in numbers, but were getting older as well.[11] A similar phenomenon took place in the United States, where the horse population peaked in 1920 (at 25,000,000) and, over the course of the next twenty years, declined to some 56% of that number (14,000,000).[12] Even on the vast steppes of the Soviet Union, so recently the scene of great cavalry battles, the number of horses was dwindling rapidly. Between 1929 and 1935, popular response to the extraordinarily brutal collectivization of agriculture reduced the total number of horses in the USSR by more than a half.[13] Unlike Great Britain, however, of Germany, the United States, and the USSR, none of them was compelled to motorize. Despite considerable decline, the horse populations of these countries were large enough to support both peacetime armies and all but the most ambitious of mobilization plans.

As late as 1928, a semiofficial German manual on the subject of higher tactics contained a design for ideal infantry and cavalry divisions that were not only larger than the infantry and cavalry divisions then serving in Germany's army, but were also much more dependent on horse transport. As these "modern" (*Neuzeitliche*) divisions were richly provided with aircraft, heavy artillery, antiaircraft guns, and a high proportion of modern heavy weapons, it is hard to ascribe this proportional decrease in motor transport to Luddite sentiments. Rather, the reason for the decrease in the number of motorcycles, cargo trucks, personnel carriers, motorized medical units, and mobile workshops seems to have been the recognition that, in places (like East Prussia or Poland) where a Germany army was likely to fight, fodder for horses was far easier to find than gasoline. The few internal combustion engines a German division could manage to feed, therefore, were to be devoted to such indispensable tasks as moving the heavy artillery.[14]

Such concerns notwithstanding, the 1920s saw two major steps in what was then called the "mechanicalization" of horse cavalry. The first was subtle, and took place without much debate or fanfare. This was the increasing use of trucks, cars, and motorcycles to carry heavy weapons, supplies, communications equipment, headquarters, and messengers. Such vehicles replaced pack animals and horse-drawn wagons, but posed no threat to the "real cavalrymen"—those who rode into battle on individual chargers. Indeed, motor vehicles used this way allowed horse soldiers a partial return to a previous era, for the motor vehicles carried the heavy weapons, ammunition, and radios that would otherwise have to be carried by horses, mules, or carts.[15] A similar evolution took place in the non-cavalry units of cavalry divisions and corps. The motorization of wagon trains, headquarters, signal units, engineer units, and, in particular, field artillery, allowed cavalry formations to march at the pace of a lightly burdened horse rather than a long column of horse-drawn wagons. The second step in the replacement of animal-power by machine-power—the complete mechanization of certain horse cavalry units—was much harder for contemporary observers to miss.

The first major power to actually convert active-duty, horse cavalry units into units armed with armored fighting vehicles was Great Britain.[16] The process of conversion began in 1928, with the temporary attachment of armored car companies of the Royal Tank Corps to two horse cavalry regiments. Over the course of the next two years, the men of the armored car companies transferred both their skills and (eventually) their vehicles to the cavalrymen. This was done one squadron at a time, with the first squadron converted being the machine-gun squadron, and "saber" squadrons continuing to serve as such until their time came to give up their horses. As reported by the commanding officer of one of these regiments (the 12th Royal Lancers), the process was a relatively smooth one. Only a small number of men, some of whom were senior noncommissioned officers with one foot in the nineteenth century, lacked the mechanical aptitude needed to make the transition from horseman to armored car driver, gunner, or radio operator.[17]

Not to be outdone by their neighbors across the Channel, the French followed suit in 1929 by mechanizing some of their own cavalry regiments. However, as they were already richly provided with armored car units, they recast five of their horse cavalry regiments as *bataillons de dragons portés*. (This might be translated as "battalions of dragoons carried in motor vehicles.") Though somewhat smaller than contemporary infantry battalions, these "dragoon" units were armed with the same sort of weapons (rifle-grenade launchers, automatic rifles, machine guns, mortars and anti-tank guns) and expected to do most of their fighting on foot. It is thus not surprising that these new units were initially used to replace the bicycle battalions that had been part of each French cavalry division for most of the decade following the end of World War I.[18]

At the time the *bataillons de dragons portés* were formed, the French military authorities made plans to provide them with cross-country infantry carriers. Indeed, it was the promise of these vehicles that undermined the main contemporary argument against the further motorization of cavalry—that horses were much less road-bound than the armored cars and other motor vehicles of the time. Most of the prototypes of the vehicles were of the half-track variety. (Thanks to recent expeditions in which intrepid French explorers had crossed the Sahara and Gobi deserts in half-track trucks, these hybrids enjoyed a great deal of interest in the late 1920s and early 1930s.) A few of the proposed cross-country vehicles used the equally novel concept of six-wheel drive. Until these were manufactured in sufficient numbers, however, the "dragoons" had to make due with trucks having very limited off-road ability.[19] More immediate gratification came in the form of motorcycles. Equipped for the most part with sidecars capable of carrying either men or heavy weapons, these motorcycles were used to transport one of the two or three rifle squadrons of each battalion.

Throughout the 1920s, the French cavalry division had been the most modern in the world. This, however, was a matter of quantity rather than of quality. Most European cavalry divisions of the day had a handful of armored cars (somewhere in the vicinity of six to twelve combat vehicles). The French led the pack with thirty-six *autos-mitrailleuses*. The creation of the *dragons portés* allowed the French cavalry division to maintain this position as the most modern or, at the very least most motorized cavalry division in the world for several more years. It also represented a qualitative difference. The *dragons portés* were not, as armored car units had been, an auxiliary to horse cavalry. Rather, each one was a reasonable substitute for a complete brigade of horse-cavalry, with a slightly smaller number of rifle squads (for holding outposts) and a similar supply of automatic weapons (for serving as a mobile reserve of firepower.)[20] "Units of dragoons carried in cross-country vehicles," wrote the anonymous author of the first paragraph of the provisional manual for these new units, "are, like the other subdivisions of the cavalry arm, characterized by firepower combined with mobility."[21]

The next step in the mechanicalization of the French cavalry division took place—on paper at least—with the design of the "Type Armée Moderne 1932" tables of organization and equipment. This was the first cavalry division in which the motorized elements (consisting of two battalions of *dragons portés*, two battalions of field artillery, one battalion of engineers, and a motorized reconnaissance battalion in trucks, motorcycles, and armored cars) dwarfed the muscle-powered ones. This disproportion was not only a matter of numbers of men and weapons, but of "footprint" as well. While the column of march formed by the two horse cavalry brigades of the 1932 cavalry division took up eleven and one-half kilometers of road space, the motorized combat units took up fifty-two kilometers, or nearly five times as much.[22] Some contemporary French military experts saw a great deal of tactical flexibility in this sort of organization. Others, particularly those concerned with what is now called operational mobility, saw a Frankenstein's monster made up of inherently incompatible parts. At the very least, the division commander would often be forced to move in two echelons, with the horsed brigades lagging far behind the motorized elements.[23]

Despite the inherent difficulty of marrying substantial motorized elements with horse cavalry, the introduction of *dragons portés* and other gasoline-powered elements to the French cavalry division sparked a continent-wide fashion for similar formations. In the course of the mid-1930s, Austria, Bulgaria, Czechoslovakia, Hungary, and Romania formed "fast" divisions of this sort, with those of Austria and Czechoslovakia having the lowest proportion of horse soldiers to gasoline-powered ones.[24] In other countries, principally Germany, Poland, and the United States, such formations were the object of serious study. As might be expected from the emphasis that German military thinking placed on operational mobility, most German military writers tended to dismiss the concept as unworkable. The idea got a much better reception in both Poland and the United States, places where French military ideas were often warmly received and the devotees of horse cavalry were particularly well placed in military hierarchies.[25]

The creation of the *dragons portés* took place at a time when France as a whole was increasingly anxious about its defense. With an increasingly powerful Soviet Union on its eastern border, Poland was no longer the counterweight to Germany that it had once been. Germany was growing bolder in its attempts to overcome, by a combination of diplomacy, thinly veiled preparations for expansion, and various secret projects, the limitations of the Treaty of Versailles. Worst of all, the number of young men becoming available for military service in France was about to shrink considerably, from 226,000 in 1934 to an average of 136,000 for the years 1935 to 1939. (This was a result of World War I, when men who would otherwise have been home fathering children were fighting and dying in the trenches.)[26]

The best-known reaction to the military crisis faced by France in the early 1930s was the construction of the Maginot Line, the much-maligned string of ultramodern forts along the Franco-German border. Far less famous, but no less central to the plan to overcome the change in the strategic environment, was a major rewriting of the plans for the mobilization and deployment of the French army. The central idea behind this reform was that the covering role (*couverture*) previously performed by the cavalry divisions, alpine troops, and units already located on the frontier would, in the future, be performed by a much larger force.[27] Where this would come from was, throughout this period, a matter of some debate. Some military writers advocated a covering force (*force de couverture*) made up entirely of professionals, whether they were native Frenchmen, North Africans, or Foreign Legionnaires.[28] A few wanted to use the entire force of men doing their twelve, eighteen, or twenty-four months of national service. Most wanted to use an even larger force, composed of both the active army and the youngest (and thus most recently trained) classes of reservists.[29] The common denominator in all of these plans, however, was the realization that this force would have to start taking up its positions in—or perhaps even on the other side of—the frontier regions of France within hours of receiving its orders.[30]

The introduction of the new covering force in the early 1930s coincided with two significant events. The first was a great increase in the level of official interest in the creation of entirely motorized divisions and army corps.[31] The second was an ambitious program to extend and improve the road network of Metropolitan France, which was already the most dense (at 120 kilometers of road per 100 square kilometers of territory) and most modern in the world.[32] Whether these were serendipitous or explicitly linked is hard to determine. What is clear is the strong logical connection between the great expansion of the covering force and a quantum leap in the motorization of the French army that took place in the early 1930s. Motorized formations of the covering force, after all, would be free of many of the tasks that had, in the past, delayed the deployment of muscle-powered units. These included the requisitioning of horses, the loading and unloading of trains, and long marches made at the pace of a walking man. Motorizing the covering force also freed the French rail network to do other things. (These included aiding the mobilization of the mass army of reservists and the gearing up of French war industries, both of which were essential to the war of rapid attrition called for in French doctrine.)

French soldiers got a preview of what entirely motorized formations might look like in 1932, at maneuvers conducted in the vicinity of Mailly. In these maneuvers, a fully motorized infantry division engaged in mock battle against a cut-down mechanized cavalry formation. The former was a regular infantry division (six battalions of infantry, five battalions of field artillery, and one of reconnaissance troops) that had traded all of its horses, bicycles, and horse-drawn vehicles for cars, trucks, buses, tractors, motorcycles, and a handful of armored cars. Apart from that, it was a perfectly ordinary French infantry division that was expected to fight in much the same way as other French infantry divisions of the day. The latter consisted of two or three battalions of *dragons portés*, one battalion of tanks, and one battalion of experimental *autos-mitrailleuses* on half-tracked chassis.[33] It was the kernel of a very different sort of division, one that would represent a significant departure from the way French soldiers had been thinking about cavalry, motorization, and tanks for the fifteen years. This new type of formation was the "light mechanized division" (*Division Légère Mécanique*).

From its inception to its untimely end in the disaster of June 1940, the French light mechanized divisions lived a double life. The prosaic argument for their existence fit well with the Cartesian outlook of most French military officers. They were, many argued, nothing more than the cavalry counterpart to the motorized infantry divisions then being formed. As such, they performed the same sort of services for fully motorized infantry that the cavalry divisions provided for the rest of the infantry divisions. (Like most infantry divisions of the time, these were moved by a combination of foot marches, bicycles, horse-drawn wagons, and motor vehicles.) A handful of French and foreign commentators, however, noted that this strict correlation did not stand up to detailed scrutiny. This was particularly true for German observers, who saw the light mechanized division as a means for conducting military operations that were far more ambitious than a mere dash to occupy a line of combat outposts.

The artillery, engineers, and service elements of the light mechanized division were very similar or even identical to their counterparts in the standard French cavalry divisions of the day. The *dragons portés* were similar in quality, but provided in larger numbers, with most tables of organization providing three or four battalions.[34] Two elements—the discovery regiments (*régiments de découverte*) and combat regiments (*régiments de combat*)—were provided with both equipment and operating concepts that were entirely new. The discovery regiments were long-range reconnaissance units, intended to travel fifty or more kilometers ahead of the main body of the light mechanized division. Their equipment consisted of particularly fast armored cars (the *autos-mitrailleuses de découverte* or AMD) and—to occupy bridges and other defiles along the path of the division—motorcycles. The combat regiments were units equipped with fast fighting tanks, of a sort that were entirely new to the French army. Because French law placed all tanks (*chars*) under the control of the Infantry, these new tanks were officially designated "combat armored cars" (the *autos-mitrailleuses de combat* or AMC).

While the French cavalry had originally considered using half-tracked armored cars as *autos-mitrailleuses de combat*, by 1935 they had settled on what would turn out to be the best French tank of the era. This was the SOMUA S-35, a tank that was better than contemporary French infantry tanks in every way (speed, armor, and armament) and inferior to the other armored vehicles of the light mechanized division only when it came to speed. As the events of 1940 would prove, the SOMUA was also a match for contemporary German tanks. Its armor was such that rounds from the principle German tank guns of the day (the 20mm gun on the Panzer II and the 37mm gun on the Panzer III) would bounce off. Its armament, a high-velocity 47mm gun, was capable of penetrating the armor on any German tank in production at the time. The only drawback of this vehicle—one that would prove its downfall—lay in the realm of human factors. While the Germans put three men in the turret of the Panzer III and IV tanks, the French put only one man in the turret of the SOMUA. Serving simultaneously as commander, loader, and gunner, this man often found himself overwhelmed by events, and much less able than his enemies to simultaneously make sense of his situation, aim the main gun, and keep it fed with ammunition.[35]

Had they been provided in small numbers, the *autos-mitrailleuses de combat* might easily be interpreted as an auxiliary to the *dragons portés*, weapons analogous to the infantry tanks that played such a central role in the tactics of contemporary French infantry units. They would thus be a means of adding the ability to capture defended terrain to the existing tactical repertoire of the *dragons portés*. (Such, after all, was the intended role of the handful of *autos-mitrailleuses de combat* slated for eventual assignment to each of the hybrid cavalry divisions.)[36] There were, however, far too many *autos-mitrailleuses de combat* (anywhere from two to four battalions-worth) in the light mechanized division for this to be their primary role. Indeed, as the light mechanized division evolved in the course of the late 1930s, the ratio of battalions of *autos-mitrailleuses de combat* to those of *dragons portés* increased considerably, from 2:4 in 1935 to 4:3 in 1939.[37] When combined with the fact that the organization of the *dragons portés* made explicit provision for the attachment of tanks from outside of the division, these numbers suggest that the light mechanized divisions had the potential to be much more than fully motorized versions of contemporary hybrid cavalry formations.[38]

This was evident to German observers, who described units of *autos-mitrailleuses de combat* as *Panzertruppen* and saw in the light mechanized division a powerful tool for waging their own particular brand of warfare. Even when the SOMUA tanks were diluted with a substantial admixture of substantially inferior H-35 two-man tanks, each *régiment de combat* was, at least on paper, more than a match for a contemporary German tank regiment was. In May of 1940, for example, a German tank regiment had, on average, thirty Panzer I tanks, forty-two Panzer II tanks, fifteen Panzer III tanks, and fourteen Panzer IV tanks.[39] The *régiment de combat* had forty-eight SOMUA tanks and forty-seven H-35 tanks. Though the German regiment had more tanks overall (101 to 95), the French had forty-eight tanks with guns that could effectively penetrate the armor of all German tanks. The Germans, however, had only fourteen tanks with guns that could effectively penetrate the armor of all French tanks.[40] This powerful advantage, however, seems to have been lost on most French soldiers of the time. Still tied to an overall doctrine that viewed the light mechanized division as little more than a fast-moving set of portable outposts, they tended to view the *autos-mitrailleuses de combat* as little more than a means of providing backup to these outposts. This would, more often than not, take the form of local counterattacks in the style of the *bataillons de chars de manoeuvre ensemble*. This second generation of French infantry tanks, while freed from direct participation in the infantry firing line, were still restricted to short-range attacks against pre-determined terrain objectives.

The French doctrine for the employment of the light mechanized divisions was faithfully executed in the second week of May 1940, when two *Divisions Légères Mecaniques* were sent forward into Belgium as part of a covering force. The *dragons portés* set up their line of outposts in areas that had been previously occupied by the long-range armored cars and motorcyclists of the *régiments de découverte*. When German reconnaissance troops attacked these outposts, the *régiments de combat* counterattacked, often inflicting great damage on the attackers. Encounters between *régiments de combat* and their German counterparts, on the other hand, were not as one-sided as a cold comparison of armored protection and armor-piercing armament would suggest. The Germans discovered that, given enough time, there were other ways to deal with a SOMUA than to penetrate its armor. In particular, a hail of projectiles fired by the semiautomatic 20mm gun of the Panzer II tank often convinced French tank crews to either abandon their SOMUAs or surrender outright.[41] The necessary time to do this was inadvertently made available by the overworked French tank commanders in their *monoplace* turrets. Trying to do the work of three men in extraordinarily trying circumstances, these young officers and NCOs not only missed opportunities to inflict damage on the Germans but also were often unable to properly deal with direct threats to their vehicles.[42]

5

THE THIRD WAY

As long as the tank was limited to the speed of a walking man, it was doomed to remain little more than an auxiliary to the infantry and a supplement to the artillery. The advent of the fast tank at the beginning of the 1920s created new possibilities. These included the possibility of tactical maneuver (such as that of a tank battalion working within the framework of an infantry division) and that of grand tactical maneuver (such as that of a tank brigade working in cooperation with an infantry division or army corps.) In the period between 1920 and 1935, the French army officially adopted the first of these possibilities, while the British army incorporated the second into its force structure and policies. At the same time, neither the French nor the British were willing to push the fast tank to the next higher level of maneuver—that of grand operations of direct strategic significance. This achievement was left to the Germans and the Soviets.

The reason that both German and Soviet officers were able to think of the fast tank as a tool for grand operations was a simple one. In contrast to the French and British, who divided the art of war into strategy and tactics, the Germans and Soviets had already begun to think in terms of an intermediate level of war—an arena in which the definitive activity was the maneuver of entire armies. As early as the 1890s, the German military theorist Sigismund von Schlichting had begun to use the adjective *operativ* to describe this level, which corresponded to what the Swiss student of Napoleonic warfare, Antoine Jomini, had called "grand operations." By the 1920s, the concept of the "operational level of war"—the arena within which generals practiced "operational art"—had found its way into Soviet doctrine. The Germans of the same decade, who lacked the desire to condense the art of war into formal doctrine, had nonetheless managed to make this idea part of their way of thinking about land warfare.

In the German case, the context for action at the operational level of war had been set by the peace that ended World War I. With its ability to field forces severely constrained by war weariness, economic exhaustion, and the Treaty of Versailles, Germany found itself faced with two great enemies. In the west, France boasted the most modern armed forces in Europe, with great fleets of tanks, trucks, aircraft, and heavy artillery. In the East, a young and vigorous Poland masked the poverty of its arsenal with laudable courage and deplorable aggression. The horrible price that France paid for victory in World War I made a French invasion of Germany quite unlikely. The Poles, on the other hand, had proved throughout the 1920s that they were willing to pounce upon any neighbor who displayed the slightest weakness.[1]

Because of the great numerical advantage enjoyed by the Poles, few German soldiers of the 1920s entertained notions of engaging them in open battle. Rather, the Germans planned to use what they called delaying resistance (*hinhaltende Widerstand.*)[2] The strategic purpose of this large-scale delaying operation was to prevent defeat—defined as the destruction of the main body of the German army in the field or the capture of a vital part of Germany—for long enough to allow some outside force to intervene on Germany's behalf.[3] Within this framework of delay, divisions and corps would defend certain areas, conduct local delaying operations, or even carry out spoiling attacks and other small-scale offensive actions.

The infantry and cavalry divisions designed for this sort of fighting consisted of both traditional (muscle-powered) units and motorized units, with a proportion of about six muscle-powered battalions for every battalion in trucks.[4] The latter carried out their actions within the framework established by the former. In particular, the motorized minority served as a mobile reserve for intervention at times and places where the muscle-powered majority was in crisis (what the Germans would later call a *Brennpunkt*) or where they traditional forces had created an opportunity for decisive action (a *Schwerpunkt*.) This might take the form of an independent attack against the flanks or rear of an enemy force, the rapid occupation of an important piece of terrain, or the rapid reinforcement of units already engaged.[5]

Even if the Treaty of Versailles had allowed the German army of the 1920s to have tanks of the type used in World War I, they would not have been able to play much of a role in battles of this sort. This is not to say that there was little interest in tracked armored fighting vehicles in the German army of the 1920s. On the contrary, if the literature on the subject is any indication, a large number of German officers followed tank developments in other countries with great interest. This was not merely because of the strong possibility that any invading army would have tanks of its own, but because of the growing belief that tanks would one day possess the mechanical characteristics that would make them useful in delaying resistance and other forms of operational maneuver.[6]

While waiting for this important technical development to take place, the Germans followed three separate but parallel paths. The first of these consisted of open inquiry, conducted by means of books and magazine articles, into tanks and the best way to use them. The second was a semi-clandestine program—officially nonexistent but evident to most foreign military observers at the time—to create combat units that used vehicles and weapons other than tanks. The third was a top-secret enterprise, conducted with the help of Sweden and the Soviet Union, to provide both prototype tanks and trained officers for future tank units.

Open discussion of armored warfare in the German Army began in earnest in 1924, with the publication of a ninety-three-page book by a young veteran of World War I, Ernst Volckheim. Volckheim's book, *The Tank in Modern War*, began with a somewhat conventional evaluation of the tanks that had been built since 1916. Contemporary tanks, he wrote, were primarily useful in trench warfare. Light tanks were particularly valuable in beating back the counterattacks that, to the Germans of the time, had been an inevitable part of any attempt to hold ground in the last three years of World War I. Heavy tanks could serve as a partial substitute for heavy artillery, facilitating the early phases of an attack. The experience of World War I had shown, however, that heavy tanks had trouble keeping up with an attack that had progressed from breakthrough to exploitation.

Though clearly enthusiastic about the long-term potential of the tank, Volckheim was concerned about the effect that overdependence on tanks might have on the infantry. He did not, for example, want to adopt the French position that infantry was incapable of assaulting prepared defenses without the aid of tanks. In this, Volckheim was very much in harmony with the mainstream of contemporary German military opinion. The experience of the spring offensives of 1918 had convinced most German soldiers that the German army already possessed the means of breaking into a well-defended trench system and moving rapidly through it and the line of artillery pieces behind it to get to "the green fields beyond." Where the German art of war was in need of help was in the next phase of attack—the exploitation of tactical victory in time to prevent the defeated enemy from establishing a new line of defense.

Volckheim began to depart from conventional thinking when he began to contemplate the types of tanks that might soon become available. He looked forward, with considerable accuracy, to tanks that were capable of operating at night, less limited by terrain, impervious to poison gas, and armed with a weapon capable of knocking out an enemy tank. He also predicted a time when heavier tanks would have the virtues then associated exclusively with the latest models of light tanks. In particular, he saw in the early versions of the American Christie tank the seeds of a future vehicle that would combine heavy armor and powerful armament with greatly enhanced speed, range, and maneuverability.[7]

Like so many denizens of the realm of intellectual provenance, the question of whether Volckheim's ideas shaped the ideas of contemporary German soldiers or merely reflected them is a slippery one. What is certain is that Volckheim's views on the best way to develop an armored force for Germany were very much in harmony with the opinions of many German military leaders of the 1920s and 1930s. In particular, Volckheim's belief that the dichotomy between speed and armor was a temporary phenomenon was in keeping with the way that the interwar German army laid the foundation for its armored formations. While waiting for engine, suspension, and transmission technology to mature to the point where well-armored, powerfully armed tanks could keep up with lighter vehicles, the German army focused its attention on the other elements of the armored force. These other elements—which would provide the majority of fighting units in any fully mechanized division or corps—were motorized infantry, long-range armored cars, motorcycle troops, and motorized antitank troops.

The framework for the development of the "other-than-tank" motorized combat units of the German army was provided by a unique organization known as the *Kraftfahrtruppen*. Usually translated as "motor transport troops," the term *Kraftfahrtruppen* might more accurately be rendered as "motor driving troops" or "motorized troops." The carriage of men and supplies was, to be sure, an important function of the *Kraftfahrtruppen*. It was not, however, the only one. An official table of organization for the *Kraftfahr* battalion of an infantry division in 1928, for example, would have shown a unit of two motorcycle platoons, three armored truck platoons, five motor transport platoons, two platoons of tanker-trucks, and two mobile workshops. (There was no permanent company organization within the *Kraftfahr* battalion of the 1920s. Rather, there were two self-contained company headquarters, each of which was capable of commanding a task force made up of several platoons.)[8] A more candid view of *Kraftfahr* units—one that showed the elements that had been forbidden by the Treaty of Versailles—would have uncovered platoons devoted to the employment of antitank guns and armored cars. Indeed, in the course of the late 1920s the classic motor transport platoons of the *Kraftfahr* battalions were increasingly displaced by these clandestine elements. In October of 1929, the chief of Organization Branch (*Organisationsabteilung*) of the thinly disguised General Staff (*Truppenamt*) issued a warning order to the commanding officers of the *Kraftfahr* battalions. As soon as the international situation permitted, the order stated, the *Kraftfahr* battalions were to reorganize themselves as combat units. Instead of a collection of legitimate and illicit platoons, the reformed *Kraftfahr* battalions would consist of four companies—one of armored trucks, one of motorcycles, one of towed antitank guns, and one of armored fighting vehicles (*Kampfwagen*). By the time that Adolf Hitler took power in Germany in January of 1933, this reorganization was well underway. Four months later, the conversion of the motor transport battalions into combat units was officially recognized by a secret order changing their nomenclature. Henceforth, the *Kraftfahrtruppen* (motorized troops) would be known as the *Kraftfahrkampftruppen* (motorized combat troops) and the *Kraftfahrabteilung* (motorized battalion) in each infantry division as the *Kraftfahrkampfabteilung*—(motorized combat battalion).[9]

Like other soldiers of the interwar period, the Reichswehr officers had initially tended to view antitank guns as an add-on to existing infantry and cavalry units. That is to say, antitank guns were included with the machine guns and mortars assigned to battalions and regiments. In 1923, this attitude took concrete shape in the form of a request to industry for the design for a dual-purpose infantry support weapon. Provided with two separate barrels, this weapon would be able to serve as both a light infantry gun and an antitank gun. In the first mode, it would fire 76mm mortar shells at low velocities. (In this respect, the proposed design was a further development of the 76mm light trench mortar of World War I, which had been modified in 1918 to permit direct fire at short ranges.) In the second mode, the dual-purpose gun would fire 37mm shells at much higher velocities.

In 1925, the German infantry and antitank guns went their separate ways. Though one could (on the margin) do the job of the other, each was a different weapon with distinct technical characteristics. The infantry gun went on to become a short-range 75mm howitzer, several of which were eventually assigned to the infantry gun company of each infantry regiment. The antitank gun became a small and handy 37mm weapon, capable of being hidden in terrain and served by a crew that was either lying down or protected by a trench. At first, the German army planned to produce two versions of this gun—a horse-drawn version for the infantry and cavalry and a motor-drawn version for the (still secret) antitank units of the *Kraftfahrtruppen*. While the former were to be deployed in platoons of two or three guns, each of which was to assigned to an infantry battalion or horse cavalry regiment, the latter were to be concentrated in powerful antitank reaction forces belonging to division, corps, and army commanders.[10]

The concept for the antitank reaction forces was that of a gladiator's net. The reaction force, kept in reserve until a concentration of hostile tanks showed itself, moved rapidly into positions that would allow it to ambush the hostile tanks. (To use the German terminology of the time, they were *Schwerpunktartig eingesezt*—"sent into action in a way that allowed them to focus their strength against the center of gravity of the enemy force.") In keeping with this concept, the reaction forces were organized as antitank battalions (variously known as *Kampfwagenabwehrabteilungen* or *Panzerabwehrabteilungen*). Each of these battalions had three companies of twelve antitank guns and a reconnaissance platoon. The task of this last named unit was to locate the concentration of enemy tanks in time for the antitank guns to move into their ambush positions.

During the first expansion of the Reichswehr in 1934 (the breaking up of the seven permitted infantry divisions in order to provide the cadre for twenty-one infantry divisions), there were not enough of the new antitank battalions to provide one for each division. In the course of the mid-1930s, however, the antitank battalions increased in number, permitting the assignment of one to each infantry division as well as leaving several left over for the new Panzer divisions and to form a general headquarters reserve. In this same period, the idea of horse-drawn antitank guns was dropped in favor of a plan to provide each infantry regiment with a full company of twelve motor-drawn antitank guns. (Cavalry regiments and motorized infantry battalions each got a platoon of three antitank guns, which were grouped with other heavy weapons in a more conventional manner.)

Because antitank guns were not on the list of weapons allowed to the German army by the Treaty of Versailles, most German antitank gun units were kept hidden from the outside world until 1935. (The exception that proves the rule was the antitank units that went to the field with dummy guns made out of wood.) The same requirement for pretense did not apply to motorcycles or armored cars. Officers of the Allied Control Commission charged with enforcing the Versailles treaty tended to see the former as nothing more than a mount for dispatch riders and the latter as a useful means for dealing with domestic disturbances. The German army was thus able to experiment quite openly with motorcycle infantry battalions, armored car companies, and motorized reconnaissance battalions consisting of various combinations of armored car and motorcycle companies.

The Reichswehr unveiled both its motorized reconnaissance battalions and motorcycle infantry battalions in September of 1932, in the course of maneuvers conducted near Frankfurt am Oder. The Blue forces, representing the defending Germans, consisted of a single infantry division. The Red forces, representing the attacking Poles, were made up of two cavalry divisions, two motorized antitank companies (with wooden guns), two motorized reconnaissance battalions, and a battalion of motorcycle infantry. Though these motorized elements were officially subordinated to the cavalry divisions, they quickly moved well ahead of the horse cavalry, astonishing the foreign observers and convincing many Germans of the futility of trying to combine horse and motor in the same formation.[11]

While the Reichswehr within Germany was quietly developing the various elements of the motorized combat troops, it was also working with prototypes for several different types of tanks. Built, for the most part, by German firms with secret contracts with the Reichswehr, these prototypes had a great deal in common with contemporary products of the Vickers Company. The specifications written in 1925 for the three competing prototypes of the *Grosstraktor* series of medium tanks were, for example, very similar to the characteristics of the revolutionary Vickers Mark I of 1924. Similarly, the multi-turret *Neubaufahrzeuge* of 1932 owed much to the Vickers Independent of 1926. Ironically, the one group of prototypes that drew its inspiration from a source other than Vickers was the series of light tanks built by the Swedish firm of Landsverk. These were improvements upon the Vollmer LK model of light tank, an indigenous German design dating from the last months of World War I.

From 1926 until 1933, the testing of German tank prototypes took place in the Soviet Union, under the auspices of a German-Soviet program of cooperation in the areas of armored warfare, chemical warfare, and combat aviation. This testing coincided with a training program aimed at giving Germany a critical mass of both potential tank unit commanders and technical experts. While this latter aspect of the clandestine tank program was a success (some of the key personalities in the later development of German armored warfare were graduates of the training program) the testing of prototypes led to somewhat disappointing results. Neither the German nor the Soviet authorities thought enough of any of the prototypes to recommend their adoption as standard equipment. The Soviets, who were in much more of a hurry to build a large tank force, ended up making direct copies of the Vickers products that had inspired the German prototypes. The Germans went back to the drawing board, incorporating many of the features of the 1926 through 1933 prototypes into subsequent designs, but ending up with a family of tanks based on very different principles.

In second half of 1934, as part of a sequence of events that would culminate in the open rejection of the military clauses of the Treaty of Versailles, the German army began to expand. At the heart of this expansion was a three-fold increase in the number of infantry divisions. Each of the seven existing divisions of the Reichswehr created two sister divisions, bringing the total number of infantry divisions to twenty-one. Within each of the seven original infantry divisions, the Kraftfahr battalions released their antitank and motorized reconnaissance units, which were then expanded into fourteen antitank battalions and seven motorized reconnaissance battalions. These new all-motorized units were then assembled into Germany's first fully motorized combat formations, the 1st and 2nd Motorized Combat Brigades (*Kraftfahrkampftruppenbrigaden*).

Whether the two motorized combat brigades were ever intended to be actual combat formations or were simply an administrative mechanism is hard to tell. German organizational practice of the era, which tended not to create tactical headquarters for units that were simply pooled, suggests that there was some tactical logic behind the structure of these formations. The fact that the antitank and motorized reconnaissance battalions were mixed up together (rather than being kept in "thoroughbred" administrative formations) also supports the thesis that the motorized combat brigades were designed to take the field as intact fighting organizations.[12] If that was the case, then the creation of small "anti-armor" formations preceded the creation of Germany's first Panzer divisions by almost a year.

While the seven infantry divisions of the Reichswehr expanded in the autumn of 1934, the three cavalry divisions allowed to Germany by the Treaty of Versailles did not. Instead, they were modified by the addition of several hundred motor vehicles of various kinds. In the 1st and 2nd Cavalry Divisions, the new motor vehicles were concentrated in motorized reconnaissance battalions of the type that had just been created for the motorized combat brigades. (These, which were to be used in much the same way as the motorized reconnaissance battalions of the 1932 maneuvers, were created by the expansion of the one company of *Kraftfahrtruppen* that had been assigned to each cavalry division.) In the 3rd Cavalry Division, the extent of motorization was far greater. Every horse in that division was replaced by a seat in a truck, staff car, armored car, or motorcycle. In keeping with this radical transformation, the Inspector of Cavalry for the German army surrendered oversight responsibility for the 3rd Cavalry Division to the Inspector of Motorized Combat Troops.[13]

While the Motorized Combat Troops were busy expanding, forming, and adopting the units needed for their three new combat formations (the two Motorized Combat Brigades and the 3rd Cavalry Division) German industry was beginning to produce respectable numbers of tanks. Between April and December of 1934, some 500 Panzer I tanks were produced by German factories. Even by the modest standards of the day, the five-ton Panzer I was a tiny tank. It owed much to the Carden-Lloyd tankette of the late 1920s, but was a little too big to be properly classed as such. It possessed, moreover, a fully rotating turret, as well as the capacity (exploited only by non-German users) to carry weapons larger than the rifle-caliber machine guns with which tankettes were armed.

Tiny or not, the new German tanks needed a home. This was created in the form of the Tank Brigade (*Kampfwagenbrigade*), an all-tank formation of six battalions. By the end of 1934, when most of the 500 tanks built that year had been delivered, the *Kampfwagenbrigade* had become the largest all-tank unit the world had seen since World War I. It was bigger than the British Tank Brigade assembled each summer on Salisbury Plain, the Soviet Tank Brigades, or the *Brigade de Combat* of the French Light Mechanized Division. Whether such a formation was suitable for the tactical or operational needs of the German army, however, was an entirely different matter.

In the summer of 1934, General Ludwig Beck, then Chief of the General Staff of the German army, spent a great deal of time studying reports about the British Tank Brigade and the various maneuvers in which it had been involved.[14] What he learned from this is hard to tell, for the most important feature of the British Tank Brigade that found its way into German tank units was very much in harmony with both the predictions of Ernst Volckheim and the failure of German industry to provide a satisfactory medium tank. That is to say, it is difficult to determine whether the German strategy of using light tanks as both surrogates for and eventual auxiliaries to the medium tanks to come was inspired or merely confirmed by the very similar British strategy of economizing on existing medium tanks. What is clear is that the standard German tank brigade of the period from late 1935 until the winter of 1940–1941 was a very close copy of the British Tank Brigade that was regularly assembled on Salisbury Plain from 1931 to 1938. In particular, the idea of the mixed tank company, in which platoons of light and medium tanks cooperated directly with each other, became an inherent part of Beck's vision for armored warfare. (While the contemporary French and Soviet armies had a considerable variety of tank types, these were not mixed at echelons below the brigade. French and Soviet tank companies and battalions were thus thoroughbred organizations, consisting only of one type of tank.)

The concept of the close support tank was another British idea that found a home in the Ludwig Beck's vision for German tank units. The original British version of this tank was a Vickers medium tank that carried a 3.7-inch (95mm) howitzer rather than the usual 3-pounder (47mm) gun. Its purpose was to fire large-caliber high explosive and smoke shells, particularly at hostile antitank guns. Enthusiasts of the "all-tank school" went so far as to argue that close support tanks freed tank units from the need to cooperate with conventional field artillery. While it is doubtful that Beck agreed with this extreme position, he was quickly convinced of the value of arming a portion of Germany's future fleet of medium tanks with a howitzer of some sort.

The third concept that Beck seems to have borrowed from the British Tank Brigade was that of using the brigade as the basic building block of larger formations. Brigades had last been used in the German army in 1919, where they had proved useful as a means for coordinating the actions of all-arms battle groups involved in street fighting. (These battle groups varied greatly in composition. Those of the famous *Landesjäger Korps* consisted of an infantry battalion, a cavalry squadron, a field artillery battery, a trench mortar platoon, and one or two machine-gun companies.)[15] Since then, German tacticians had seen little need for a single-arm unit larger than a regiment (of two or three battalions) or a combined-arms formation smaller than a division. The formation of the single-arm Tank Brigade, the two-arm Motorized Combat Brigade, and the combined-arms (but very small) 3rd Cavalry Division in the autumn of 1934 suggests, however, that Beck was very interested in experimenting with building blocks of nontraditional shapes and sizes. A glimpse of Beck's thinking in this respect can also be seen in Heinz Guderian's grossly unfair criticism of Beck as an obstacle to progress where armored formations were concerned. A better view is provided by Beck's own writings, which include memoranda and reports of war games, as well as his contribution of the oft-quoted edition of the German field service regulations known as *Truppenführung*.[16]

Ludwig Beck's intensive investigation of the proper way to deal with mechanized forces coincided with the publication of an important (but now largely forgotten) book, Ludwig Ritter von Eimannsberger's *Tank Warfare* (*Der Kampfwagenkrieg*.)[17] Like Beck, Eimannsberger thought in terms of both British-style, all-tank tank brigades and fully motorized antitank brigades. Eimannsberger referred to the antitank brigade described in his book as a *Jäger* Brigade, providing it with three battalions of motorized light infantry and seventy-two antitank guns (See Figure 5.1).[18] (The German Motorized Combat Brigade of 1934 had about half the infantry of this Jäger Brigade but 108 antitank guns.) Taking advantage of the relative ease with which one can create a formation on paper, Eimannsberger went a step further than Beck had done. He combined two of his all-tank tank brigades, one of his Jäger brigades, and various supporting elements to form a hypothetical Tank Division (*Kampfwagen Division*).[19] Whatever the source of inspiration—whether reading Eimannsberger or listening to Heinz Guderian or some combination of those factors—Beck's creation of his various mechanized brigades was soon followed, in October of 1934, by his ordering the General Staff to conduct a theoretical study of possible armored divisions. The study concluded, in the summer of 1935, with a staff ride conducted by Beck himself. The scenario for the staff ride began with a hypothetical invasion of southern Germany by the armed forces of Czechoslovakia.[20] A portion of the defending German forces, consisting of three armored divisions and two infantry divisions, responded to this invasion with a counterattack against the rear areas and lines of communication of the invading Czechoslovak army. The infantry divisions were conventional ones

Figure 5.1
German Motorized Combat Brigade 1934 and Ludwig Ritter von Eimannsberger's Jäger Brigade 1934

German Motorized Combat Brigade - 1934

Motorized Reconnaissance Battalions

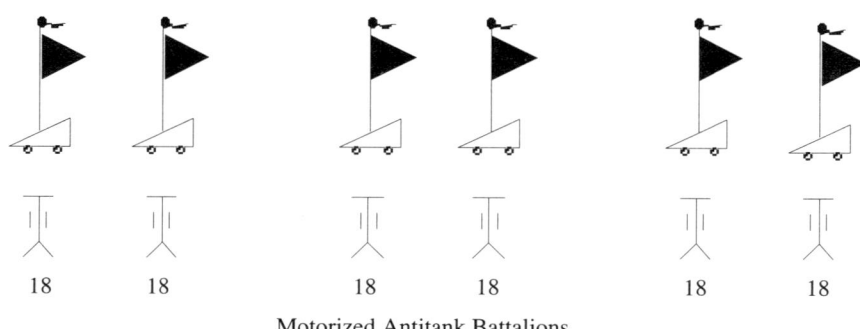

Motorized Antitank Battalions

Ludwig Ritter von Eimannsberger's Jäger Brigade – 1934

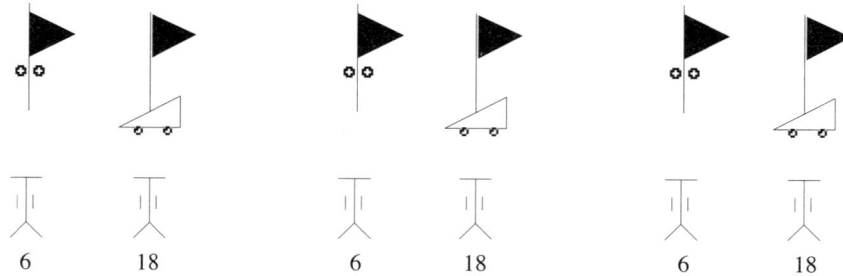

Motorized Infantry and Antitank Battalions

for the day. The armored divisions each consisted of a tank brigade of four tank battalions, a motorized infantry brigade, and a field artillery regiment, as well as separate reconnaissance, engineer, and signal battalions.

At the beginning of the operation the bulk of the combat elements of the three armored divisions were still stretched out for miles along the roads behind the German front lines. Beck therefore recommended that the forward tank battalions (as well as the artillery of the armored divisions) be subordinated to the army corps commanding the conventional elements of the counter-attack force. He even went so far as to suggest that the forces might be profitably subordinated to one of the two infantry divisions that made up that corps. This, he argued, would aid the infantry divisions fulfill their task of completely breaking into the Czechoslovak position, destroying the infantry and artillery units in that position, and breaking through to the area behind the forward Czechoslovak divisions. Once this was done and the Germans attempted to exploit their tactical victory, Beck believed that control of the tank and motorized artillery units should revert to the control of the armored corps.

Beck's belief in the utility of subordinating parts of the armored corps to infantry formations was reinforced by an event that happened in the course of the staff ride. Two hours before the German counterattack was scheduled to begin, the Czechoslovak forces launched a spoiling attack. In such a crisis, Beck argued, voluntary cooperation between the forward elements of the armored corps and the infantry formations was not sufficient. Only "clear lines of subordination" could ensure the kind of concerted action needed to avoid disaster.[21]

Beck's comments on the internal organization and techniques of the armored corps were very much in keeping with his emphasis on flexible command relationships. In the one big attack of the exercise, the commander of the armored corps arrayed his forces in three waves. The first consisted of two armored brigades; the second of a single armored brigade; and the third of the motorized infantry brigades. Given this arrangement, Beck wondered whether it might not be better to place the first two armored brigades (and perhaps even the third) under a single commander, thereby creating a single all-tank formation of eight or even twelve tank battalions.[22]

The organizational flexibility that Beck displayed in the 1935 staff ride reflected Beck's vision of an army that could, if needed, easily create fully motorized formations of various types. These would enable Germany to fight the fast moving, decisive campaigns of offensive maneuver that German soldiers liked so well. At the same time, Beck did not want Germany forced into an offensive strategy by an army that was designed primarily for offensive operations. Rather, he wanted to give German strategists a variety of means for reacting to an invasion or other international crisis. In this respect, Beck had much in common with the elder Helmuth von Moltke (1800–1891), whose plans for war included defensive and delaying maneuvers, as well as the fast-moving offensive campaigns for which he is best known.[23]

In the months following the 1935 staff ride, German motorized formations underwent a complete metamorphosis. This was accomplished partially by the creation of new units and the recasting of existing ones, but mostly by the reshuffling of battalions created in the great expansion of 1934. The Motorized Combat Brigades, Tank Brigade, and 3rd Cavalry Division were disbanded. Their component battalions, along with newly motorized infantry units and horse cavalry units that have been converted into tank units, provided the building blocks for an entirely new set of motorized formations. The most spectacular of these were the three Panzer divisions, built on the model used in Beck's staff ride. There was also the Berlin Reconnaissance Brigade (of three motorized reconnaissance battalions) and the 1st Light Brigade (consisting mostly of recently motorized infantry units.) One of the fourteen antitank battalions was sent to each of the Panzer Divisions. The rest joined infantry divisions, thereby making a considerable contribution towards the goal of providing each infantry division with a fully motorized antitank battalion of its own.[24]

The twelve tank battalions in service at the end of the 1935 reformation of German motorized formations were still uniformly equipped with Panzer I tanks, a situation that led to heated discussion in the pages of the German military press. In December of 1935, however, Ludwig Beck made it clear that German reliance on this tiny tank was merely a temporary expedient. In a memorandum written that month, Beck explained his vision for the near-term development of the German tank battalion. There was, he wrote, to be a single type of tank battalion in the German army, one that could serve to advantage within the framework of a Panzer division as well as in other organizational structures.[25] Two-thirds of these tanks were to be medium tanks capable of action against other tanks. (This, Beck thought, would probably translate into a model armed with a 37mm antitank gun and protected by 25mm-thick armor.) The remainder (one-third) of the tanks in each tank battalion were to be auxiliaries to the "antitank tank"—scout tanks armed with machine guns and close support tanks armed with howitzers.[26]

Beck's vision for the all-purpose tank battalion coincided with his plan for the further expansion of the German army. This involved the creation of fifteen new infantry divisions, two mountain divisions, and three motorized cavalry divisions, as well as numerous smaller organizations. At the same time, four existing infantry divisions would be fully motorized. The tank element of this expanded force was to consist of forty-eight tank battalions. Twelve of these would be assigned to the three Panzer divisions. The rest would be grouped by fours into standard tank brigades.[27] These would be administratively assigned to an army corps, but operationally independent.[28]

It was these latter brigades that could be used to form ad hoc armored divisions, employed as independent units, or split up into independent regiments and battalions. At no point, however, did Beck permit the possibility that tank battalions would be employed in a wide variety of ways from using the peculiar requirements of service within an armored division as criterion by which equipment, organization, and training would be judged. Indeed, Beck's argument for the organization of all tank units into brigades was based primarily on the need to facilitate the organization of ad hoc armored divisions and corps.[29]

The concept of an all-purpose tank battalion was very much in keeping with Beck's fondness for strategic and organizational flexibility. Easily transferred from one sort of division to another, the single-type tank battalions (and the standard regiments and brigades assembled from them) tied the German army to no particular strategy. Both the radical vision of an elite army of mechanized formations and the more pedestrian dream of a product-improved version of the German army of World War I were compatible with Beck's armored battalions. That is to say, single tank battalions could be attached to infantry divisions or corps. They could be assigned to mechanized cavalry formations or formed into armored brigades subordinated to an infantry corps. They could also be used to reinforce permanent armored divisions, or, formed into armored regiments and brigades that, in turn, would be used as the nucleus of ad hoc armored divisions.

Expressed in terms familiar to other armies of the time, a German tank battalion would be able to serve much the same function as a French *bataillon de chars de manoeuvre ensemble*. It could also serve in the same role one of the three mixed battalions within the British tank brigade, or one of the fast tank battalions within a Soviet mechanized brigade. Likewise, a German tank brigade (of four battalions) could perform the same sort of tasks as the British Tank Brigade as a whole or one of the all-tank Soviet tank brigades. Indeed, the only contemporary tank function that the German tank battalion of the 1930s would not fulfill was that performed by the light infantry tanks that the French and the Soviets subordinated to infantry regiments and battalions.

Ludwig Beck's fondness for the creation of standard building blocks extended to motorized units other than that of the tank: the motorized rifle battalions, regiments, and brigades; motorized artillery battalions and regiments; motorized reconnaissance battalions and regiments; engineer battalions; antitank battalions; signal battalions; and reconnaissance troops. All of these units were designed with an eye towards direct cooperation with tank units within the framework of an armored division.[30] Not all the units of each type, however, were assigned to armored divisions. This was true even of the motorized rifle brigades, which were units of truck and motorcycle-borne infantry specially trained and organized for work with tank brigades.[31] Three of these brigades were allocated to the armored divisions. The remaining six brigades were to remain independent; capable of being assembled into a mobile operational reserve for an army and of being used, with other units, to form fully motorized cavalry divisions.[32]

Beck's vision for fully motorized cavalry divisions may have had some connection to the contemporary French idea of the "light mechanized division" (*division lègere méchanique*). It is intriguing, for example, that Beck referred to such formations as "light" (*Leichte*) divisions. Unfortunately, Beck's surviving memoranda lack the level of detail needed to support or deny this supposition. Nonetheless, the creation of such divisions—with their armored car, tank, and motorized infantry elements—would be entirely consistent with Beck's "building block" approach to organization. Such a vision would likewise be in keeping with the formation, in 1935, of an independent, fully motorized, reconnaissance brigade (1st Light Brigade) and the creation, two years later, of three light divisions.[33]

Beck distinguished between the motorized rifle regiments associated with armored warfare and the motorized infantry divisions he was also in the process of organizing. The former were known as *Schützen*, a term that had been borrowed from elite German rifle units of the early nineteenth century and were to be formed, not only by the motorization of infantry units, but also by the conversion of horse cavalry.[34] Beck did not determine, a priori, how these units were to be organized, Rather, he authorized the formation of experimental Schützen units in which more than half of the men were transported in motorcycles, as well as *Schützen* brigades, regiments, and battalions with organic armored car platoons.[35] Responsibility for raising and training the *Schützen*, moreover, rested not with the infantry branch but with the General Oswald Lutz, an officer who, throughout the interwar period, had been closely connected to both motorization and mechanization in the German army.[36]

The German motorized infantry divisions were, by way of contrast, nothing more than ordinary infantry divisions that, for rapid movement behind the lines, had been provided with trucks and other motor transport. They were thus similar in conception to contemporary French motorized infantry divisions and nearly identical in organization, weaponry, and tactical capabilities, to muscle-powered German infantry divisions of the time. Indeed, so clear was this distinction between operational movement by truck and tactical movement by foot that Beck actively considered keeping the majority of trucks in an echelon that could be withdrawn from one division and assigned to another.[37]

6

BEYOND THEORY

A number of prominent commentators on the Second World War have questioned whether the conquest of Poland in September of 1939 was a genuine *Blitzkrieg*. Writing soon after the war, both B. H. Liddell Hart and Heinz Guderian complained that the gasoline-powered units were tied too closely to the muscle-powered ones. Later, Mathew Cooper and Len Deighton have argued, for much the same reason, that the start of the Blitzkrieg era can only be said to begin with the invasion of France in 1940. Most recently, a number of German historians have taken the position that the first true Blitzkrieg did not take place until Operation Barbarossa, the German offensive against the Soviet Union that began on 22 June 1941.

On the surface, this argument is an artificial one, an exercise in the creation of categories so small that each operation ends up in a class by itself. On a somewhat deeper level, however, there is much to be gained from a close comparison of the various Blitzkrieg campaigns. At the very least, such an examination helps to dismiss the false image of the Blitzkrieg as a formula, an idea that was fully formed before it was applied and then applied consistently as a standard package. Rather, the many differences between the campaigns underscore the great degree to which the Blitzkrieg was less an act of institutional creation than the result of rapid adaptation at a number of levels.

Much of the argument that the Polish campaign was less than a full-fledged Blitzkrieg is based on the initial distribution of forces. A look at an organizational diagram for the German army that crossed of the German-Polish frontier on 1 September 1939 shows fifteen motorized divisions and forty-five divisions moved primarily by animal power. Rather than segregating the motor-driven divisions from their muscle-powered counterparts, however, the German authorities combined both to form mixed armies, and, in many cases, even mixed corps. The result is the appearance of a German army High Command intent on hitching of the racehorse of the world's most modern divisions to the plow of walking infantry and horse-drawn artillery.[1]

When the initial locations of these formations are placed on a map, much of the evidence that the German authorities were intent on "penny-packeting" their motorized forces disappears. A sizeable proportion of these divisions, seven out of fifteen, were assigned to the Tenth Army. Three more were assigned to the neighboring Fourteenth Army. As the Tenth Army formed the initial main effort (*Schwerpunkt*) of the German invasion force and as the motorized forces of the Fourteenth Army spent much of the campaign directly cooperating with the Tenth Army a fair case can be made that the Germans intended their motorized formations to serve as a concentrated force with an important, even decisive, mission.

Further evidence in support of this argument may be seen in the way that German gasoline-powered formations were organized after the first few days of the Polish campaign. In the flurry of attachments and detachments that took place soon after the battles on or near the German-Polish and Slovak-Polish frontiers, eleven of the fifteen motorized divisions were employed as part of motorized army corps. The three original light divisions went to war with their parent XV Motorized Corps. The four motorized infantry divisions likewise operated under the direct control of their peacetime commands, the XIV and XIX Motorized Corps. (The latter corps, commanded by Guderian, also included an armored division.) The two Austrian motorized divisions, the 2nd Panzer Division and the 4th Light Division spent the bulk of the campaign together, as part of newly formed the XXII Corps, which was a motorized corps in all but name.[2]

Of the four remaining German motorized divisions, two were improvised divisions assembled, on mobilization, from independent tank regiments, units of the infant *Waffen SS*, units detached from other formations, and other odd pieces. The 10th Panzer Division, an understrength formation with only three-fifths of the infantry, one-half of the tanks, and one-third of the artillery of other armored divisions, served as part of the reserve of the German High Command. It was later committed to a number of corps, including Guderian's XIX Corps. *Panzerverband Kempf* was made up of units that had been conducting autumn exercises in East Prussia. Stranded on the outbreak of war, it fought as part of an ordinary army corps.[3]

The last two armored divisions formed, with two ordinary infantry divisions, the XVI Army Corps. As was the case with the other German corps that contained both motorized and muscle-powered formations, the first task of the XVI Army Corps was to break through the thick belt of wooded terrain that covered the German-Polish frontier in its area of operations. Once it passed this barrier, the second task of the corps would be to operate in the vast expanse of more open ground that stood between the it and the Polish capital of Warsaw. Given the vulnerability of tanks in such terrain and the ability of woods to "swallow" the five Schützen battalions that the two armored divisions could together deploy for such work, using muscle-powered infantry divisions to clear a path for the mobile troops made perfect sense. Once in the "green fields beyond," the XVI Motorized Corps could shed the slow-moving infantry divisions and take full advantage of its mobility.[4]

How this could have been done can be seen in the example of the three motorized divisions of the XXII Corps. All of these divisions were, when they crossed the German-Polish frontier, subordinated to muscle-powered corps. The two divisions moving through mountainous terrain (the 2nd Panzer Division and the 4th Light Division), began the campaign in the company of an Austrian mountain division and under the command of the Austrian XVIII Army Corps.[5] The division moving through flatter, but more heavily forested terrain (the 5th Panzer Division) was accompanied by two infantry divisions and was subordinated to the VIII Army Corps. However, once they were in less confining terrain, the gasoline-powered divisions parted company with the muscle powered-formations, forming the all-motorized XXII Corps under General of Cavalry Ewald von Kleist.[6]

Why the XVI Motorized Corps failed to convert itself into a fully motorized organization seems to be the result of the outstanding performance of one of its component infantry divisions. Making forced marches of as many as sixty-five kilometers (a little more than forty miles) a day—a rate made possible by the sensible practice of transporting foot soldiers' backpacks in wagons or trucks—this infantry division was generally able to follow the two armored divisions to the very gates of Warsaw. While the other infantry division of the XVI Motorized Corps was detached as soon as the corps entered the great Polish plain, the uncanny ability of the men of the hard-marching infantry division to use animal power and secondary routes to keep up with their more modern comrades resulted in their continued membership in what otherwise would have been an "armored division only" motorized corps.[7]

In those few cases where a motorized division was part of an otherwise muscle-powered corps, this fact seems to have done little to inhibit full advantage being taken of their operational mobility. In the German army attacking out of East Prussia (the Third Army), the rapid lateral movement of Panzerdivision Kempf allowed the entire army to shift its main effort and thus avoid getting bogged down in strong Polish fortifications.[8] Far to the south, in the army attacking through the Carpathian Mountains, the 2nd Panzer Division made a similar move in order to take the important Jablonka Pass in a *coup de main*.[9]

Despite the peculiar conditions faced in Poland, the unprecedented degree to which armored and motorized units were concentrated, and the overall success achieved by German arms, Heinz Guderian was not satisfied with the arrangement. In a letter to Liddell Hart after the war, he wrote that he had "always proposed deep thrusts operating independently of the infantry corps." This, he explained, would have required the assembly of an actual Panzer army.[10] What this *Panzer* army was supposed to have done, however, is another question. The five motorized corps that took part in the Polish campaign were able, in the course of less than two weeks, to drive through the full depth of the German sphere of influence in Poland. Had they gone any deeper, they would have run into the Soviet forces scheduled to attack Poland from the east. As the Soviet attack on Poland was one of the chief foundations of the German plan, this would have resulted in few, if any, benefits for the Germans. Indeed, as things turned out, the capture of Brest-Litovsk by Guderian's own XIX Motorized Corps only resulted in Guderian's having to turn that city over to the Soviets.[11]

If Guderian's imaginary Panzer army was not to thrust so deeply, then it would have ended up doing what the four motorized German corps did anyway. More specifically, if it were not to drive east across the full width of Poland, the Panzer army could only be assigned one other independent mission: the capture of Warsaw. As the costly failure of the 4th Panzer Division to gain even a toehold in that city indicates,[12] that operation might well have resulted in a minor setback for the German war effort and a major embarrassment for the German tank enthusiasts. The Panzer army would thus have had to satisfy itself with more shallow maneuvers. As the logical aim of such maneuvers would be the isolation of Warsaw and other pockets of Polish resistance, the action of the Panzer army would have to be rapidly exploited by the action of muscle-powered units. For soldiers as stubborn as the Poles of 1939 proved to be, having one's lines of communications crossed by an armored unit is merely a nuisance. Having them occupied by infantry divisions is a far bigger problem. In short, it is hard to imagine Guderian's wished-for Panzer army acting much differently than the four motorized corps actually did.

The irony of Guderian's complaint was that the German use of armored and motorized forces in Poland corresponded closely to the model promulgated in his prewar writings. Tanks were concentrated in tank battalions. The tank battalions served, to a degree far greater than might be expected from Germany's peacetime distribution of tank battalions and Guderian's postwar complaints, with fully motorized divisions. These divisions, in nearly complete accord with both the spirit and letter of prewar organization, most often served as part of fully motorized corps.

Of the thirty-four German tank battalions that participated in the Polish campaign, all but two fought as part of motorized divisions. Those that had not been part of such divisions in peacetime were attached to them on mobilization. The independent 4th Panzer Brigade, for example, provided two battalions to each of the armored divisions that were improvised for the campaign. The other independent battalions (save the two assigned to muscle-powered formations) were used to reinforce armored and light divisions. As a result of this latter decision, half of the light divisions were as well supplied with tanks as the two improvised armored divisions. As the light divisions (with these extra tank battalions) both formed part of the "light" XV Motorized Corps, that corps ended up with a tank force (six tank battalions) that was only slightly less impressive than that of the corps provided with two armored divisions (having eight or nine tank battalions).

It was perhaps because of this that the "light" corps was not employed as cavalry, with its armored car and motorcycle units forming a wide but fragile screen in front of the German army. Instead, the three light divisions of the XV Motorized Corps were formed into two separate, but mutually supporting, fighting columns. One of these columns, consisting of the 2nd and 3rd Light Divisions, was under the direct command of the headquarters of the XV Motorized Corps. The other was formed by the reinforced 1st Light Division and acted under the direct control of the Tenth Army. Although variously provided with motorcycles and armored cars, each of these columns had, with three tank battalions, a tank force comparable to that of a Panzer division. This arrangement lasted until the end of the second week of the campaign, when the need to deal with two distinct pockets of Polish resistance resulted in the 1st Light Division being employed a hundred or so kilometers away from the XV Motorized Corps.[13]

Between the end of the Polish campaign and the beginning of the German invasion of the West, the organization of the German motorized forces underwent a number of minor changes, almost all of which consisted of a reshuffling of units and resources that already belonged to the *Schnelle Truppen*. Non-divisional tank battalions—both those of the independent tank brigades and those that had been wholly autonomous—were reassigned in order to formalize the conversion the four light divisions into Panzer divisions. The four motorized infantry divisions were slimmed down by the removal of three infantry battalions from each of them. These battalions, in turn, were used to bolster the strength of the infantry brigades in the original Panzer divisions.

The actual expansion of the motorized troops during the winter of 1939–1940 was thus modest. Much of it took place under the auspices of Hitler's guard organizations. The combat troops of the SS, which had provided many of the elements of Panzerverband Kempf in 1939, had grown into two motorized infantry divisions and an independent motorized regiment. The army equivalent of these units, the *Großdeutschland* organization, was formed, with three infantry battalions and a battalion of heavy weapons, as a heavily reinforced motorized infantry regiment. Four additional motorized infantry battalions were formed into an independent motorized infantry brigade.

The number of tank battalions increased only slightly, from thirty-four to thirty-nine. As all but two of these were incorporated into armored divisions, Guderian's ideal of the concentration of all tank units in armored formations had come close to complete realization. These two non-divisional tank units, moreover, had extremely specialized missions. One had been formed for the largely amphibious Scandinavian campaign. The other, which was conducting experiments with such things as flamethrower tanks, belonged to an instructional brigade.[14] It could thus be said that, at least for the time being, Guderian had won the battle to tie Germany's tanks closely to Germany's armored divisions.

Indeed, the strength of the tank enthusiasts in the German army of the winter of 1939–1940 can be seen in an attempt by the die-hard horse cavalrymen to reestablish muscle-powered army cavalry. This was to be done, not at the expense of the Panzer divisions, but by depriving the infantry divisions of the horsemen and cyclists of their reconnaissance battalions.[15]

(These reconnaissance battalions had been formed on mobilization by breaking up the peacetime cavalry regiments.)[16] Thus, though the 1940 edition of a popular German textbook on higher tactics devoted more space to army cavalry than armored divisions and continued to refer to the latter as an "expedient," the only threats to German plans for motorized divisions, corps, and armies would come, not from other German soldiers, but from materiel shortages and enemy action.[17]

Though relatively modest, the organizational changes of the winter of 1939–1940 facilitated the employment of fully motorized corps. With significantly larger infantry brigades, the armored divisions were better able to use their own resources to deal with broken terrain and field fortifications. If additional help were needed, the smaller motorized infantry divisions formed a handier and more compact means of providing additional infantry and field artillery strength. When combined with the fact that the road network in France and the Low Countries was one of the most modern and most extensive in the world, these reforms greatly reduced the need to use muscle-powered formations as a means of escorting fully motorized formations through woods or mountainous country.

It was largely because of this new capability that the Germans were able to make use of the densely wooded and extremely hilly Ardennes region as the main route for their gasoline-powered formations. Of the sixteen motorized divisions available to the German army for the campaign in the west, ten attacked through the Ardennes. Of these, eight (five armored and three motorized infantry) divisions formed *Panzergruppe von Kleist*, an organization that was, in all but name, a small army.[18] The other two divisions (the 5th and 7th Panzer divisions) made up the independent XV Motorized Corps, a small corps that was to enter French territory through the northern tip of the Ardennes while Panzergruppe von Kleist cut its way through the center of that ancient forest.

A sense of the size of Panzergruppe von Kleist can be obtained by looking at the amount of space needed for its deployment. In the days before the launching of the German attack, each division was assigned an assembly area near Germany's western frontier. The armored divisions destined to attack first—the 1st, 2nd and 10th Panzer divisions—were assigned assembly areas that stretched for forty to sixty kilometers along roads leading into Belgium and France. The assembly areas of other motorized formations, some of which were more than 200 kilometers west of the frontier, were superimposed upon networks of roads that fed into these main routes. Each of these covered an amount of ground comparable to that covered by the long, thin assembly areas of the forward armored divisions (about 400 square kilometers).[19]

As was the case with other motorized formations in the 1940 campaign, the initial crossing of the German frontier was made by units of muscle-powered infantry and mountain divisions. These advanced, like the divisions of Schlieffen's great wheel of 1914, on a nearly solid front. This served three purposes. First, it gave the muscle-powered formations the head start they would need if they were to effectively cooperate with the motorized troops. Second, the fact that the French, Belgians, and Dutch were being attacked on a broad front made it considerably more difficult for them to concentrate combat power against the motorized units. Third, the use of non-motorized formations as trailbreakers economized on the fully motorized divisions (formations that were simultaneously critical to the success of the German plan and in relatively short supply).

Thanks in part to the work of muscle-powered divisions, as well as to the relative weakness of the French and Belgian forces in the area, the movement of Panzergruppe von Kleist through the Ardennes was relatively uneventful. Its first big job—what might be called the maiden battle of the world's first fully motorized army—occurred at the western edge of the Ardennes. This task, the passage of the Meuse River near the city of Sedan, was given entirely to units other than tank battalions: Schützen battalions, assault engineer battalions, antiaircraft gun battalions and antitank units, and a considerable force of field artillery.[20] It was not until the motorized infantry brigade forming the main effort of Panzergruppe von Kleist had created a bridgehead on the French side of the Meuse, and other motorized infantry units had made secondary crossings, that the tanks came into their own. This was in keeping with the predictions of the now obscure German theorists of the 1930s, officers like Alfred Baentsch, who had argued that massed tanks could be effectively unleashed only after the initial breach had been made by the infantry and the artillery.[21]

The crossing of the Meuse at Sedan was replicated at two other points. At Monthermé, Schützen and engineers of the 6th Panzer Division used the debris of a blown-up bridge to shelter their infiltration across the Meuse. At Dinant, the lead elements—Schützen and engineers from the 7th Panzer Division—achieved similar success. In all three cases, the first breach was made without significant assistance from the tank battalions. (There are some reports that German tanks were used as direct fire artillery to knock out or suppress French bunkers. In most cases, however, the weapons used for that work seem to have been 88mm dual-purpose guns and self-propelled 150mm infantry guns.) Thus the role of the tanks, as Lutz, Baentsch, and many other German soldiers of the interwar period had predicted, was not so much to make the breach, but to exploit it.[22]

The wisdom of letting the infantry of the armored divisions lead the attack against prepared positions was demonstrated, not merely by the success of every attack in which the technique was used, but also by the failure of the breakthrough attempts in which it was not. In two cases, German corps commanders tried to attack in the manner prescribed by Guderian in *Achtung Panzer!*, with tank brigades leading the attack and the Schützen, mounted on their trucks and motorcycles, held back in readiness to exploit the breach. In the other case, the task of making the initial breakthrough was given to muscle-powered infantry divisions.

The German attacks that failed are rarely discussed in the English literature of the 1940 campaign. This may be because of their tendency to ruin the story of the mechanized juggernaut that overwhelmed Western Europe in a matter of weeks. A more likely reason is that these failed attacks all took place in the second half of the German campaign in the west, in the course of the operation that began with the attempted breakthrough of the Weygand Line on 5 June 1940. Though it was this operation that brought France to her knees, and proved far more expensive for the Germans than the conquest of the Low Countries,[23] it took place after the collapse of the Dunkirk pocket. As that is the point in time at which most British troops left the continent, it is also the point at which most English-language accounts of the campaign begin. This is unfortunate, for the while the operation that began on 10 May provided a marvelous object lesson in what armored and motorized forces could do, the operation that began on 5 June illustrated the limitations of these new arms.

The first phase of the 1940 campaign in France and the Low Countries (the one that had begun with the German crossings of the Meuse on 10 and 11 May) lasted less than three weeks. In those three weeks, the Germans had managed to conquer all of Belgium and the Netherlands as well as a slice of northern France. They had also succeeded in expelling most of the British Expeditionary Force from the Continent and defeating a substantial portion of the French field army. (This included all three *divisions légères mécaniques* and three of the four armored divisions.) The victory gained was, nonetheless, only a partial one.

While the fighting still raged to the north, the French were hard at work establishing a new barrier behind the Somme and Aisne Rivers. Named for the new French commander-in-chief, Maxime Weygand, this line began at the English Channel and ran east until it connected to the still-unbroken Maginot Line. Between these two pillars stood an impressive number of French infantry divisions. Thanks to the efforts of the now-mobilized French war economy, these were often better equipped than the infantry divisions that had fought in May. Moreover, because of the rapid dissemination of "lessons learned" from the failure of French forces to stem the initial breakthroughs, these divisions could make use of novel techniques for dealing with German tank attacks.

The fully motorized forces that had taken part in the operation beginning on 10 May 1940 were reshuffled for the attack that started on 5 June. Guderian's XIX Motorized Corps, so recently subordinated to Panzergruppe Kleist, became a Panzergruppe in its own right. The remaining four motorized corps headquarters (plus a newly created one) were used to create five motorized corps of a standard pattern. With one exception, each corps consisted of two armored divisions and a motorized infantry division. The exception, which consisted solely of two armored divisions, was made necessary by the lack of a fifth motorized infantry division (See Figure 6.1).[24]

Two of the five motorized corps were assigned to Panzergruppe von Kleist. Another two were put under the command of *Panzergruppe Guderian*. The remaining corps, the XV Motorized Corps of Hermann Hoth, was assigned directly to an otherwise muscle-powered army. As might be assumed from the distribution of forces, each of the Panzergruppen was assigned to lead a major breakthrough. The XV Motorized Corps was assigned to make a smaller breakthrough, the main event within a supporting attack.

Figure 6.1
Organization of German Motorized Corps June 1940

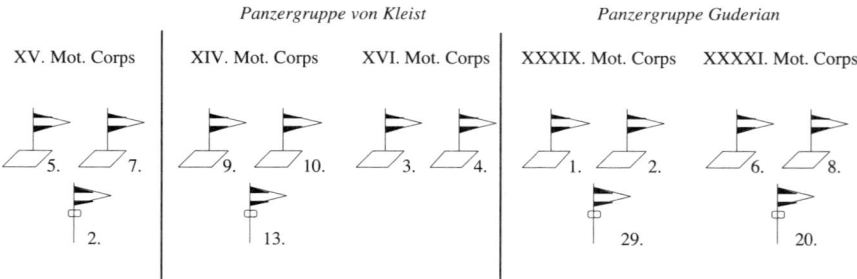

Like that of 10 May, the attack of 5 June was launched on a broad front, with muscle-powered infantry divisions making aggressive, but necessarily shallow, attacks all along the line of the Somme. In many cases, these attacks made better progress than those of the motorized formations, most of which ran into some nasty surprises. At Amiens, the problem was the French "hedgehog" tactics, which allowed German tanks (but none of the other elements of the attacking armored divisions) to pass between a series of strong points. This left the German tanks, short on fuel and out of ammunition, stranded in an empty field while the infantry, engineers, and antiaircraft units fought fierce battles to clear a path through the strong points.[25] At Peronne, the same technique led to similar results. Within two hours of leaving their assembly areas, many of the German tanks had passed beyond the hedgehogs and were now among the French batteries. This still left the French strongpoints, some of which were well protected by minefields, without artillery support but otherwise intact.[26]

Only at Abbéville, on the western edge of the Weygand Line, did a German attack result in unqualified success. There, the XV Motorized Corps used its Schützen to cross the Somme, and, without the slightest pause, began its long ride down the Channel Coast. The best-known member of this corps, Erwin Rommel, contributed to this victory in his usual manner, leading his armored division from the front and allowing nothing to stop the forward movement of his command.[27] By 9 June, the XV Motorized Corps had crossed the River Seine at a number of points, capturing the ancient city of Rouen and isolating the great port of Le Havre. Three days later, this latter city, along with the last remaining British combat troops in France, surrendered.[28]

Farther east, in an attack that started on 9 June, the four armored divisions of Panzergruppe Guderian encountered difficulties of a different sort. Both Guderian and his immediate superior, General List of the Twelfth Army, agreed that infantry units should lead the attack across the Aisne. While Guderian argued that these should be Schützen from the same divisions as the tanks that would exploit the breakthrough, List commanded that the initial breaches be made by the muscle-powered infantry divisions already in sector. This way, List believed, the combat power of the armored divisions could be preserved for subsequent operations.

Subsequent events would show that List was right about the need to preserve the combat power of Guderian's Panzergruppe, which would face two weeks of hard fighting once it got south of the Aisne. List was overoptimistic, however, about the ability of his walking infantry to get across the river. The

French defense along the Aisne, though ultimately futile, was the best executed French operation of the campaign. In contrast to the defenders of Sedan, the French divisions south of the Aisne were full of infantrymen with a taste for close combat, gunners who realized that the bark (or, more precisely, the wail) of the *Stuka* was worse than its bite, and officers who knew when to throw out the book. As a result, when the German infantry made a penetration, they were met with immediate and violent counterattacks. When they assembled for an attack, their assembly areas were bombarded by French artillery.[29] As a result, of the eight German attempts to create a bridgehead on 9 June, only three succeeded.[30]

Three small bridgeheads were enough, however, to get two armored divisions (the 1st and the 2nd Panzer Divisions) across the Aisne. Once on the south bank, these divisions pushed forward energetically, beating back counterattacks by ad hoc French armored units. What was far more important, the breakthrough convinced the French leadership that the battle to hold the Aisne had been lost. French divisions that had had some success in beating off German attacks along the Aisne were now ordered to give up their positions and retire to the next river line, that of the Marne.[31] This not only made it possible for the rest of Panzergruppe Guderian to cross the Aisne but also created the very sort of fluid situation in which German soldiers in general, and German soldiers on wheels and tracks in particular, liked best.

7
MIXING IT UP

For most of the world, the lesson of the Battle of France was the primacy of the tank. For the Germans who won the victory, the many insights gained included a greater appreciation for the possibilities of fully motorized formations and, at the same time, a new sense of the limitations of the tank. The result was that, while the other armies rushed to increase their tank arsenals, the Germans focused on those arms intended to cooperate with tanks within the framework of the armored division or motorized corps. This gave the German army the ability to fight campaigns of a type envisioned only by the most radical of the mobile warfare enthusiasts of the interwar period. Moreover, in the course of these campaigns, the Germans discovered that the future of the tank depended not only on its being employed as part of an all-arms, fully motorized formation but also on the closer integration of those arms at the unit level.

After the end of World War II, Guderian and a number of the other German tank enthusiasts accused Hitler of watering down of the German armored force during the winter of 1940–1941. The doubling of the number of German armored divisions (from ten in the summer of 1940 to twenty in the summer of 1941), these generals argued, was achieved only at the cost of greatly weakening the tank component of each division. This, some of the German generals added, was a great handicap during Operation Barbarossa, the German invasion of the Soviet Union that started on 22 June 1941.[1] From the point of view of absolute numbers of tanks, the first half of this criticism is based on fact. From the point of view of the lessons of the campaign in France, the state of German resources at the time, and the task faced by the German armored divisions in the Soviet Union, it is misplaced.

On 10 May 1940, the ten German armored divisions had fielded approximately 2,100 tanks. On 22 June 1941, the twenty German armored divisions fielded some 3,000 tanks.[2] The average number of tanks in each armored division was reduced from 210 to 150 and the number of tank battalions in a typical division was reduced from four to three. Almost all of the tanks lost to each division in this process were, however, of the lightest and oldest types, the Mark I and Mark II. In May of 1940, each German armored division had, on average, 142 of these tanks. In June of 1941, this average number was reduced to 47. The number of the Mark IV "close support" tanks in each division was also reduced, but by a number so small as to be insignificant. While there had been twenty-seven Mark IV tanks to each armored division in 1940, there were but twenty-four in 1941.

What was far more significant than the great reduction in the number of light tanks and the tiny reduction in the number of Mark IV tanks was a considerable increase in tanks of the third category, the "medium" vehicles armed with 37mm guns. In May of 1940, German armored divisions contained 590 tanks of this sort. In June of 1941, there were 1,570. The total number of these vehicles (the German-built Mark III as well as the Czech-built 38t and 35t) fielded as part of armored divisions was thus nearly tripled.[3]

This reorganization represented considerable progress towards the goals that Ludwig Beck had laid out in 1937. Beck had wanted two-thirds of Germany's tanks to be medium tanks like the Mark III, 38t, or 35t. In June of 1941, a little more than one-half of the tanks in the German armored divisions fit that category. Beck had wanted howitzer-armed "close support" tanks on the British model to assist the "mediums" with such tasks as firing smoke shells to blind the enemy and high-explosive shells to knock out enemy antitank guns. The number of Mark IV tanks available to the German armored divisions in June of 1941 was more than sufficient for this set of duties. Finally, Beck had wanted light tanks to serve as "scouts" for the larger, less nimble vehicles. While the divisional allotment of these vehicles had been considerably reduced in the reorganization of the winter of 1940–1941, there were still far more of them in each tank battalion than the relative handful that Beck had considered necessary in 1937.[4]

The net reduction in the two lightest models of German tank was, moreover, more than compensated for by other changes in the German armored divisions. Fourteen out of the twenty armored divisions were provided with enough armored personnel carriers to carry a rifle company from one of the motorized infantry regiments. Two more armored divisions mounted an entire rifle battalion in such vehicles and one, the 1st Panzer Division, had two battalions of fully "armored" motorized infantry.[5] With eighteen armored vehicles, more than twenty machine guns, and the ability to dismount three full rifle platoons and the standard allotment of company heavy weapons, one of these armored infantry companies could easily fulfill all the missions assigned to a company of Mark I tanks. In addition, a company of armored infantry could do what light tanks could not. This included attacking small enemy parties hiding in woods or villages, providing security for tanks in broken terrain, and, most important of all, combating enemy antitank guns.[6]

Lest this use of the armored infantry for direct cooperation with tank units weaken the infantry brigades of the armored divisions, these were increased by about 25%. In the 1940 campaign, these brigades had, with one exception, consisted of four battalions of rifle troops, variously mounted in trucks and on motorcycles.[7] In the expansion of the winter of 1940–1941, these brigades were augmented and reorganized. The new standard, which was uniformly applied, called for a brigade consisting of two truck-borne regiments (each of two truck-borne battalions) and one motorcycle battalion. (Rifle companies and battalions carried in armored personnel carriers replaced truck-borne companies and battalions on a one-for-one basis.)[8]

Given the experiences of 1939 and 1940, this maintenance of the strength of the infantry brigade was prudent. The little embarrassments that had marred the otherwise spotless record of the German armored formations of the first year of the war had rarely been caused by a lack of tanks. The ambush of the tanks of the 4th Panzer Division in the woods near Czestochowa, the difficulties suffered by the tanks of that same division when they tried to enter Warsaw by themselves, and the breakdown of the breakthrough attempt at Amiens could all have been prevented by an extra battalion or two of infantry. Moreover, the river crossings and bridgehead breakouts so necessary to freedom of maneuver of the armored divisions had been, without exception, achieved by infantry components of those divisions.[9]

The modest increase of the motorized infantry within the armored division was matched by a similarly modest increase in the number of motorized infantry units serving outside of armored divisions. In the winter of 1940–1941, the German army formed six new motorized divisions and strengthened the four existing ones. With seven battalions of infantry (six carried in trucks and one on motorcycles), three battalions of artillery, an antitank battalion, and all of the usual division services, the motorized divisions were an important complement to the armored divisions, doing for the latter what the organic infantry brigades of the armored divisions did for the tank regiment. Where terrain was unsuitable for the armored division, the motorized division could take its place, freeing the armored division for employment elsewhere. When an armored division sped forward to seize an opportunity, the motorized division was, ideally, right behind it, doing all those things that permitted the commander of the armored division to concentrate on the task ahead of him rather than worry about the dangers behind him.

When the four motorized infantry divisions (of varying composition) of the *Waffen SS* are taken into account, the German forces in the Soviet Union included fourteen motorized infantry divisions. Compared to the ratios of motorized-to-armored divisions in the Polish (four-to-ten) and Western (six-to-ten) campaigns, the number of motorized divisions available for service in 1941 seems reasonable. Compared to the distances a motorized corps was expected to travel in the Soviet Union, however, the increase in the number of motorized divisions is far less impressive. After all, the further an armored division traveled, the greater the gap between it and the "walking" divisions that followed. The greater the gap, the greater the number of tasks that only a fully motorized formation could fill.

In the campaign of 1941, the armored divisions were often scores of kilometers, and, in some cases, hundreds of kilometers, ahead of the muscle-powered formations. This gap was often, for energetic Soviet commanders, a gift of time. With the danger posed by the armored division passed and the next wave of Germans hours or even days away, they could prepare their defenses, arrange for large numbers of their comrades to escape from the pocket that the Germans were trying to form, or, paradoxically, retreat into the depths of the pocket. As a result, the German infantry divisions marching in what they had thought was the wake of a fully motorized corps often found themselves fighting considerable Soviet forces. These battles, in turn, often tempted German commanders (up to and including Hitler) to order armored divisions to slow down or, in some cases, to come to the rescue of the hard-pressed infantry.[10] In a campaign whose success was based on the maintenance of an extraordinarily high tempo of operations, these delays were nothing short of disastrous.

Had they been available in sufficient numbers, motorized infantry divisions would have been well suited to interfere with such counteractions.

As with other things relating to warfare in the east, however, the Germans greatly underestimated the distances that they would be asked to cover and the scale of forces needed to effectively deal with those distances. Felix Steiner, who commanded a motorized infantry division during the 1941 campaign, later argued that about twenty-five or so additional motorized infantry divisions would have been needed to provide a proper connection between the armored divisions and those built around regiments of walking infantry. This, Steiner admitted, would have required ruthless exploitation of the auto industries of both Germany and occupied Europe.[11]

Though largely dependent on horse-drawn transport, the muscle-powered formations contained a considerable number of trucks, cars, and motorcycles. As had been the case in the 1940 campaign, ordinary infantry and mountain divisions used these, as well as captured vehicles and a variety of bicycles, to form mobile "advanced detachments" (*Vorausabteilungen*.) In the 1st Mountain Division, for example, elements of this sort were used to form *Vorausabteilung Lang*. Composed of three fully motorized antitank companies, a fully motorized combat engineer company, a platoon of motorcyclists, three rifle companies on bicycles, and a battery of 150mm howitzers, this was an advanced detachment led by (and named for) the commander of the division antitank battalion. Unlike the Vorausabteilungen of 1940, the German advanced detachments of 1941 were hard put to keep up with the armored and motorized infantry divisions driving on ahead of them. The distances were simply too great.

One of the many ironies of the 1941 campaign was that horse cavalry divisions of the type fielded by the Reichswehr during the interwar period might have proved a useful means of filling the "mobility gap" between fully motorized and walking divisions. The Germans had used their single brigade of horse cavalry in this way during the second half of the battle of France, where it rode in the wake of the fastest moving of all German formations in that campaign, General Hoth's XV Motorized Corps.[12] Expanded into a division (the 1st Cavalry Division) in the winter of 1940–1941, this same organization played a similar role during Barbarossa, serving as part of Panzer Gruppe Guderian.[13]

Trained to move on horseback but fight on foot, the German cavalrymen of 1941 were, strictly speaking, mounted infantrymen.[14] Even when the need to detail men to serve as horse-holders is taken into account, the division built around eight battalions of these cavalrymen, had a "bayonet strength" that was only slightly inferior to that of motorized infantry division. The greatest weakness of the German cavalry division (its relative lack of antitank guns and the heavier sorts of field pieces) could easily have been fixed by the attachment of independent antitank and artillery battalions from the general headquarters pool.[15]

The reason the Germans didn't field additional horse cavalry divisions was not, as one might suppose, Guderian's hostility towards horse cavalry.[16] Rather, the advocates of horse cavalry in the German army of the late 1930s had tended to focus on the mission of operational reconnaissance. Cavalry divisions and corps, the cavalry enthusiasts imagined, would range *ahead* of the rest of the army. The idea that cavalry formations might serve a force that followed *behind* other parts of the army did not receive much attention. Though they kept themselves busy trumpeting the virtues that would have made cavalry so useful in Russia, the members of the German cavalry "club," like the rest of the German army, were not mentally prepared for a campaign in which distances were measured in hundreds of kilometers.

The attack against the Soviet forces in Poland, Byelorussia, and Ukraine that began on 22 June 1941 placed unprecedented demands on the German armored and motorized infantry divisions. In the course of the first *month* of fighting, the fully motorized formations involved in the operation penetrated into Soviet held territory to a depth of 600 to 750 kilometers. When compared to the 250 or so kilometers traveled by most German armored divisions in three weeks of the first phase of the 1940 campaign and the similar distances covered by the same formations in Poland, this is an impressive achievement. When we consider the pattern of the fighting, which often required the armored divisions to turn away from their routes in order to complete the encirclement of a pocket of defending Soviets, the deed is more impressive still. Finally, when the primitive nature of the Soviet roads is taken into account, the fact that the German armored divisions traveled as far as they did is only a little less than miraculous.

A good deal of this miracle can be attributed to the powers of improvisation possessed by ordinary German soldiers and NCOs. Products of a society that respected education, skill, and craftsmanship and members of an army that valued initiative over routine, men whose names will never grace the pages of history books found ways to obtain the food, fuel, ammunition, transport, and spare parts needed to keep their units moving. The other part of this miracle can be credited to the German leadership. True to the German teaching that fully motorized formations should not be tied to closely to muscle-powered ones, they managed to preserve the armored and motorized divisions from secondary tasks that might have kept them from moving forward. Thus, while armored and motorized divisions crossed the border in the company of walking infantry formations, they parted company with the *Fußvolk* as soon as the opportunity presented itself.[17]

As before, the armored and motorized divisions spent most of the 1941 campaign, and, in particular, most of the first month of the campaign, as part of fully motorized corps of two, three, or four divisions. Recently been rechristened *Panzer Korps,* the fully motorized corps were provided with recently formed corps headquarters.[18] The older motorized corps headquarters were converted into the headquarters of fully motorized "armored groups" on the model of *Panzer Gruppe von Kleist* of the 1940 campaign. As the commanders of the motorized corps of 1940 became the commanders of the armored groups of 1941, this conversion of headquarters preserved the human relationships essential to command in fast-changing situations. Like the one armored group of 1940, the new armored groups were, in all but name, fully motorized field armies and, in October of 1941, were redesignated as Panzer armies.[19]

As might be imagined, the wear and tear on the German motorized forces that plunged so deeply into the territory of the Soviet Union was considerable. By the end of the first month of the campaign, even if the Soviets had not resisted at all, hard driving on dirt tracks, with little time allowed and almost no facilities available for maintenance, would have taken its toll. The winter that followed close on the heels of the final phase of the German campaign of 1941 would likewise have required little human assistance to deprive the armored divisions of much of their equipment.

As it was, Soviet resistance was often fierce, and though often characterized by inept tactics and the total absence of any plan of campaign, benefitted from considerable material advantages. Not the least of these was the availability of a new main battle tank that combined the mobility of a German medium tank with the armor and weaponry of the French Char B. This was the famous T-34. Initially outnumbered by less capable models, both heavy tanks that were less mobile and light tanks that were not as well armed, the T-34 was rarely employed in groups of more than five or six. It could thus be dealt with by such expedients as the forward deployment of the handful of 100mm field guns and 88mm antiaircraft guns available to the motorized corps.[20] As the Germans understood very soon after encountering it, however, the new tank rendered obsolete all German tanks save the Mark IV. Until suitably improved by additional armor and the replacement of its 75mm howitzer with a suitable antitank gun, the latter tank had merely been made obsolescent.

German Mark III tank, with long-barreled 50mm gun. Photo courtesy of the Department of Defense.

German Mark IV tank, with long-barreled 75mm gun. Photo courtesy of the Department of Defense.

As is well known, the eventual German response to the discovery of the T-34 was the creation of the Panther tank. A year would pass before the T-34 would become a common sight on the Eastern Front. Two years would be needed for significant numbers of Panther tanks to find their way into tank battalions. In the mean time, another change in the tactical environment took place. With winter and increasingly strong Soviet resistance taking their toll on man, beast, and the internal combustion engine, the German army stopped moving. The position warfare that the Germans had tried so hard to avoid set in. Though situation maps still showed the jaunty flags representing armored divisions and motorized corps, the formations they represented had been reduced, like the rest of the German army at the front, to small battle groups capable of little more than self-defense and small-scale attacks.

The motorized forces rebuilt on the sturdy framework of the survivors of the first winter in Russia bore little outward resemblance to the force that had taken the field in 1939. The tanks that had played such a big part in the Polish campaign, the tiny Mark I, the Mark II, the 38t, and the 35t, had all but disappeared from frontline service. Those light tanks that remained served in highly specialized roles, such as command, recovery, reconnaissance, and engineer vehicles.[21] The motorcycle, which, on 22 June 1941, had carried 20% of the infantry strength and 30% of the reconnaissance troops of each armored division, was quickly disappearing. The motorcycle battalions of armored and motorized infantry divisions were amalgamated with the reconnaissance battalions of those divisions. While some of these still included one or two companies mounted on motorcycles, two-wheeled motor transport was increasingly replaced by a combination of *Volkswagens*, trucks, and armored personnel carriers.[22]

The tanks that remained in the armored divisions were the Mark III and IV. Improved with additional armor and longer, more powerful guns (50mm and 75mm, respectively), these tanks were still, on balance, inferior to the T-34. What was worse, they were slow to come off the production lines. Thus, while Herculean efforts had been made to recover the many tanks that littered the paths that the armored divisions had taken in the 1941 campaign, most of the nineteen German armored divisions on the Eastern Front had to make do with one or two understrength tank battalions.[23] The motorized infantry was likewise reduced in strength. Officially, the only infantry unit lost by each armored and motorized infantry division was the single motorcycle battalion. The amalgamation of this unit with the division reconnaissance battalion, however, masked the fact that remaining infantry battalions (four for an armored division, six for a motorized division) had been shrunk considerably.[24]

The armored divisions that emerged from this reorganization, though smaller, were much more intensively armed than their predecessors. The reduction in the number of motorized infantrymen increased the proportion of infantry heavy weapons (antitank guns, infantry guns, mortars, heavy machine guns) to riflemen. The towed 37mm antitank guns of the division antitank battalions were replaced with 50mm and 75mm antitank guns, many of which were self-propelled. (By the end of 1942, self-propelled 75mm antitank guns were a common sight in German armored divisions.) As anti-aircraft battalions were increasingly made a permanent part of armored divisions, 88mm guns became available to further bolster the antitank strength of those formations.

This proliferation of antitank weapons was not a purely German phenomenon. On the Soviet side, purpose-built antitank guns, field guns and infantry guns pressed into service as antitank guns, mines, antitank rifles employed *en masse,* and a large variety of grenades were provided to the troops at the front. Together, these antitank weapons accomplished what the "tank cannot survive on its own" school of the late 1930s had prematurely predicted. By the end of 1942, there were so many of these weapons that the Germans had to radically revise the way that they handled their armored divisions. The essential element of this change was a lowering of the echelon at which tanks cooperated with the other arms present within the armored division.

The close combination of the various arms was not a new practice for the Germans. Far from it, the degree to which German fighting men from different units, different arms, and even different branches of service cooperated with each other had long been the envy of foreign observers. This ability was closely related to "mission tactics" (*Auftragstaktik*) the German philosophy of command and control, with its emphasis on the duty of subordinates to do whatever was required by the situation. That is to say, "mission tactics" required soldiers to solve problems with whatever resources were at hand, even if these resources originated from a different unit or arm.[25]

The German capacity for intimate cooperation between units of different arms was also related to the long-standing fondness of German officers for the command of *Detachements,* all-arms task forces of brigade size with independent missions.[26] "The whole of our training in time of peace, including the Autumn Maneuvers," lamented one Prussian general of the late nineteenth century, "rests essentially upon the practice of detachments, and only a few hours are devoted to the exercises of the division, which is the proper fighting body. Even our greatest maneuvers, those of one corps against another, belong still in a certain respect to the operations of detachments. . . ."[27]

Despite this tradition, there was little mixing of the elements of German tank and motorized infantry brigades until 1940.[28] In most instances of the campaigns of 1939, and some in 1940, each brigade had its own axis of attack, thus it may have been separated from the other by a considerable distance. The experience of General Ritter von Thoma, commander of the tank brigade of the 2nd Panzer Division in the Polish campaign, was typical. "That division was in General von List's Army on the extreme southern wing of the Carpathians. I was ordered to advance on the Jablonka Pass, but suggested instead that the motorized brigade should be sent there, while I carried out with my tank brigade a flanking move—through thick woods and over the ridge."[29]

Within each brigade, regiments and battalions of the same arm cooperated directly, and intimately, with each other as well as with the artillery, engineers, and antitank troops. There were also instances where infantry companies (particularly those in armored carriers) were attached to tank units and when tank companies were attached to motorized infantry regiments and brigades.[30] As a rule, however, the tank and motorized infantry brigades remained, to employ a term the Germans of the time were fond of using, *thoroughbred,* until 1940.

The notable exception to this general rule was provided by the 4th Light Division. From the very beginning of the Polish Campaign, this formation operated as three all-arms task groups. Referred to variously as *Regimentsgruppen* (regimental groups), *Verfolgungsgruppen* (pursuit groups), and *Kampfgruppen* (battle groups), each of these groups were built around the headquarters of one of the three maneuver regiments—the two cavalry Schützen regiments and the reconnaissance regiment. Assigned forces varied greatly, with Schützen battalions, artillery battalions and batteries, the motorcycle and armored car squadrons (from the reconnaissance regiment), engineer companies and platoons, antitank companies and platoons, and elements from the division's single tank battalion combined in nearly all possible ways. The one general rule was that tanks were generally employed as single companies. Indeed, though the 4th Light Division took part in fifty-eight engagements in the course of the Polish Campaign, there were only two cases where the tank battalion was employed as an intact unit.[31]

The old habit of forming *Detachements* was extended, without much fanfare, to the armored divisions in the course of the 1940 campaign in France. Immediately after the breakthrough at Sedan, for example, the 1st Panzer Division converted its armored and motorized infantry brigades into two nearly identical organizations, each with two battalions of tanks, two battalions of infantry, and a share of the divisional artillery, engineers, antitank troops, and services.[32] It was not until 1942, however, that the barrier between the tank and infantry elements of the armored division broke down completely, with the nearly universal replacement of the single-arm regiment or brigade with all-arms battle groups (Kampfgruppen.)

What an ideal battle group, one formed with the best weapons available, might have looked like can be seen in the example of *Kampfgruppe Strachwitz,* a battle group of *Großdeutschland* Division that went into action in March of 1943. Led by Count Hyacinth von Strachwitz, one of Germany's most daring tank commanders, the battle group consisted of two tank battalions, four motorized infantry battalions, a company of combat engineers, an antitank company, and four batteries of field artillery.[33] Though commanded by a lieutenant colonel aided by the small staff of the headquarters of a tank regiment, this battle group was, in fact, almost as large as the armored divisions of 1940 and somewhat larger than most German armored divisions of the 1943. It follows that the battle groups formed in divisions less favored than *Großdeutschland* were considerably smaller.

One technique, favored by General Frido von Senger und Etterlin when he commanded the 17th Panzer Division, for using battle groups in ordinary armored divisions, was to divide the division into two very different battle groups. The tank group, consisting of tank units, armored infantry units, and attached assault guns, was organized as the division commander's "arm of decision." The infantry group, consisting of the unarmored elements of the division, had the mission of finding the enemy, occupying his attention, and probing for weaknesses. Once a critical weakness, such as a poorly protected flank, was discovered, the tank group would be sent forward to exploit it.[34]

Generally, the tank group was not to be sent into action until the infantry group had discovered (and perhaps influenced) the true shape of the battlefield. This was necessary to prevent the tanks from running into what the Germans sometimes called *Pakfronts* (antitank gun fronts). Consisting of far more than antitank guns, and, rarely arranged as a solid front, Pakfronts were, in fact, large traps designed by the Soviets to catch and destroy German tanks. Attacking in the manner of the Blitzkrieg years of 1939 to 1941, German tanks would have been easy prey for Soviet Pakfronts. By the time that their leaders had realized that they had blundered into a trap, the tank units would have been hemmed in by mines, shot at from all directions by a variety of antitank guns, pounded by artillery, and perhaps subject to swift counterattack. A force rich in infantry, on the other hand, was less vulnerable to the antitank weapons, much less likely to penetrate far enough to spring a trap, and, most of all, far more capable of observing its surroundings.

The one exception to the German policy of leading with the infantry took place when the Soviets were kind enough to expose their own flanks. This occurred during enemy attacks, during that short window of opportunity between the time the enemy tanks had passed through an area and the time that flank defense had been properly established.

> The employment of tanks leads to the greatest success when, sent into action and controlled by the "all arms" leader, they are used to strike the enemy in the flank, soon after the latter has begun an attack and before his antitank weapons have established firm antitank positions. In addition, in this last case, the attack must, with a view to direction and timing, be ordered by the all arms leader on the spot. (With this last method the weak forces of the worn-out 17th Panzer Division annihilated one enemy division at Kuteinikowskaja on 5 January 1943 and another at Bol Talowaja on 27 January 1943.)

The aforementioned technique of the 17th Panzer Division could be used in two ways. If the division was intact, the tank regiment and motorized infantry brigade would serve as the nucleus of the tank and infantry groups. If the division was already broken up into all-arms battle groups, each battle group would be formed into tank and infantry groups of its own. In the former case, the division commander would serve as the all arms commander, the man who, among other things, decided when the time was ripe to send the tank group into battle. In the latter case, an all arms commander who was independent of both the tank and infantry groups had to be found for each battle group At no time, the commanding general of the 17th Panzer Division stressed, should the commander of either the tank group or the infantry group attempt to simultaneously serve as the all arms commander.[35]

The senior artillery officer (such as the commander of the division's artillery regiment) would remain close to the all arms commander. Subordinate artillery commanders would locate themselves with the leaders of the tank and infantry groups. In this way, which borrowed a great deal from traditional German artillery practices, the artillery could be used for two purposes. When targets of interest to the battle as a whole presented themselves, the senior artilleryman could order the batteries to fire upon them. When, on the other hand, the targets could not be seen by the senior artilleryman or were only of local interest, they could be dealt with by subordinate artillery commanders.[36]

The bulk of the artillery available to support the various battle groups formed within armored divisions consisted, through the end of the war, of conventional howitzers and guns towed by a variety of trucks and tractors. Beginning in 1942, however, small numbers of self-propelled artillery pieces became available. By early 1943, it was common for one of the three artillery battalions of an armored division to be entirely equipped with self-propelled pieces. In the experience of the 17th Panzer Division, these self-propelled artillery units proved particularly useful as a means of cooperating with tank groups that had advanced into the depth of an enemy position. Given enough time, towed artillery could displace forward. In battles of this sort, however, time was of the essence.[37]

The great advantage of the self-propelled artillery battalion was not so much the time saved in attaching and detaching the howitzers from their tractors, but a combination of a large number of little efficiencies. For example, the armor that protected the essential vehicles of the self-propelled unit, those that carried the commander and other forward observers, the signalers, the officer in charge of the gun line, and, of course, the pieces themselves, was not very thick. It was thick enough, however, to preserve the battalion from the type of fire (whether from small arms or the near misses of large shells) that tended to drive the unarmored gunners to the ground. This same armor, combined with the fact that the key vehicles were either tracked or half-tracked, also allowed self-propelled artillery units to follow more closely behind attacking tanks. This increased the chances that battery commanders could see the tank battle and intervene at the appropriate time and place.[38]

Even when the rest of an artillery unit cooperating with tanks was not armored or even motorized, there was still considerable advantage to providing artillery commanders and other artillery observers with armored vehicles. While such vehicles did exist, purpose-built mobile observation posts were rare. In most cases, the vehicle that carried the man who controlled the artillery fire was either a tank or an assault gun. As many of the commanders of assault gun units had been initially trained as conventional artillerymen, they were usually happy to lose the services of one of their 75mm guns in order to gain the use of a much larger number of 105mm and 150mm howitzers. Even when observers from the supporting artillery unit were not available, the assault gun units contained many men qualified to call for artillery fire. Tank unit commanders were often harder to convince. As late as May of 1944, General Guderian (then serving as Inspector of Armored Troops) felt obliged to remind tank men that the loan of one tank to an artillery observer was a fair trade for the suppression of enemy antitank defenses.[39]

The great disadvantage of the self-propelled artillery was the tendency of the motorized mounts to break down. Even though the chassis used for most German models of self-propelled artillery pieces were well-proven ones taken from mature tank types, they were far more prone to mechanical trouble than the carriages of towed guns. For that reason, German self-propelled batteries were provided with six pieces rather than the customary four. When all six pieces were in working order, moreover, the Germans found that there were some advantages to the larger batteries. In rapid movement, the batteries had to displace often. With six pieces in a battery, a half-battery of three pieces could remain in firing position while the other three pieces moved forward. Six pieces could also provide wider smokescreens and denser concentrations of high explosive. As self-propelled batteries were rarely close enough to combine their fires on the same target, this extra firepower was important.[40]

Not all of the leaders of German armored troops were impressed with the new self-propelled artillery. Herman Balck, who had commanded the 1st Schützen Regiment of the 1st Panzer Division in 1940, the 11th Panzer Division in 1941 and 1942, and the overgrown Großdeutschland Division in 1943, had little use for such weapons. In an interview in 1979, he said that they were "very large and visible and vulnerable to being found by air reconnaissance."[41] Balck also noted that while a towed gun whose prime mover was out of action could be pulled by another vehicle, mechanical trouble in a self-propelled piece disabled both the mount and the howitzer. Balck's solution, laid out in his proposal for reorganizing the Großdeutschland division in 1943, was to provide part of the artillery with fully-tracked prime movers.[42]

Apart from this point, Balck's ideal armored organization reflected the same concerns as the improvisations that Senger und Etterlin made. Noting that the Großdeutschland division was so big that it could easily be divided into two "ordinary" armored divisions, Balck proposed that Großdeutschland be divided into three permanent battle groups, two of which would be well provided with motorized infantry and one of which would be almost entirely armored. These three groups, which Balck called brigades, were to have been supported by a reconnaissance battalion, a pioneer battalion, an artillery regiment, and an antiaircraft battalion. Whether the resulting formation was to be called a division or a corps, Balck noted, didn't matter. The important thing was the way in which the various arms cooperated with each other.

Balck's ideal armored brigade consisted of three tank battalions, a single battalion of armored infantry, a battalion of 105mm howitzers towed by fully-tracked vehicles, a battalion of self-propelled antiaircraft guns, and a company of combat engineers mounted in armored carriers. The infantry brigades were the mirror image of this organization. The three tank battalions were replaced by three motorized infantry battalions, the armored infantry battalion was replaced by a battalion of assault guns. The engineer company, artillery battalion, and antiaircraft battalion were armed with similar weapons as their counterparts in the armored brigade. Instead of armored vehicles, however, they were mounted in trucks and other soft-skinned, mostly wheeled motor vehicles.[43]

In a sense, Balck's proposed organization was an updated version of one of the common configurations for a motorized corps of the Blitzkrieg years (one armored division and two motorized infantry divisions). Balck's brigades were not just smaller than the corresponding gasoline-powered divisions of 1939 through 1941, they were much more tightly integrated. Interarm cooperation was no longer just a matter of divisions and brigades working with each other. Rather, Balck's proposal provided for the direct and frequent cooperation between battalions and even companies of different types. The distinction between large units of armored troops and motorized infantry, moreover, was no longer so stark. Rather than being a matter of formations with radically different capabilities, the gulf between large armored and motorized units had narrowed to become a matter of emphasis and proportion. Thus, while Balck's ideal armored brigade had lots of the best tanks Germany had to offer and enough infantry to protect those tanks from immediate threats, the motorized infantry brigades had a sufficient number of assault guns to provide direct protection to the motorized infantry.[44]

Balck's proposal did not go very far. Germany could not afford to provide such a rich array of weapons to a single division, no matter how favored. Nonetheless, the ideas behind Balck's organization soon found their way into the structure of the German motorized forces. In the summer of 1943, most of the motorized infantry divisions in the German army were authorized tank battalions. As tanks were in short supply, most of these battalions were, in fact, equipped with assault guns. This expedient notwithstanding, the difference between armored divisions and motorized infantry divisions were getting progressively smaller. The tables of organization promulgated in September of 1943 called for armored divisions with two battalions of tanks and four of motorized infantry and motorized infantry divisions with one battalion of tanks and six of motorized infantry.[45]

There were, of course, a number of other differences. German armored divisions were provided with armored personnel carriers, self-propelled artillery, self-propelled antiaircraft guns, and self-propelled infantry guns. Armored divisions were more likely to have actual tanks, rather than the turretless assault guns, in their tank battalions. The antitank guns in the division antitank battalion were more likely to be self-propelled and, of the self-propelled guns, the ones in the armored divisions were more likely to be of the well-armored (tank hunter) types.[46] These differences were nonetheless so small that armored and motorized infantry divisions (since renamed *Panzergrenadier* divisions) could increasingly be considered variations on the same theme. This was particularly true of the armored and Panzergrenadier divisions of the Waffen-SS, which, as the power of the SS "state within a state" grew, got an increasing share of first-class equipment.[47]

The final step in the evolution of the two principal types of German motor-driven formations of World War II was an even closer association between the armored infantry and tank battalions. Two of the three armored formations that the Germans experimented with in the last year of World War II, the independent armored brigade and the Type 1945 armored division, were built around the pairing of a tank battalion with a battalion of armored infantry. In the case of the armored brigade, this pairing constituted the bulk of the organization. Apart from it, the only other units were the engineer and reconnaissance companies and the rear services. In the case of the Type 45 armored division, the "mixed armored regiment", as the pairing was called, was the armored heart of a much larger organization that also included a battalion of assault guns, four battalions of motorized infantry, and the usual combat support and service troops.[48]

These plans barely saw the light of day. Only one of the seven independent armored brigades that were formed in the fall of 1944 escaped immediate amalgamation into an armored or Panzergrenadier division. No divisions seem to have been completely reorganized as Type 45 divisions. The important thing about these ideas is thus their inspiration rather than their implementation. They reflected attempts by the writers of tables of organization to come to grips with a situation that the men at the front had understood for a long time. The tank could do its duty on the modern battlefield only when it cooperated intimately with other arms.

8

THE ARMORED GUERILLA

The Russo-German War of 1941–1945 was, among many other things, a great eater of tanks. The response of the Soviet Union to this phenomenon was to obtain, by a combination of importation and manufacture, more tanks. Lack of resources, however, prevented the Germans from doing the same. Their response to the growing shortage of tanks was to develop other sorts of armored fighting vehicles that, despite their outward resemblance to tanks, could be both produced and employed with greater economy. Though overshadowed by the more spectacular Panther and Tiger tanks, these vehicles—assault guns; tank hunters; self-propelled antitank, infantry, and anti-aircraft guns; and cannon mounted on armored personnel carriers—achieved impressive results in difficult situations. The key to this success were tactics that had far more in common with those of guerilla warfare than they did with those of the Blitzkrieg years of 1939 through 1941.

The first vehicle of this sort to enter the German inventory was the inappropriately named assault gun. The honor of inventing this weapon is usually accorded to Erich von Manstein. Unlike many of his colleagues, Manstein was not convinced that the storm troop tactics developed during World War I were sufficient to give German infantry divisions the attacking power that they needed to break the deadlock of the trenches. The spring offensives of 1918 had shown, Manstein believed, that the German infantry was too dependent upon massive artillery support.[1] This made the stockpiling of large amounts of artillery ammunition a prerequisite for a breakthrough of a well-defended front. The need to stockpile, in turn, made possible the repetition of the phenomenon that had prevented the success of the spring offensives of 1918. That is to say, as fresh troops from the enemy strategic reserves were able to establish a new defensive line faster than the Germans could amass the materiel needed to break through that line.[2]

Manstein's solution to this problem was to advocate a new type of artillery—infantry guns mounted on the armored chassis of light tanks. Infantry guns had, from the very start, been an integral part of storm troop tactics. Moving them through the twenty or so kilometers of a defended zone was, however, a problem that was only imperfectly solved by drag ropes and teams of horses. An armored chassis also permitted the assault gun to be employed with far greater flexibility than an infantry gun mounted on steel or wooden wheels. Assault guns could, for example, move from one end of a division's sector to the other in a matter of minutes, even if under fire. Traditional infantry guns, on the other hand, tended to spend the entire battle in one or two firing positions. As a result, assault guns could be used by a division commander to rapidly form and shift his main effort (*Schwerpunkt*). Infantry guns could only be used as "main effort" weapons (*Schwerpunktwaffen*) by battalions and regiments, units whose zones of action were so narrow that infantry guns could change targets without changing fire positions.[3]

Manstein chose a short-barreled 75mm howitzer as the main armament of the assault guns. This weapon had much in common with both the infantry guns of World War I and the lighter infantry guns then being developed for the use of the German infantry. (The heavier versions were 150mm howitzers.) Like these other weapons, the howitzer carried by the first German assault guns was primarily a means of shooting high-explosive shells at targets such as machine gun nests, antitank guns, houses, and even enemy tanks. It was also an efficient means of small concentrations of smoke—too weak to constitute a proper smoke screen but sufficient to prevent enemy observers from using a particular vantage point.

In some respects, Manstein's assault gun was similar to the contemporary British, French, and American conceptions of an infantry tank. Manstein, however, was far less bound by regimental and arm of service boundaries. The product of an army that used such terms as "infantry artillery" and "cavalry artillery," Manstein was more interested in the tactical and operational characteristics of weapons. The assault guns that he imagined were to be capable of serving as mobile antitank guns as well as machine gun destroyers. Manstein even imagined these weapons being capable of using indirect fire.

Like the infantry tanks of other armies, Manstein's assault gun would fight in close proximity to friendly rifle squads and machine guns. For this reason, it would rarely be called upon to provide its own local security. That is to say, any antitank gun close enough to fire upon it would have to advertise its position to German infantrymen a few meters away. The fact that German infantrymen would always be nearby, Manstein argued, allowed the assault gun to dispense with a fully rotating turret. This, in turn, made it possible to mount a relatively large gun on a relatively small chassis. It also made it possible for the assault gun to be produced far more easily (and thus cheaply) than tanks carrying equivalent firepower.[4]

Though primarily concerned with boosting the combat power of infantry regiments, divisions, and corps, Manstein was not averse to the use of his assault guns as part of independent armored formations. His argument for the weapon, after all, was neither an attempt to deprive the German army of its independent armored force nor to diminish the tank brigades then being formed to cooperate with infantry formations. If other units had to be sacrificed to make room for the assault guns, Manstein's preferred victims were divisional antitank and field artillery battalions. In other words, Manstein was by no means proposing a substitute for the tank or a competitor for the independent armored force. Rather, he was advocating that Germany acquire even more armored vehicles than either Beck or Guderian had deemed practical.[5]

Manstein first proposed the assault gun in the fall of 1935, when he was serving with the operations branch of the general staff in Berlin. General Beck was hard to impress. "My dear Manstein," he is reported to have said, "this time you missed the target." The overall commander of the army, Baron Werner von Fritsch, was more encouraging. The difference between how the two generals, who tended to agree on most things, seems to have been a function of their background. Both Beck and Fritsch were artillerymen. While Beck had served in artillery units that had been part of infantry divisions, units designed to participate in massive bombardments, Fritsch had been a horse artilleryman, commanding fast-moving batteries attached to cavalry divisions. Fritsch was thus better able to imagine guns that moved rapidly into position to fire a few well-chosen shots.[6]

In the autumn of 1937, General Fritsch promulgated a plan to provide, within twenty-four months, a battalion of twelve or so assault guns to each active infantry division.[7] By the end of 1940, each reserve division was also to be so equipped. In addition, an assault gun battalion was to be assigned to each armored division and an assault gun platoon included in the reconnaissance battalion of each fully motorized division. Like the plans to provide each German infantry division with six field artillery battalions and each army corps with a tank brigade, this project could not long survive Hitler's decision to step up the pace of German rearmament. Quantity rather than quality was the order of the day and only a handful of assault guns were built. Few, if any, took part in the Polish campaign, and only thirty assault guns (organized into five six-gun batteries) served in the west in 1940.[8]

By the summer of 1941, the number of assault guns had increased nearly tenfold. Eleven battalions (of twenty-one assault guns each) and five independent batteries (of seven assault guns each), brought the number of such weapon in use to 266.[9] While this was far from the originally prescribed allotment of one battalion per division, it was enough to give both the German artillery (which operated the weapons) and the German infantry (which benefitted from their employment) a taste for the new weapon. The use of the assault gun battalions as part of the general headquarters ensured that they would be employed at a wide variety of places and with a wide variety of units in a relatively short period of time. It was thus not long before after-action reports and letters from the front were full of requests for additional assault guns.

The popularity of the assault gun was enhanced by its usefulness as an antitank weapon. Like the infantry guns that were their immediate ancestors, the assault guns were coming into widespread use just at that point in time when enemy tanks were proving hard to deal with. The short barreled 75mm gun initially carried by the assault guns were a less than perfect means for dealing with heavier Soviet tanks that made their appearance during the summer of 1941. Even when firing the hollow-charge projectiles that were sometimes available, these weapons were rarely able to destroy a T-34 or other first-line Soviet tank with a frontal shot. Hits against the flanks and rear of these tanks, particularly multiple hits, were another matter indeed. The poor training of the Soviet crews, the fact that their fighting (as opposed to command) tanks were not equipped with radios, and the Soviet habit of going into combat with buttoned-up commanders made it relatively easy for assault gun units to set up situations where this was possible.

Though they fit in well with the situation at hand, these ambush tactics were a natural and nearly painless continuation of traditional German artillery tactics. From the days of Frederick the Great there had existed a subculture within the German artillery who favored a quick dash by a single battery to deliver a few shots at the right time and place over daylong bombardments by hundreds of guns. The gunners who made up this sub-culture were, for the most part, associated with the horse artillery.

Frederick the Great had invented horse artillery as a secret weapon to use in pitched battles. His vision of the new arm was that it should serve as a sort of fire brigade—a unit to be held in reserve until needed to respond to either crisis or opportunity. By the end of the nineteenth century, however, German horse artillery had become closely linked with the cavalry. In particular, the purpose of horse artillery was to provide artillery support to cavalry formations operating apart from the main body of an army. Though no longer associated with main battles, the idea of a "stitch in time that saved nine" (a small amount of artillery that could intervene rapidly) remained.

In 1877, the German artillery general Adolph von Schell wrote the following about the horse artillery of his day.

> Artillery requires time for the proper development of its action, but in a cavalry action every moment is precious, and the time available for the work of the guns passes very rapidly. We must make the most of it and avoid wasting precious moments in long movements. The time for producing an effect being so short we must take care not to lose a moment of it through a lengthy firing to ascertain the range or any want of skill in shooting. The tactics of horse artillery must be simple, the determining of the range rapid, and its skill in shooting of a very high standard of excellence.[10]

How General von Schell's ideal worked in the mobile campaigns of the first season of World War I can be seen in the following report of the commander of the horse artillery battalion (*Reitende Abteilung*) of the 15th Field Artillery Regiment. Attached to a cavalry division, the horse artillery was cooperating with other elements of that division—horse cavalry and Jäger—covering the advance of the Sixth (Bavarian) Army into Lorraine.

Having just been told by cavalrymen that a large force of French cavalry, artillery, and cyclists was on a collision course with his division, the German horse artillery battalion commander commanded his three batteries to gallop forward to a hill that offered suitable firing positions. Riding ahead of his guns, the battalion commander quickly reached the hill, took a look at the targets that presented themselves, and made his plan. He then rushed back to the road where his gun teams were straining to climb the hill, oriented his battery commanders, and gave his order. "Haste is urgent. Here's a chance to get a few Iron Crosses. Fire upon everything that is standing or moving down there. Right battery, cyclists. Center battery, artillery. Left battery, cavalry."[11]

The batteries began to fire as soon as they were in position. Moving along roads or standing in open fields, the French cavalrymen, cyclists, and artillerymen were easy targets. The physical effect of the fire, though considerable, was not nearly as great as it might have been if the German battalion commander had taken the time to find better positions for his guns, to make better range estimations, and organize a "time on target" mission. The time needed to take such measures, however, would have permitted the French to advance into the wooded hills (then occupied by the German cavalrymen). This, in turn, would have resulted in a bloody, retail battle that would then have prevented the German cavalry division from fulfilling its mission of facilitating the advance of the infantry that would follow in a day or two.

German horse artillery was never formally separated from the field artillery. From the early nineteenth century, through the First World War, and up until the eve of the Second World War, horse artillery batteries and battalions were formed as supernumerary elements of selected field artillery regiments. On mobilization, the horse artillery units reported to cavalry brigades, divisions, or corps. In peacetime, they trained with the ordinary field artillery batteries of their regiments.[12]

For this reason, as well as the fact that no distinction was made between horse artillery officers and other field artillery officers, there was considerable cross-fertilization within the larger field artillery community. Horse artillerymen learned the techniques appropriate to the relatively leisurely pace of a major battle while field artillerymen became familiar with the faster pace of cavalry engagements. The only difference in transportation was that horse artillery gunners rode into battle on the backs of the horses that pulled the guns while the field artillery gunners rode on the limbers or in wagons.[13]

The tactics that the German field artillery took into World War I were also affected by the peculiar fashions of the German army of the time. At a time when the exploitation of technology was permitting more and more Germans to enter the middle classes, and the middle classes to erode the power of the aristocracy, the German officer corps served as a refuge from the grim, leveling tendencies of mathematics, steel, and artificial dyestuffs. For this reason, officers of all branches—to include the artillery and engineers—tended to neglect the technical aspects of their work in favor of the dynamic ones. Thus, German gunnery in 1914 was universally rated as inferior to that of the French artillery, and, in the opinion of one distinguished observer, inferior to that of the British, Russians, and Austro-Hungarians. The ability of German artillerymen to deal with fast-moving tactical situations, however, was unsurpassed.[14]

The fruit of this phenomenon could be seen throughout the First World War. Though much of the German artillery of that war fought from fixed positions, there were times when batteries of both horse and field artillery were called upon to fight differently. During the French Champagne offensive of September 1915, for example, a field artillery battalion of 105mm howitzers (three batteries of four pieces each) was deliberately kept out of the weeklong artillery duel that preceded the French attack. When the change in the pattern of fire signaled that the French infantry attack was about to begin, the battalion moved forward. Instead of deploying his sixteen pieces, the battalion commander moved them into a covered and concealed *Lauerstellung* about three kilometers away from the closest French units.[15]

The original purpose of putting the artillery battalion in the Lauerstellung was to ambush any French cavalry that might try to exploit a breakthrough by the French infantry. (For that reason, the Lauerstellung was established near the most likely route that such a cavalry force might take—a major north-south highway leading straight into the German rear areas.) The cavalry attack never materialized. In its place came an attack by French infantry that, despite horrible losses, threatened to carve a gap in the German line. The cause of the gap was the nearly complete destruction of those German units that were defending from fixed positions. The danger was that the French might use the gap as a means of penetrating deeply into the German position, cutting off those portions of the German line that were still holding on, or both of these.

On order from the colonel commanding the divisional artillery, the German artillery battalion moved rapidly out of its Lauerstellung. After passing through a zone subject to continuous interdiction fire, the battalion reached the southern outskirts of the town of Sommepy. There the batteries deployed and took up firing positions that had been preselected by the battalion commanders. Seeing that the French infantry had just advanced across the crest of a ridge 1,600 meters away, they began to fire in support of the hard-pressed German infantry on the rear slope of that crest.[16] Once engaged, the German field artillery battalion lost its power of maneuver. Moving horse-drawn artillery over ground dominated by enemy artillery, after all, was an enormously risky business. As a result, the battalion had become, like scores of other artillery battalions involved in the battle, an instrument of position warfare rather than mobile warfare. The timely intervention of this battalion, however, did more for the Germans than the actions of those battalions that were unable to respond to the changing situation.[17]

The same could be said of the horse artillery battalion of 1914. Once engaged, it was no longer mobile. The horses would be separated from the guns and provided with the best protection that the local terrain might offer. The guns themselves would be under fire. Although this posed little danger to the men who were actually working the guns—the gun shields were proof against both small arms fire and shrapnel balls—it made moving the guns a very dangerous proposition. The *Sturmgeschütze* of World War II had no such limitations. Their armor permitted them to cross zones that were subject to enemy indirect fire with near impunity. The tactical advantages of this were huge. They could enter a battle that had already "gone hot." Likewise, if they could be better used elsewhere, the Sturmgeschütze could withdraw despite heavy indirect or small arms fire. In other words, the German assault artillery of World War II enjoyed many of the benefits of the horse artillery of a previous generation without having to put up with the extreme vulnerability of horses.

The additional degree of mobility provided by the tracked carriage of the Sturmgeschütze combined with this armored protection to make the use of the Lauerstellung a central feature of assault gun tactics. This was particularly true when it came to using Sturmgeschützen as antitank weapons. The habit of hiding the guns until the moment when they could be used decisively translated easily into the practice of hiding small groups of assault guns behind the main line of resistance in order to catch penetrating enemy tanks in the flanks or rear. Indeed, this technique may have been responsible for the fact that the assault guns of the Großdeutschland Division were, at least in 1942, far more efficient tank killers than the Mark III and Mark IV tanks of the same unit during the same period.[18]

Clever tactics were not the only virtue that the German assault gunners drew from their initial training as artillerymen. A major contributor to the success of the assault guns was the fact that their crews were far better shots than their counterparts in the armored branch were. Part of this can be credited to the simple fact that the officers commanding Sturmgeschütze units took gunnery seriously. Another part is the result of the practice of finding range by bracketing. By the time of World War II, this technique had been in regular use by German artillerymen for over a century.[19] German tank gunners, by way of contrast, were taught to "walk" their shots onto a target, much in the way that a machine gunner or an eighteenth century artilleryman might have done.

When combined with such mechanical advantages as greater reliability, lower silhouette, and better observation for the vehicle commander, the superior tactical and technical training of the German assault gun crews made the assault gun a far more survivable vehicle than contemporary German tanks. Indeed, a comparison of armored vehicle production figures for the latter part of World War II with figures derived from reports of vehicles on hand leads to the surprising conclusion that the life expectancy of a German assault gun was seven times greater than that of a German tank. That is to say, while a turreted tank could expect to serve for about a month before being destroyed, an assault gun lasted for seven months before it had to be replaced.[20]

This remarkable difference in life cycle led to a great expansion of the role of the German assault gun. In addition to being used in an increasing number of assault gun battalions formed under the auspices of the German artillery, assault guns were used to partially replace the towed antitank guns of infantry division antitank battalions. They were also used to stiffen armored reconnaissance units and, increasingly, to replace some of the tanks in the tank battalions of armored divisions and all of the tanks in the tank battalions of Panzergrenadier divisions.[21] In these latter units, the assault gun crews belonged, not to the artillery, but to the armored troops or, in the case of the assault gun companies of infantry division antitank battalions, the infantry.

It was during this period that Guderian reversed his uncharitable opinion of the assault gun. Rather than trying to preserve armored chassis for the production of tanks, he found himself competing with the artillery and infantry for control of the assault guns that came off the production lines. He even sponsored the design and production of an assault gun optimized for service as an antitank ambush weapon. With the official nickname of *Hetzer* (which may be loosely translated as "ambusher") and the less formal moniker of "Guderian's duck", this weapon mounted a 75mm gun on a light tank chassis in a way that produced a compact vehicle that was relatively easy to hide.

How the assault gun served in the antitank role can be seen from the experience of Tank Hunter Company 1045, an assault gun company serving as part of an infantry division antitank battalion.[22] The weapons employed were Sturmgeschütze III, with long-barreled 75mm guns mounted on the chassis of the Panzer III tank. The report is taken from the *Nachrichtenblatt der Panzertruppen*, a newsletter published by the Inspector of Armored Troops.

The company was held in readiness as the division reserve. After half an hour of intense artillery preparation (*Trommelfeuer*), the enemy attacked in the late morning with 30 tanks (late model T-34 and KV1) and ground attack aircraft. With portions of five or six divisions, he sought to force a breakthrough. The terrain was extraordinarily favorable for the enemy. In particular, patches of woods offered opportunities for gun positions and assembly areas.

The company went into action with nine assault guns and, on the first day, was able, within three hours, to shoot up or destroy the following: sixteen late model T-34 tanks, one KV 1 tank, two T-34 tanks (mobility kills), seventeen machine guns, two mortars, two artillery forward observers and their radios, one antitank gun, and one infantry gun. On the second day: two T-34 tanks, one self-propelled gun, twenty-one machine guns, three antitank rifles, two mortars, and two antitank guns.

The tanks were shot up at ranges of 600– 800 meters. One assault gun shot up in fifteen minutes a column of five tanks.

The enemy tanks didn't have time to get off any aimed shots. The rest of the tanks were hunted down individually. One T-34 was shot up with three shots at a range of 1,000 meters.

High explosive shells had an outstanding effect against unarmored targets. The provision of machine guns and submachine guns to the assault guns has proved itself advantageous, because these weapons allow enemy infantry and antitank teams to be suppressed or kept at a distance.

It should be mentioned that in the fields where the fighting took place the grain had been gathered into haystacks. During a counterattack, the Russians used incendiary ammunition and set fire to three assault guns which had used these haystacks for concealment.

Soon after the first 30 minutes of combat the Russians came on our radio net and, using the code name of the company commander, attempted to get position reports from the individual assault guns and to give orders. The company commander was forced to change the frequency three times during the attack.

All that remains to be said is that, after such heavy losses of tanks, the enemy no longer employed armor to accompany his infantry attacks, but rather dug them in near the line of departure.[23]

Even when employed as part of a tank battalion, assault gun units continued to employ their peculiar tactics. In the case of a mixed battalion of tanks and assault guns whose tactics Guderian considered exemplary, the assault guns were, whenever possible, used for direct cooperation with the Panzergrenadier units and as mobile antitank guns. In the attack, the assault guns formed, with attached Panzergrenadier platoons, the second wave of the tank battalion. This served two purposes. First, it allowed the assault guns to assist the Panzergrenadiere to mop up in the wake of the tank attack. Second, putting the assault guns in the second wave provided a reserve for such contingencies as an enemy counterstroke against the flank of the German attack.[24]

The fact that the German assault gun was a weapon designed to cooperate directly with infantry did not by itself solve the classic problems of cooperation between foot soldiers and armored vehicles. If the infantry kept its distance from the assault guns, the assault guns would be deprived of the benefits of close support. There would be no one to spot land mines or antitank guns and no one to protect against the brave Russian with a bundle of grenades or satchel charge. If, on the other hand, the infantry got too close to the assault guns, they would deprive themselves of the infantryman's greatest advantage—his ability to hide in even the smallest fold in the ground. In addition, proximity to an assault gun would expose the infantry to all of the gratuitous fire that assault guns attracted—artillery, small arms, and mortar fire, not to mention near misses from antitank weapons.

Part of the answer to this problem was the proper training of the infantrymen that accompanied assault guns into battle. Though steps were taken in this direction, such training would have to compete with the many other skills needed by German infantrymen. Thus, while steps were taken to train German infantrymen in the techniques of cooperating with assault guns, the heart of the solution was an organizational change. One of the early attempts at this was the formation, in April of 1943, of the Assault Gun Escort Company (*Sturmgeschütz Begleitkompanie*) of the Assault Gun Battalion 189 (*Sturmgeschütz Abteilung 189*). Assault Gun Battalion 189 was a garden variety assault gun battalion, with three batteries of ten assault guns (Sturmgeschütze III with the long 75mm gun). At the time of the formation of the Escort Company, the chief distinction of Assault Gun Battalion 189 was its position as the organic assault gun battalion of the 78th Assault Division (*78. Sturm-Division*). This was an experimental formation whose purpose was to test a new "capital intensive" approach to infantry combat.[25]

Like many units formed to meet the needs of the Eastern Front, the Escort Company was "unofficial."[26] That is to say, rather than being formed according to a table of organization provided by the army high command and thus being assembled from men and equipment "force fed" from the rear, the Escort Company was formed from resources already present in the 78th Assault Division. The majority of men who ended up in the Escort Company were from the 1st Company of the division Training School (1./*Ausbildungs Schule*), another "unofficial" unit. True to its name, the Training School was a unit in which soldiers—recruits fresh from their training regiments in Württemberg, veterans recovered from their wounds, and soldiers combed from noncombat units—were trained in the peculiar methods of the 78th Assault Division. (Most German divisions of the time had Field Replacement units that performed the same function. The practice dated back to 1916, when divisions established Field Recruit Depots to train incoming soldiers in skills peculiar to trench warfare or even a particular sector of the front.)

The idea behind the formation of the Escort Company was to provide each assault gun battery with its own platoon of close-support foot troops. This platoon would be intensively trained in the techniques of working with assault guns. It would thus allow the ordinary infantrymen to do their own job while depriving them of any excuse for bunching up around the assault guns. This is not to say that the Escort Company relieved the infantry entirely of the burden of cooperating with assault guns. The order that established the company made it clear that there would be times when the assault guns would need the direct assistance of large units of both infantry and pioneers. In such cases, however, the Escort Company would be able to serve as a sort of buffer between the assault guns and the ordinary infantrymen and pioneers. While taking care of the more demanding forms of close support themselves, the leaders of the Assault Gun Escort Company would be able to explain, in language that the latter could understand, how the infantry and pioneers might best help the assault guns.

Because of this mission, there was a one-to-one correspondence between the elements of the Escort Company and the subdivisions of the Assault Gun Battalion. Just as the Assault Gun Battalion was divided into three batteries, each of which had three platoons of three assault guns, the Escort Company was divided into three platoons of three squads. Just as each escort platoon was permanently associated with an assault gun company, each escort squad was linked to an assault gun platoon. The majority—eleven out of thirteen—of the men of each escort squad were infantrymen initially trained as riflemen and light machine gunners. These men were equipped with the chief weapons of the German infantryman of 1943—light machine guns (with two MG42 light machine guns in each squad), hand grenades, and bolt-action carbines. In addition, each squad had a combat engineer and a pathfinder. The combat engineer was primarily concerned with the art of locating, avoiding, and disabling land mines. The pathfinder was an experienced assault gun crewmember who was adept at recognizing terrain that was unsuitable for assault guns.[27]

The training of the Escort Company included techniques for protecting assault guns against enemy antitank sappers; using infantry fire to suppress antitank gunners and antitank riflemen; liaison between assault gun units and infantry companies, platoons, and squads; the use of signal flares fired from pistols ("Very lights"); locating mine fields and negotiating important terrain features (trenches, creeks, bridges, bogs, cliffs, etc.); reinforcing bridges, roads, and the ground so that they might support the weight of assault guns; and the recovery and destruction of crippled assault guns. Particular attention was also paid to the use of artillery and infantry heavy weapons to suppress antitank weapons and various means of designating targets.

Assault Gun Battalion 189 was not the only assault gun battalion to organize an escort company. By June of 1944, the practice was made official. Tables of organization published in that month called for a type of "assault artillery brigade" that consisted of three large assault gun batteries (of fourteen assault guns each) and one "battery" of escort troops. (The practice of referring to battalion-sized assault gun units as brigades had been introduced in 1943 to confuse the enemy about the strength of German forces. The term *battery* reminded all present that the escort troops were, despite all appearances to the contrary, still artillerymen.) While many of the unofficial escort companies had included such things as antiaircraft weapons and, in a few cases, even Mark II light tanks, the official tables called for the escort batteries to be composed of three platoons of "grenadiers" and one of combat engineers.[28] While the latter were provided with trucks, the grenadiers were expected to do their traveling on the outside of the assault guns.[29]

The grenadiers of the escort battery could assist the assault guns in a number of ways. At the most prosaic level, they relieved the assault gun crews from the need to stand watch over their vehicles. (This was particularly useful when an assault gun had broken down far from the rest of the unit.) More importantly, the grenadiers compensated for some of the inherent weaknesses of the assault guns. They could spot mines and other dangers that would otherwise be invisible to the assault gun crews. They could identify and designate targets. They could protect the assault guns from infantry antitank teams. Moreover, even when it was too dangerous for the grenadiers to ride on top of the assault guns, they could use their light machine guns to provide covering fire for the attacking armored vehicles.[30]

In order to facilitate this intimate degree of cooperation, each platoon of thirty-six grenadiers was permanently associated with a battery of assault guns. Teams of three or four grenadiers were further linked to a particular armored vehicle, so that each grenadier went into combat riding his "own" assault gun. Though the pattern of organization permitted the association of an intact grenadier squad to each assault gun platoon, this arrangement made it difficult for the grenadiers to practice traditional German squad tactics. While the light machine gun central to those tactics was still present, it had been supplanted as the primary infantry weapon by the recently introduced assault rifle.[31]

While deliberately disguising the size of assault gun units, the term brigade was, in one sense at least, appropriate. Employed as the "fire brigade" of a corps or army, an assault artillery or assault gun brigade was routinely accorded a degree independence far greater than that normally given similarly sized units equipped with other sorts of weapons. (Assault gun brigades were assault artillery brigades that lacked escort batteries and, in some cases, were authorized only ten assault guns per battery.) When it went into action, the assault gun brigade was rarely attached to an infantry regiment or even an infantry division. Instead, the brigade was assigned the task of cooperating with a particular infantry unit in order to fulfill a mission. When that mission was complete, the brigade withdrew from the fight in order to prepare itself for the next assignment.

Though Manstein's plan for an assault gun battalion in every division was never fulfilled, his belief that assault guns would preserve tank formations for concentrated employment turned out to be correct. What was true for assault guns, moreover, was also true for the large variety of self-propelled, direct fire weapons that, as the war progressed, played an increasingly larger role in the German war effort. Those vehicles that most resembled the assault guns, with fully tracked chassis, an armored roof, heavy frontal armor, and a powerful antitank gun (a long 75mm gun or better) were known as "tank hunters" (*Panzerjäger*). Vehicles with powerful antitank guns but less armor were rather more prosaically known as "self-propelled antitank guns" (*Panzerabwerkanonen auf Selbstfahrlaffetten*).[32] Other vehicles mounting direct fire weapons were likewise christened with names like "self-propelled antiaircraft gun," "self-propelled infantry gun," or "cannon on armored personnel carrier."[33]

As might be imagined, the tank hunters were employed in much the same manner as assault guns. That is to say, the tank hunters combined quasi-guerilla tactics with aggressive, offensive cooperation with other arms. The crews of other sorts of self-propelled direct fire weapons had to be more circumspect. Lacking the frontal armor of the tank hunters and assault guns, these weapons were (once emplaced) employed in much the same manner as their towed counterparts. In the defense, they were used as ambush weapons. In the attack, they supported the advance of tanks, assault guns, infantry, and engineers from covered firing positions. In either the attack or defense, the chief advantage of the self-propelled weapons was the speed with which they could move from one firing position to another. As the Germans were often outgunned by their enemies (particularly in the last three years of the war), this ability to change firing positions was an important one.[34]

In contrast to the assault gun, which was purpose-designed in response to a high level mandate, the less well armored self-propelled weapons tended to be improvisations. Some, like those of Major Becker's assault gun battalion of the 21st Panzer Division of 1944, were even built by the units that used them.[35] The chassis were provided by tanks, primarily German, French, and Czech, which had become obsolete early in the war. The guns, on the other hand, tended to be of types that still had a lot of life in them. These included the standard 150mm infantry gun, 75mm antitank guns, the famous 88mm antiaircraft gun, and the 76.2mm field gun that was captured in such great numbers from the Soviets.

The longstanding German fondness for the intimate cooperation of fire and movement had, as early as 1915, led them to use a variety of direct fire, large-caliber weapons that they called "infantry guns." By World War II, light (75mm) and heavy (150mm) versions of these weapons were present in almost every German infantry regiment. Because of this heritage, German soldiers had no difficulty using antitank and antiaircraft guns in ways other than those implied by their names. In June of 1940, for example, four 88mm antiaircraft guns, nine or more antitank guns, and eight or so infantry guns supported the attack of a single engineer company against the Maginot Line fort of La Ferté.[36]

Not surprisingly, the first formations to be equipped with self-propelled infantry guns were armored divisions. In the 1940 campaign, six of the ten armored divisions were each provided with a company of six 150mm infantry guns mounted on the chassis of a Mark I tank. Though the resulting vehicle was mechanically unreliable, poorly protected, and top-heavy, it performed

An "armored guerilla"—German assault gun with long-barreled 75mm gun. Photo courtesy of the Department of Defense.

yeoman service in the various crossings of the Meuse and the reduction of the stubborn French hedgehogs south of Amiens.[37] In the latter battle, the ungainly 150mm pieces were joined by more graceful self-propelled weapons, the 20mm, 37mm, and 88mm guns belonging to antiaircraft battalions. Though most of these latter weapons belonged to the air force rather than the army, the Germans experienced few difficulties integrating them into the retail battles fought by infantry squads and platoons.[38]

The advent of the T-34 gave a great boost to both the supply of and demand for self-propelled weapons. The block obsolescence of nearly all of the tanks that had served Germany so well in 1939, 1940, and 1941 made a large number of chassis available. At the same time, the fact that the enemy possessed large numbers of first-class tanks made the German army very attentive to the problem of antitank warfare. One of the many measures taken was the employment of the majority of the available chassis to mount antitank guns capable of dealing with the T-34. Between April of 1942 and March of 1944, for example, 200 heavy (150mm) infantry guns and 315 light (105mm) field artillery howitzers were affixed to the chassis of light or medium tanks. During that same period, 2,901 first-class antitank guns were made into self-propelled weapons.[39] (These numbers include neither assault guns nor weapons improvised at the front.)

Beginning in 1943, the chassis of first line tanks such as the Panther and Mark IV were also pressed into service as mounts for heavier weapons. The principle results of these marriages were the Hornet (*Hornisse*) and the Bumble Bee (*Hummel*). The former was an antitank gun of 88mm, the latter a 150mm artillery howitzer. As before, the self-propelled antitank guns greatly outnumbered other sorts of weapons. Between January of 1943 (when production started) and March of 1944, 570 Hornets and 180 Bumble Bees were produced. Even when the ninety ammunition carrier versions of the Bumble Bee are taken into account, there is no doubt about the priorities of the German production program.[40]

The majority of the self-propelled antitank guns in German service seem to have been assigned to divisional antitank battalions of armored Panzergrenadier divisions. In the former case, the tables of organization implemented in September of 1943 provided for one of the three companies of the single divisional antitank battalion to be provided with self-propelled guns. The other two were equipped with either assault guns or tank hunters. In the latter case, all three companies of the antitank battalion were provided with self-propelled antitank guns. The infantry units of both types of divisions seem rarely to have been provided with such weapons. Instead, those mounted in trucks were generally provided with towed antitank guns while the armored infantry had 75mm guns mounted on armored personnel carriers.[41]

Self-propelled antitank guns rarely found their way into walking infantry divisions. Assault guns and tank hunters, on the other hand, were assigned to the antitank battalions of muscle-powered divisions in ever increasing numbers from 1943 through the very end of the war. For the last two years of the war, tables of organization for most types of infantry divisions called for a divisional antitank battalion that consisted of one company of towed antitank guns, one company of tank hunters or assault guns, and one company of antiaircraft guns. The relatively long life expectancy of the assault guns, as well as the large numbers that were manufactured, helped to make this goal a reality.

The importance of a single company of a dozen or so assault guns to a German infantry division was increased by a paucity of other sorts of antitank weapons. Apart from assault guns and tank hunters, the only first-class antitank weapons in most German infantry divisions were towed 75mm or 76.2mm antitank guns. These, however, were in short supply. In a report from October of 1943, the infantry representative on the army general staff noted that, over two full years after the unveiling of the T-34, German infantry divisions serving on the Eastern Front possessed an average of only *nine* such antitank guns.[42] (By way of contrast, a typical French division in the 1940 campaign possessed fifty-eight purpose-built antitank guns whose power to damage German tanks was similar to the effect of a first-class antitank gun on a T-34 tank.)

As these few first-class antitank guns were generally assigned to the divisional antitank battalion, the shortage of such weapons put most infantry battalions and regiments in a difficult position. Possessing only obsolete antitank guns, converted French field guns, and low-velocity infantry guns, these units had to adopt guerilla tactics of their own. While the actual techniques varied greatly, the essential idea was to let the Soviet tanks overrun the German position. Once within the position, the tanks could be fired on from the flanks or the rear or attacked by infantry antitank teams.

While the Germans eventually got very good at this, the results were less than encouraging. Physically and psychologically exhausted by the harsh conditions on the Eastern Front, many German soldiers succumbed to "tank terror." Even when they maintained their composure, German infantry units were only able to cope with small numbers of Soviet tanks. In the middle of the maze of trenches, mines, and smoke that formed the typical German platoon position of 1943 or 1944, one or two T-34s were easy prey for an intrepid man with a teller mine or antitank grenade. For a battalion of such tanks, however, such a trap was hardly an obstacle at all. At best, the act of breaking the thin crust of the defense served to show the division commander where he might best employ his handful of first-class antitank guns.[43]

The problems of relying on improvised methods to kill tanks can be seen in figures collected by the Germans near the end of World War II. During the first three months of 1944, German forces on the Eastern Front reported the destruction of 7,351 tanks. Details about the manner in which these tanks were destroyed were provided for 4,764 tanks. Of these latter tanks, 25.7% were destroyed by German tanks, 26.9% by assault guns and tank hunters, and 29% by heavy (75mm or better) antitank guns. Tanks destroyed by infantrymen, engineers, and rear area troops in close combat accounted for only 8.3% of the reported losses. These, moreover, were outnumbered by the tanks destroyed by miscellaneous means, a category that included land mines, infantry guns, and artillery pieces.[44]

Even if the German "body counts" that made these statistics possible can be believed, the figures are somewhat misleading. A tank destroyed at a critical time and place is far more important than many knocked out in the course of less important operations. The confidence gained by troops that managed to kill even one tank in close combat, moreover, was doubtless an important boost to morale. Finally, it is reasonable to assume that most of Soviet the tanks knocked out in close combat were those that had been employed in small numbers as infantry support tanks. Knocking these out put the attacking Soviet infantry at a considerable disadvantage and often led to the collapse of the Soviet attack.[45]

As a rule, however, the task of dealing with enemy tanks on the Eastern Front was largely a matter for fire brigades. Small breakthroughs brought out the handful of assault guns or tank hunters of the divisional fire brigade. A larger danger resulted in the dispatch of an assault gun battalion. Major breakthrough attempts required the services of a larger battle group, a division, or even a full-scale corps. (It was no accident that the newspaper of the Großdeutschland Division, an organization that was an armored corps in all but name, was called *Der Feuerwehr/The Fire Brigade*.) There was even a short-lived attempt to create an elite force of two fully motorized army corps, one from the army and the other from the SS, to serve as a theater-level reaction force.[46]

How one of the larger German fire brigades operated is well illustrated by a battle that took place in the summer of 1943 along the banks of the Mius River, in the region of Stalino-Gorlovka. The Germans were defending the river line with a string of worn-out, battle-weary, and understrength infantry divisions. Behind this line was an armored division organized into two battle groups. One of these contained the bulk of the motorized infantry and artillery. The other consisted of a tank battalion, an assault gun battalion, an artillery battalion (with forward observers mounted in tanks), and a single understrength infantry battalion in armored personnel carriers.

The battle started when a Soviet force of three infantry regiments and twenty-five tanks crossed the river by means of a ford and quickly established a bridgehead that was three kilometers wide and nearly 1,500 meters deep. The German infantry division in the sector was able to prevent the force from breaking out of the bridgehead, but lacked the means to launch an effective counterattack. This task was given to the tank-heavy battle group of the armored division held in reserve.

Knowing that the Soviets were in the habit of rapidly reinforcing success, particularly where bridgeheads were concerned, the commander of the battle group attacked as soon as he could. On the day after the Soviets had begun their crossing of the Mius, the German battle group struck. Reinforced by the artillery of the local infantry division and acting in concert with ground-attack aircraft, the battle group was able to locate and eliminate the dug-in tanks and antitank guns that formed the backbone of the Soviet defense. Once these were gone, the Soviets lost heart and evacuated the bridgehead.[47]

That the German battle group was able to deal with the Soviet antitank guns despite its relative lack of infantry seems to have been a function of the unusually open terrain in which the battle was fought. The ground was open and slightly undulating, with neither forests nor built-up areas in which to hide antitank guns or the defending tanks. Thus, while the Soviet tanks and antitank guns were thoroughly dug in, they were relatively easy for the German tank crews and forward observers to find.

Not all German fire brigade actions were as successful as this one. Nonetheless, during the long years between the revival of the Soviet ability to conduct offensive operations in the spring of 1942 and the collapse of the Third Reich in 1945, German fire brigades performed countless miracles. Though they sometimes arrived too late to save the infantry that had stood in the way of the Soviet tanks, they rarely failed to strike a mortal blow to the Soviet units that had broken through. However fast it might be, however, a fire brigade could not be in two places at one time. Once the Soviets realized this and made full use of their vast superiority in manpower and equipment to exploit this vulnerability, the fate of the German forces in the East, and with them, the fate of the German nation for the next fifty years, was sealed.

9

A FAMILY RESEMBLANCE

The defeat of France in June of 1940 came as a great shock to the United States Army. This was a function, not only of the implication that America would soon become embroiled in another European war, but also of the longstanding American fondness for French military methods and ideas. That the French collapse had discredited the French approach to staff organization, the writing of orders, the conduct of large unit operations, or the employment of artillery was apparent only to the most perceptive American officers of the time. That the French approach to the employment of armor was bankrupt, however, was clear to all with even a passing interest in the subject. The corollary to this, the bankruptcy of the approach to armored warfare practiced in the United States Army for over twenty years, was also painfully evident. As a result, American armor was created anew at the very moment that the U.S. Army began to mobilize for its entry into World War II.

With the failure of the French approach to armored warfare evinced by the debacles of May and June, the most obvious model for the new American armored force was the German one. Appreciating what German armored forces had accomplished and understanding why they had been successful were, however, two different things. Thanks to the diligence of exchange officers and military attachés, a number of American military leaders were knowledgeable about German military ideas and practices.[1] Nonetheless, information about the actual operations of German armored formations came largely from German propaganda. Spiced by the excuses of those defeated, this propaganda tended to stress the role of German wonder weapons (most of which were entirely imaginary), greatly exaggerate the size of German forces, and downplay the role of the less glamorous contributors to German victories.[2] The American armor enthusiasts, both those who had been laboring in the vineyards of doctrine during the long years of peace and those who had been recently converted, were thus reduced to trying to replicate a force that they knew very little about.

In some cases, this misinformation proved to be a blessing in disguise. The wildly erroneous supposition that the entire German army was powered by internal combustion engines did much to suppress the cult of the horse in the U.S. Army. The similarly false belief that all German tanks carried guns with calibers of 75mm or more led to the requirement that all American medium tanks carry similar weapons.[3] This ensured that, at least for the first two and one-half years of the war, American-built tanks would, unlike their perennially under-gunned British counterparts, have adequate firepower. This same overestimation of the number and size of German tanks gave birth to the tank destroyer organization, a uniquely American organization whose units, though often mishandled, proved more than useful.[4]

Generally, however, inaccurate information about the Blitzkrieg hobbled the development of American armored formations. The greatest mistake in this regard was the underestimation of the role played by German infantry. The fact that German infantry had led the way in all successful breakthroughs was not reported. The fact that infantry battalions tended to outnumber tank battalions within the German armored divisions was not emphasized. And, because the American focus was on the division rather than the corps, the fact that German armored divisions of the early years of World War II habitually fought in the intimate company of motorized infantry divisions was generally ignored.

These mistakes were compounded by a phenomenon that may be described as doctrinal bait and switch. Eager to learn as much as possible about armored warfare, the American armor enthusiasts of 1940 and 1941 turned to the only models that they knew. The most powerful of these had come out of the many British efforts, both literary and experimental, of the interwar period, as well as more recent British experiences in North Africa. The effect of the British models, moreover, was cumulative. That is to say, British ideas that had been absorbed by Americans in the early 1930s laid the foundation for subsequent absorption of later versions of the same ideas. Indeed, one can argue that the Americans of 1940 and 1941 took so readily to British models not only because they were the most readily available but also because many of the underlying notions were already familiar.

While the British models of the period before 1941 offered a great deal of variety where things such as tank types and armament, artillery, engineers, and reconnaissance were concerned, they all shared an important common denominator. When compared to the German armored formations of 1940, as well as nearly all armored formations of the last two years of World War II, they were painfully short of infantry. Between 1937 and 1940, the various patterns of British armored division had but one or two infantry battalions to support no fewer than six (and sometimes as many as nine) battalions of armored fighting vehicles.[5]

Prior to the reform that took place in the winter of 1940–1941, the six or more tank battalions of a British armored division were organized into two armored brigades. All other combat units—motorized infantry, field artillery, antiaircraft guns, and antitank guns—were formed into a "support group," which was designed to fight as a separate echelon (See Figure 9.1). "The duty of the support group," wrote the author of *Royal Armored Corps Training Instruction Number 1*, "is to provide a pivot from which armored action may be developed, to assist the armored brigades in unsuitable country, and to take over ground won by armored action."[6]

The first American armored divisions, formed in the second half of 1940, bore a mild resemblance in structure, and a strong resemblance in concept of employment, to their British counterparts. The notion of the division fighting as two separate echelons was as central to the American

Figure 9.1
Comparison of British and U.S. Armored Divisions 1940

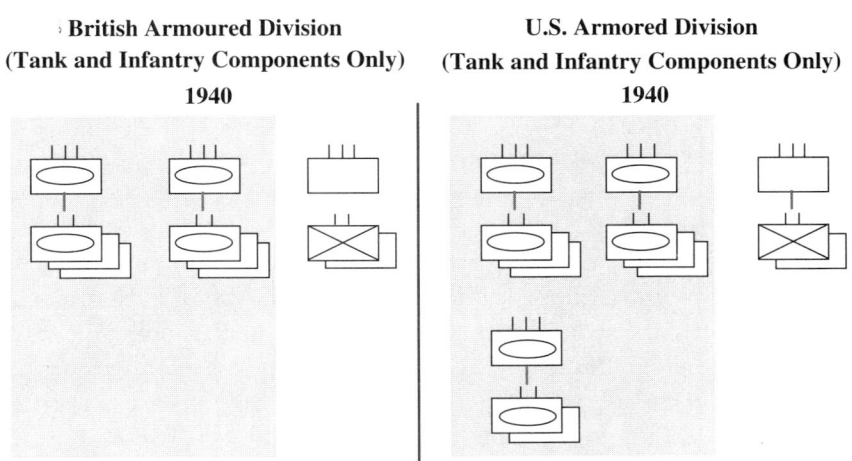

armored division as it was to the British. In the American case, all eight of the armored division's tank battalions were assigned to a single armored brigade, creating a formation with over 350 tanks. The two infantry battalions and a single antitank company formed a small infantry regiment. Reinforced with a field artillery battalion and additional antitank guns, this regiment served the same purposes as the British support group[7]

The chief difference between the British and American armored divisions of 1940 was the role allotted to field artillery. Both provided a single field artillery battalion with a comparable number of field pieces to the support group, but differed greatly when it came to providing field artillery to the armored echelon.[8] The Americans gave two field artillery battalions (for a total of twenty-four 105mm howitzers) to their armored echelon. Intended primarily to protect American tanks from hostile antitank guns, these howitzers were an organic part of the armored brigade.[9] British tanks, on the other hand, were expected to go into action without any direct help from their own field artillery.[10] Their chief defense against hostile antitank guns were the howitzers mounted in their close support tanks.

The American attitude towards the relationship between field artillery and tanks may have dated back to the closing weeks of World War I. At a time when the Germans were fielding an increasing number of antitank guns, some American formations adopted the French practice of setting aside a portion of the field artillery of an attacking force to the exclusive task of combating those weapons[11] The British attitude seems to have deeper roots. As early as 1917, some British leaders seem to have seen the tank as a weapon that might be able to attack well-defended positions without the aid of a preliminary bombardment.[12] This attitude flourished in the interwar period, fed by influences that included the writings of the "all-tank" school of thought, the difficulties of representing artillery fire in field exercises, and the proliferation of weapons such as the Birch gun and the close support tank.

Differences concerning the role of field artillery notwithstanding, British influence on the way that Americans thought about armored warfare remained strong until late in 1942, when the landings in North Africa gave American armored divisions their first taste of combat. Until then, American attachés and liaison officers followed British developments, particularly those in North Africa, with great interest. For one reason or another, however, it took quite a few months before lessons learned by British armored forces in combat were applied to the benefit of the still mobilizing Americans. The changes made by the British in 1940 and 1941 (setting the tank strength of each armored division at six battalions and increasing the number of infantry battalions to three) were thus not reflected in American tables of organization until March of 1942.

By the time that the Americans had completed this reform, the British had started a program that would add even more infantry, both absolutely and in proportion to tanks, to the armored division. This took the form of replacing one of the two armored brigades in every armored division with an infantry brigade, creating a formation of four infantry battalions and four tank battalions.[13] This, for the first time in the English-speaking world, created an armored division in which the number of infantry battalions was equal to the number of tank battalions. It was not until September of 1943 that American armored divisions would undergo a similar reapportionment to yield a formation with three tank battalions and three infantry battalions (See Figure 9.2).

As had been the case with reorganization of the German armored divisions in the fall of 1940 and the British reorganizations of 1940 and 1941, most of the tanks lost in this American reform of 1943 were light models. In 1940, light tanks—of the model named for the Civil War cavalryman J. E. B. Stuart—had equipped six out of the eight tank battalions in the standard U.S. armored division. In 1942, their number had dropped considerably, but

Figure 9.2
Comparisons of British and U.S. Armored Divisions 1941–1943

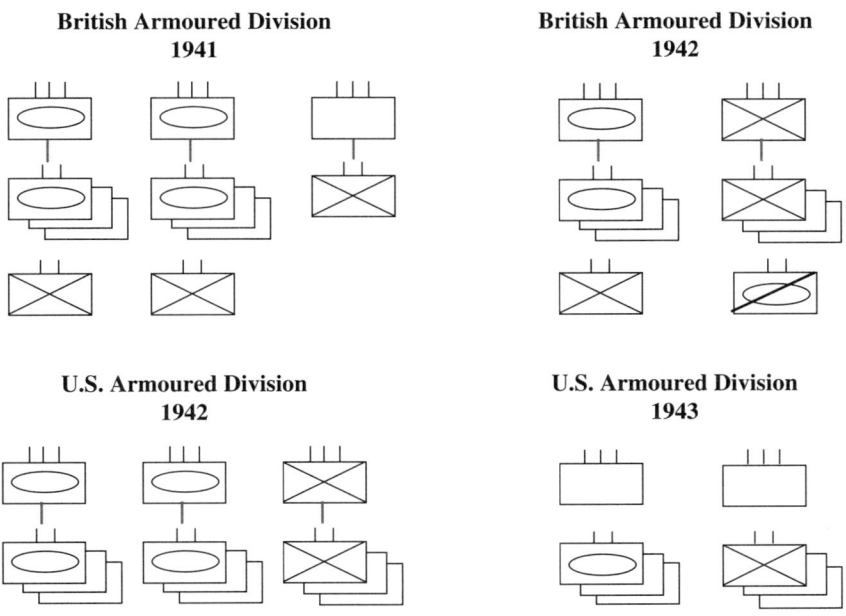

they provided the principal equipment of two out of six tank battalions. The 1943 reorganization, however, deprived the light tanks of their own battalions, relegating them to a supporting role within medium battalions, which had one company of Stuarts for every three equipped with medium tanks.

Though an element of imitation was certainly present, it would be a mistake to dismiss the 1943 reform of the American armored division as a repetition of the kind of exercise in imitation that had taken place in 1940 and 1941, or, for that matter, a mere reshuffling of battalions. Indeed, the 1943 reform was, if anything, a kind of declaration of independence for American armor. The principal and uniquely American feature of this reform was the elimination of permanent tank, infantry, or field artillery units larger than a battalion. Instead of regiments or brigades, the battalions would fight as part of "combat commands," ad hoc groupings whose composition would depend entirely upon the task at hand.[14] To command these groupings, each division organized two small headquarters, known as "Combat Command A" and "Combat Command B." An even smaller headquarters, called "Combat Command R" (for "reserve") served as a holding tank for any units not assigned to one of the other two combat commands.[15]

The combat command system permitted a degree of cooperation between tanks, infantry, and artillery that was unprecedented in any Allied armored division. Indeed, as late as 1944, some British armored divisions were still practicing the tactics of separate brigades, something the Germans had abandoned by the end of 1941. In September of 1944, for example, in an attack on the Gothic Line in Italy, the 2nd Armoured Brigade of the 1st Armoured Division was sent into the attack while its companion infantry brigade remained in the rear. The result was both failure and the loss of fifty-three tanks.[16] Worse still was the practice of sending the armored and infantry brigades of an armored division into battle at two entirely different locations. This happened to the 11th Armoured Division during the fighting in Normandy in 1944. On the first day of Operation Goodwood, the armored brigade (29th Armoured Brigade) of that division lost 126 tanks.[17]

The British tactics of separate brigades was mitigated by the institution known as the motor battalion. This was an infantry battalion, usually drawn from an elite (Rifle or Guards) regiment, which had been made an organic and inseparable part of an armored brigade. While the internal composition of these battalions varied greatly, they were usually provided with a higher proportion of automatic weapons—Bren guns, Vickers medium machine guns, and 3-inch mortars—than other infantry battalions. The men of motor battalions were also more likely to be carried in small trucks (and, towards the end of World War II, armored half-tracks) than in the lorries (motor trucks) of other motorized infantry battalions. This allowed motor battalions to provide a vehicle to every squad, rather than every platoon, as was often the case with the lorried infantry battalions.

British motor battalions began World War II in the support groups of armored divisions, with the official allocation being two motor battalions per division. When, late in 1940, a third motorized infantry battalion was added to the standard armored division, the motor battalions were assigned to the armored brigades. Nonetheless, it was a while before division and brigade commanders were able to free their motor battalions from the notion that "tanks conquer, infantry occupies."[18]

Writing in January of 1941, an American officer observed that

> Their motor battalion is unarmored. Hence, where armored maneuver is contemplated, they hold the battalion to the rear in reserve. They propose to use it to mop up villages, woods, etc., which have been overrun by the tanks to provide a safe route for other unarmored units to move forward. Another mission for the Motor Battalion will be that of advancing to hold an important defile or bridge, through or over which the tanks are to pass. Lastly, they expect to use it to form an outpost behind which the tanks may bivouac. It is not expected that the motor battalion will follow the tanks too closely into battle. It will organize its own bivouac against both air and ground attack and then move forward by bounds, as the situation warrants.

In the course of 1942 and 1943, the British learned the value of closer cooperation between the motor battalions and the armored elements of the armored brigade. The fact that there were three armored battalions for each motor battalion, however, usually meant that there was not enough motorized infantry to go around. Indeed, the standard practice in most British armored brigades at this time seems to have been the assignment of one company of the motor battalion to each of the three armored battalions.[19]

One solution to this problem, recommended by Field Marshall Montgomery in a pamphlet he published in December of 1944, was to make British brigades resemble American combat commands.[20] This called for the reshuffling of armored and motorized infantry battalions so that each brigade had two of each, as was done by the British 11th Armoured Division after Operation Goodwood.[21] A further extension of this solution, adopted by the Guards Armoured Division, was to marry tank battalions to infantry battalions to form permanent battle groups. Within these battle groups, some tank and infantry companies remained thoroughbred organizations. Others were linked to each other on a permanent basis, with explicit affiliation between armored and infantry units down to the level of the individual tank and infantry squad.[22]

The ability of the Guards Armoured Division to do this, however, was an accident of the British regimental system. In sharp contrast to all other British armored divisions, the Guards Armoured Division had infantry and armored battalions drawn from the same regiments. It was thus possible, for example, to link the 1st Battalion of the Grenadier Guards (an infantry unit) with the 2nd Battalion of the Grenadier Guards (an armored unit) to form the Grenadier Guards Battle Group. With officers who were all members of the same "club," with similar social backgrounds and outlooks, and men who had, at the very least, all been recruited and trained at the same depot, inter-arm cooperation of the most intimate sort was relatively easy to achieve. The same, however, could not be said of other British armored divisions, which drew their armored and infantry battalions from a wide variety of regiments.

Although the tendency towards many of the elements of methodical battle has deep roots in the American military tradition, American armored divisions seem to have been less susceptible to the tactics of separate brigades than their British counterparts were. One reason is the tendency of the American soldier of World War II to see his division, rather than a battalion or regiment, as the focus of loyalty and source of identity. Another is the fact that, from the very beginning, the American armored force cultivated a cult of combined arms, drawing its officers from all branches and combining the crests and colors of the other branches to create its own heraldic devices. A third contributor to inter-arm cooperation within American armored divisions was the peculiar character of American armored infantry.

Thanks to the miracle of industrial mobilization, the United States was able, from the very beginning, to put *all* of the infantry of the armored division in armored, half-tracked vehicles. Inspired by the vehicles of the French *dragons portés*, these half-tracks gave the American infantry the ability to work with tanks on terms that were far more intimate than was the case in most other armies. Indeed, every American armored infantry battalion was able, at least insofar as equipment was concerned, to fill a role that in the German army was restricted to the minority of Panzergrenadier units that were provided with

US M4 ("Sherman") tank, with long-barreled 76mm gun. Photo courtesy of TACOM Archives.

US M4 ("Sherman") tank, with long-barreled 75mm gun. Photo courtesy of TACOM Archives.

armored half-tracks. As a result, even when, in 1941 and 1942, American armored divisions were hampered by the official assumption that their commanders would employ the tactics of separate brigades, the equipment of the armored infantry made a strong case for integration at a lower level.

This advantage notwithstanding, some American commanders held on to the tactics of separate brigades as long as their British counterparts. Still wed to the notion of an armored division divided into "armored" and "support echelons," they put all of their infantry into one combat command and all of their tanks into the other. More often than not, the result of this antiquated arrangement was a bifurcated battle in which neither the infantry nor the tanks were able to properly support each other. Once they understood this arrangement, the Germans would often allow the American tanks to get as far forward as they liked, and then launch a counterattack against the American infantry.[23]

A far happier arrangement was that of Major General Lunsford E. Oliver's 5th Armored Division. While training for the Normandy invasion, this division merged its tank and armored infantry battalions to form what Oliver called "married companies." The basic element of these companies was a "married squad" made up of one Sherman tank and one squad of armored infantry in a half-track. An administrative as well as a tactical unit, each married-squad trained, lived, ate, and fought together. Tasks such as digging foxholes (which were sometimes placed under tanks), standing watch, and performing maintenance were shared without reference to the original branch of service of the squad member.[24]

One or two married companies, under the command of a tank or armored infantry battalion headquarters, formed the nucleus of what was known as a column or task force. Reinforced with a battalion of field artillery, and a platoon each of tank destroyers, armored cars, engineers, self-propelled 105mm cannon, and 81mm mortars, these columns, could, and did, act with considerable independence. Two of these columns, one heavy (with two married companies) and one light (with one married company), made up one of the Fifth Armored Division's standard combat commands.[25]

From the point of view of getting the most work out of any of the combat elements of the division, this arrangement was very inefficient. It would have been very difficult to assemble the artillery, tanks, or infantry of the division for the breakthrough of a fortified line or the clearing of a major town. General Oliver's peculiar organizational scheme was, however, ideally suited to the work of the 5th Armored Division, which consisted almost entirely of pursuit. The Germans, both motorized and muscle-powered, that stood in the path of this division fought in a manner that combined the traditional tactics of rear guards with those of guerillas. Small German units, ranging from three man light machine gun or antitank teams to company-sized battle groups, used techniques such as ambushes, long-range attacks by machine-gun or mortar fire, and opportunistic counterattacks, in an attempt to force the Americans to slow their rate of advance.[26] The task of the Fifth Armored

Division was thus to overcome these relatively minor obstacles with the least possible delay. This, in turn, required that all necessary means be immediately available to the lowest possible echelon of command.

The radical integration of tanks and armored infantry as practiced by the 5th Armored Division was rarely, if ever, imitated by other American armored divisions fighting in the last year of the war in Europe. Instead, the combat command remained the principle echelon at which tanks and armored infantry cooperated with each other. The degree of cooperation was sometimes extended by what was to eventually become known as *cross-attachment*. Tank and armored infantry battalions would trade one or two of their component companies, producing mixed battalions with two or three companies of one arm and one or two companies of the other. Occasionally, cross-attachment was practiced as far down as the company level, with, for example, a platoon of ar mored infantry being attached to a tank company. For the most part, however, the American commanders seem to have preferred to avoid breaking up tank and armored infantry companies.[27]

10
BREAKTHROUGH

Reduced to its essence, the story of the evolution of the tank during World War II is one of simplification. The multitude of categories that had existed at the beginning of the war slowly gave way to the class of vehicle that would dominate armored warfare for the subsequent half-century—that of the main battle tank. Some of these categories, such as light infantry tanks, cavalry tanks, and tankettes, failed to survive the first two years of the war. Others, such as howitzer-carrying support tanks, retained their niche until 1945. One category, the heavy infantry tank, even enjoyed a renaissance of sorts, playing an important role in the middle period of the war and even managing to father a variety of interesting, if short-lived, offspring. In the end, however, even these precocious oddities fell prey to the notion that a single type of tank—what Field Marshal Bernard Montgomery called the "capital tank"—could fulfill a wide variety of functions.

In the United States, the impetus towards the creation of the capital tank was largely industrial. That is to say, proposals for the building of specialized tanks were routinely rejected on the grounds that it was far better to mass produce a large number of general purpose tanks than to handcraft a smaller number of optimum solutions to various battlefield problems. A similar phenomenon occurred in the Soviet Union. Though Soviet officials tried, at first, to produce the full panoply of armored fighting vehicles called for in prewar mobilization plans, factory managers found it much easier to produce large numbers of T-34 tanks. In Great Britain, where a bewildering array of different tank types were produced in relatively small lots, the impetus towards the capital tank came less from the tank-building industry than from the armies in the field. In particular, a tank fleet composed largely of capital tanks was the natural—and all but necessary—complement to the organizational scheme used by the British army during the last three years of World War II.

Between 1920 and 1935, most Britons involved with armored vehicles displayed a marked preference for speed over protection. Thus, as engines became more powerful and transmissions more efficient, designers who could have used the extra power to increase the thickness of armor on tanks usually opted to make their creations faster. In the mid-1930s, however, this consensus began to break down. Designers, theorists, and practical soldiers all began to worry about such things as the increasing power of purpose-built antitank guns and the possibility that British infantry might once again have to fight a Continental opponent. The result of these worries was the creation of a new type of armored vehicle, variously known as the "heavy infantry tank," the "infantry tank," and the "I tank."

The British infantry tanks had much in common with the R-35 tanks that the contemporary French army was building to replace the six-ton Renaults left over from World War I. They were sufficiently well armored to be proof against the small caliber (25mm, 37mm, 40mm) antitank guns of the day. Because of this, they were much slower than other types of tanks being designed at the time. The two major areas of difference between them concerned armament and turret design. While the French gave the R-35 a single-man turret (*tourelle monoplace*) that carried a low-velocity 37mm gun, the British provided their tanks with a much larger three-man turret and a two-pounder (40mm) high-velocity antitank gun. (As had been the case with other British tanks of the time, about 10% of infantry tanks were close support versions armed with howitzers rather than antitank guns.)[1]

The difference in turret size made British infantry tanks much larger than their French counterparts. At the same time, the larger crew and more powerful armament made the British infantry tank a vehicle that could do much more than knock out hostile machine guns. The antitank guns provided considerable protection against contemporary fast tanks, including all tanks of the armored divisions then being formed in Germany. The 3-inch (77mm) and 3.7-inch (95mm) howitzers of the close support variants could fire both high-explosive shells and smoke projectiles. (As was the case with the fast tanks that the British army was building in the late 1930s, the proportion of close support tanks to tanks carrying antitank guns was somewhere between one-in-five and one-in-six.)[2]

The introduction of the infantry tank concept into the British army represented a dramatic departure from orthodoxy. In the late 1920s and early 1930s, the de facto policy of the Royal Tank Corps had been to focus all of its efforts on the development of independent formations equipped entirely with fast tanks of one sort or another. After 1935, these efforts were split between two types of tank and two types of organization. The new generation of fast tanks (now called cruiser tanks) remained with the independent formations that would soon evolve into the armored brigades of the first British armored divisions. The infantry tanks were formed into army tank battalions for direct cooperation with infantry brigades and divisions. (On the eve of World War II, these battalions were assembled into army tank brigades).[3]

The simple dichotomy between infantry tanks and cruiser tanks lasted until October 1942. In that month, each of the five armored divisions in the British army was reformed by the replacement of one of its two armored brigades with an infantry brigade.[4] This created armored divisions that were far better suited to the conditions that they would face in the close terrain of Tunisia, Italy, and Northwest Europe. It also created the problem of how best to employ the five spare armored brigades that had been withdrawn from their parent divisions. One possible solution to this problem was to use the redundant armored brigades as a means of temporarily reinforcing armored divisions that found themselves in need of additional cruiser tanks. Another was to exchange the cruiser tanks of the homeless armored brigades for infantry tanks, thereby converting them into army tank brigades. A third solution was to reequip the armored brigades with tanks that were more heavily armored than cruiser tanks and, at the same time, faster than infantry tanks. A brigade equipped with such tanks would be a true "swinger brigade"—one that could effectively reinforce both infantry formations and armored divisions.

The great deficiency of the first solution to the problem of redundant armored brigades was the fact that the British army was quickly losing interest in the type of fast-moving, wide-ranging, cavalry-style operations for which the cruiser tank had been optimized. (In that respect, the British decision to refrain from an aggressive exploitation of their victory at El Alamein was the harbinger of things to come.) The chief drawback of the second solution was the fact that the British army already possessed seven army tank brigades. Converting five of the ten armored brigades into army tank brigades would have tipped the bureaucratic scales in favor of the latter. That is to say, a British army with twelve army tank brigades and five armored brigades would be far less hospitable to an independent Royal Armoured Corps than one with seven army tank brigades and ten armored brigades. The second solution would also have conflicted with supply. The infantry tank that had served so well in the first three years of the war (the famous Matilda) had, thanks to the widespread introduction of the German 50mm antitank gun, lost its near invulnerability to hostile fire. The Matilda's replacement (the Churchill) was proof against the new German weapon, but it was suffering significant teething problems.

The third possible solution to the problem of the five spare armored brigades was alien to British doctrine of the day. Nonetheless, it had one great advantage. The tank that was needed to make it work (the U.S. Sherman) was about to become available in very large numbers. As a bonus, the main armament of the Sherman was a 75mm gun capable of firing both antitank and high-explosive rounds. Just as the tank itself was a compromise between armored protection and speed, the 75mm gun was neither a proper howitzer nor a proper antitank gun. Nonetheless, at a time when British antitank guns were all but useless against soft targets and the 3.7-inch howitzer had a very limited ability to damage hostile tanks, this sort of compromise had many advocates.

As things turned out, the British army adopted a fourth solution to the problem of the five armored brigades that needed a new home. Two were converted into army tank brigades. The remaining three retained their status as armored brigades and an organization similar to that of the armored brigades of armored divisions. As for the Sherman tanks, they were distributed among the armored brigades as a means of making up for some of the deficiencies of the cruiser tanks. At first, they served to reinforce the close support tanks. By 1944, however, the Sherman had displaced the cruiser tanks to the point that the latter were little more than an auxiliary vehicle that played a role similar to that of the light Stuart tanks in a U.S. armored division.

The triumph of the Sherman tank within the British army was, in part, a matter of efficient use of industrial resources. Acquiring large numbers of American-built tanks allowed the British tank factories to concentrate on rebuild work—correcting the deficiencies of the Churchill tank, converting garden-variety tanks into specialized vehicles, and upgrading the armament on existing vehicles. The Sherman also had the cardinal virtue of being better suited to the great increase in the size and power of antitank guns that took place in the last three years of World War II. This was partially a matter of the relative ease with which Sherman tanks could be modified to carry high velocity weapons such as the U.S. 76mm gun or the British 17-pounder. It was also a matter of overkill. German antitank weapons of the first class—high-velocity weapons with calibers greater than 50mm—were so powerful that only a very heavy infantry tank could be made proof against them. In other words, the proliferation of the German 75mm gun did to the Churchill what the introduction of the German 50mm antitank gun did to the Matilda.

The increasing role played by the Sherman tank in British armored brigades was very much in keeping with Field Marshal Montgomery's fondness for the concept of the capital tank. It was not, however, in keeping with the kind of battle that Montgomery liked best to fight. General Giffard Martel, the officer in charge of combat development for British armored forces for most of World War II, was of the opinion that this type of battle required large numbers of infantry tanks. Indeed, he argued that the key to flexibility was having armored brigades that had two sets of equipment—cruiser tanks for exploitation and infantry tanks for set-piece battles. This "golf-bag" approach, which was widely used by units of the Royal Artillery during the last year of World War II, would have allowed the employment of infantry tanks that were "true to type"—as invulnerable to the 75mm antitank guns of 1944 and 1945 as the Matilda had been to the 37mm antitank guns of 1940.[5]

While the proliferation of 75mm antitank guns deprived the British infantry tanks of 1944 and 1945 of their invulnerability, it did not entirely eliminate the advantage conferred by their heavy armor. One reason for this was the German soldier's habit of forgetting to turn in old weapons when he was issued new ones. This meant that the first-class antitank weapons of specialized antitank units, as well as those mounted in tanks, tank destroyers, and assault guns, were supplemented by a wide variety of obsolescent antitank guns, infantry guns, and captured weapons of all sorts. The closer that Allied tanks got to German infantry positions, the greater were the chances that these weapons would come into play. A further danger to Allied tanks came in the form of various handheld antitank weapons. These included the German answer to the American bazooka (the *Panzershreck*), the single-shot rocket propelled grenade (the *Panzerfaust*), and a variety of hand grenades, rifle grenades, and mines. While the British infantry tanks were not entirely free of danger when attacked by these weapons, they were much less susceptible to their effects than the Sherman. Put more simply, most of the relative advantages of the infantry tank were a positive function of proximity to the enemy.

The obvious corollary of the evolution of the infantry tank into a close-combat tank was a change in main armament. The antitank weapons with which most infantry tanks were originally armed were entirely unsuited to the task of closing with German infantry. This became obvious as soon as the campaign for North Africa moved out of the open desert of Libya into the heavily compartmentalized terrain of Tunisia—a development that resulted in an ingeniously simple solution. Rather than wait for tank factories at home to come out with either a more suitably armed infantry tank or a better-protected version of the Sherman tank, British soldiers in Tunisia took matters in their own hands. Making use of 75mm guns and gun mountings from battle-damaged Sherman tanks, they converted 120 of their Churchill tanks into vehicles that were much better able to deal with the danger from close-range German antitank weapons.[6]

The 75mm gun was much better suited to the needs of a close-combat tank than the 2-pounder and 6-pounder antitank guns with which most production models of the Churchill tank had been equipped. It was not, however, the best solution available. In particular, the 75mm gun, which had evolved from the standard American field piece of World War I, was still a weapon that had been designed to hit soft targets at relatively long ranges. What was needed was a weapon that sacrificed most of its range on the altar of sheer weight of high explosive. The 3.7-inch (95mm) howitzer of the close-support versions of the Churchill was more like this weapon than the 75mm gun. An even better solution was found in a 290mm mortar that bore the classic name of *Petard*. Where the 75mm gun fired a 15-pound (7-kilogram) shell containing less than 3-pounds (1.5 kilograms) of high explosive, the Petard fired a 50-pound (23-kilogram) projectile loaded with a 40-pound (18-kilogram) bursting charge.

Strictly speaking, the Petard was a tool for combat engineers. Its original purpose was less to attack Germans in defensive positions than to destroy obstacles of various sorts, particularly the type of beach obstacles encountered during the ill-fated raid at Dieppe on 19 August 1942. These obstacles included classic antitank obstacles such as concrete pyramids ("dragon's teeth") as well as surf-zone obstacles capable of tearing the bottom out of landing craft. Nonetheless, as any projectile capable of destroying these obstacles was also an excellent means of blowing large holes in concrete fortifications, British and Canadian combat engineers quickly embraced the bunker-busting potential of the new weapon.

The Petard was developed in tandem with the tank that was to carry it—the AVRE (Armored Vehicle Royal Engineers). This was a Churchill that had been modified by the removal of its antitank gun and the redesign of its crew compartment. In addition to serving as a platform for the Petard, the Churchill AVRE was also capable of placing very large explosive charges against walls and dropping various kinds of bridging material—whether hardwood planks or tightly wrapped bundles of logs—into ditches and narrow waterways. By the time of the Normandy landings in June of 1944, 180 standard Churchill tanks had been converted into AVREs. This was more enough to equip the three armored combat engineer battalions (field regiments) of the 1st Assault Brigade, Royal Engineers, of the 79th Armoured Division.[7]

Like the AVRE, the 79th Armoured Division was a direct consequence of the soul-searching that followed the Dieppe raid. It was not, strictly speaking, a division at all. Rather, it was a framework for the maintenance, deployment, and bureaucratic protection of a variety of specialized combat units. In addition to the 1st Assault Brigade, the 79th Armoured Division served (at various times during the last two years of World War II) as the parent formation for units equipped with flamethrower tanks (Crocodiles), mine-clearing tanks (Crabs), bridging tanks, heavy armored personnel carriers (Kangaroos), searchlight tanks, and amphibious tractors.[8]

While the searchlight tanks and the amphibious tractors did not come into their own until the river crossing operations of the last six months of World War II,[9] the other specialized vehicles of the 79th Armoured Division played important roles in various phases of the Normandy operation. During the landing itself, the Churchill AVREs and other engineer tanks cooperated to clear a path for the conventional forces that landed on the two British beaches. (In his official report, General Dwight Eisenhower not only gives these vehicles credit for the relatively low casualties suffered by the British landing force, but blames the American high casualties on their absence from Omaha Beach.)[10] In the days that followed, the Crocodiles and Kangaroos joined the engineer tanks in the effort to move off of the beach and into the "green fields beyond."

The definitive task of the AVREs was to clear a path through the obstacles that the Germans had constructed on the landing beaches. The same Petard that was so useful in this original role, however, was also capable of performing other services as well. Soon after the AVREs landed, for example, their crews realized that the Petard was an excellent means of destroying bunkers, pillboxes and other concrete fortifications. (Where guns and howitzers firing smaller projectiles needed to "post a letter"—get a direct hit on a firing slit or other opening—in order to have an effect on well-built fortifications, the "dustbin" fired by the Petard could gouge a large hole of its own in the concrete.)[11] Once they got inland, the AVRE crews also used the Petard in much the same way as a conventional mortar. That is to say, Petard rounds fired at high angles were dropped into places masked by buildings, walls, or terrain. This capability was of particular value for protecting the flanks of tank/infantry teams advancing through built up areas.[12]

The cooperation between AVREs and other specialized tanks was greatly facilitated by the overlap in the capabilities of the weapons that they carried. The 3.7-inch (95mm) howitzers carried by close-support Churchills were not, for example, as efficient a means of blowing things up as the Petards of the AVREs were. On the margin, however, they could do much of the work ordinarily assigned to Petards, thus allowing the AVRE to concentrate on duties that only it could perform. The same can be said of the relationship between the 3.7-inch howitzers and the 75mm guns carried by the Crocodiles and Crabs. When the latter were not performing their specialized functions of throwing flame or clearing mines, they could provide covering fire for elements that were closing with the enemy.[13]

Specialized tanks with weapons that fired large high-explosive rounds were often pressed into service as "ordinary" infantry tanks. The Churchill AVRE was particularly prized in this role, as was the close-support variant of the standard Churchill. The reason for this was the nature of the threat most often faced by British infantry in Normandy. With German tanks husbanded for large-scale counterattacks or concentrated to defend against major Allied operations, the German defenders that attacking British battalions were most likely to encounter on any given day were heavily armed infantrymen. Because the British foot soldiers had far fewer mortars than their German counterparts did and were entirely bereft of general-purpose machine guns and infantry guns, tanks were the most important source of close-range high-explosive shells available to them.

In major operations, such as the Epsom and Goodwood set-piece attacks, the relationship between tanks and infantry was reversed. The proliferation of antitank weapons meant that attacking British tanks could not do much unless their own infantry managed to clear the woods and villages where those weapons tended to lurk. In a combined arms battle (one in which the Germans could protect their own positions with artillery and mortar fire) getting this infantry into a position where it could assist the tanks forward was a difficult proposition. The trucks that carried most of the Allied infantry were far too vulnerable to shell fragments and small arms fire.

The thinly armored half-tracks enjoyed a degree of protection that was only slightly better than that of trucks. A far better solution to this problem was found in the form of an improvised armored troop transporter with the picturesque (and aptly descriptive) name of *Kangaroo*.

The Kangaroo was actually a Canadian invention, the fortunate but unintended consequence of the desire of the Canadian forces landed at Juno Beach to optimize their field artillery for the breakout from the Normandy bridgehead. This artillery had, for the landing itself, been equipped with the American-built Priest, a 105mm howitzer mounted in the modified hull of an American medium tank. As soon as they were able, the Canadian gunners exchanged these weapons for British 25-pounder gun-howitzers, towed field pieces with longer range, a higher rate of fire, and greater flexibility. This rendered surplus the Canadian Priests, which, on the suggestion of General G. G. Simonds, then commanding the Canadian II Corps, were deprived of their howitzers and converted into armored personnel carriers.[14]

The great virtue of these "defrocked Priests" was that they were as well armored as the main battle tanks of the time. This meant that, in sharp contrast to armored infantry in half-tracks, the squad carried in each Kangaroo could go anywhere that a tank could. This advantage proved decisive in the first battle in which the Kangaroos were used, a limited objective night attack designed to secure a piece of high ground south of Caen. Because of the poor visibility (made worse by dust, artificial smoke, and the glare of headlights), neither the Canadian attackers nor the German defenders had a very good view of the battlefield. As a result, most of the action consisted of Germans firing blindly at the noise made by similarly impaired armored vehicles. Had the accompanying infantry been carried in trucks or even lightly armored half-tracks, the German interdiction fire would have prevented their forward movement. For infantry in Kangaroos, however, this essentially random fire was little more than a nuisance.[15]

Though this attack was aimed at the seizure of terrain rather than the destruction of a particular enemy unit or the achievement of a breakthrough, it was, by British standards of the time, uncharacteristically deep. The offloading point for the infantry was five kilometers beyond the forward edge the German position and thus almost in the area occupied by the German field artillery.[16] This meant that, instead of having to fight their way into the depths of the German position, the Canadian and Scottish infantry carried in the Kangaroos were directly delivered into an area where the enemy was highly vulnerable to infantry attack.

Canadian success convinced the British authorities to follow suit and, for most of the rest of the war, the Allied forces operating in the northern portion of northwest Europe could call on the services of about 300 Kangaroos, all of which had been converted from self-propelled guns or tanks built on the standard American medium tank hull and chassis.[17] In the next few months, a further 177 tanks or self-propelled guns were transformed into Kangaroos by British army workshops in Italy.[18] Altogether, these Kangaroos could simultaneously carry a total of six or so infantry battalions.

Instead of being assigned to British and Canadian armored divisions, however, the Kangaroos in each theater were kept in general reserve. In northwest Europe, this meant that they were organized into two regiments (one Canadian and one British) that came under the control of the same 79th Armored Division that served as the holding organization for nearly all unusual armored vehicles (know as "funnies") in that theater. There were a number of benefits to this arrangement. Kangaroos could be concentrated for use en masse, in areas where their particular virtues were both needed and appreciated. Kangaroo units could return to a home base, trade lessons learned, get their vehicles repaired, and provide the workshops with direct feedback on modifications to the basic design.

The chief drawback to the policy of concentrating Kangaroos was the lost opportunity to integrate them into the armored divisions. Like the other funnies, the Kangaroos remained in a world of their own, often attached to, but never fully a part of, other formations. Anecdotal evidence suggests, moreover, that Kangaroos were more often used to support infantry divisions rather than armored divisions.[19] Indeed, Field Marshall Montgomery, in his pamphlet *The Armoured Division in Battle*, mentions armored troop carriers only in reference to what he calls "set piece battles," which he described, with characteristic understatement, as "not a role for which the armoured division is entirely suitable."[20]

Though invariably effective, the Kangaroo was never present in sufficient numbers to change the way that the infantry units of most British, Canadian, or American infantry divisions cooperated with tanks. For the most part, these units used tanks to do what their German opponents routinely expected their infantry guns (both 75mm and 150mm), mortars (both 81mm and 120mm), and tripod-mounted machine guns to accomplish.[21] These tasks included dominating open ground and urban streets as well as the provision of covering fire during river crossings and other sorts of attacks. There were many occasions, however, where tank-infantry cooperation was more sophisticated. One particularly interesting technique, developed by the U.S. 1st Infantry Division and its attached 745th Tank Battalion was to assign a four-man infantry escort to each tank of a tank platoon that was cooperating with an infantry battalion or company fighting in a suburban area. These riflemen provided close security, exact information about the location of friendly infantry, and liaison with other friendly units. In a town such as Aachen (Aix-la-Chapelle), where large, well-built buildings provided German antitank teams with many places to hide, the number of infantry escorts was increased by a factor of three, resulting in a team consisting of two tanks and a full platoon of riflemen.[22]

A similar pattern of cooperation between tank and infantry units emerged with the U.S. forces (both Army and Marine Corps) that fought in the Pacific. The fighting that took place in the first three years of the struggle to defeat Japan was such that American commanders saw few opportunities to do much more than attach a tank battalion to each infantry division. The nature of the terrain was such, moreover, that these battalions were usually broken up into companies and even platoons for direct attachment to infantry regiments, battalions, and companies.[23] This practice was continued through the last year of the war, even though the fighting had shifted from small, jungle-covered islands with little in the way of roads or other infrastructure to larger, somewhat more developed pieces of land.

To fight the battle for Okinawa, the largest land battle in the Pacific theater, the U.S. Army and Marine Corps landed six infantry divisions, each of which controlled a battalion of tanks and a battalion of armored amphibious tractors. In addition, the army component included three companies of armored cars and a tank group headquarters. Colonel Hiromichi Yahara, operations officer of the Japanese force defending Okinawa, feared that these forces would be assembled into a powerful armored formation and used to make a decisive breakthrough of the Japanese defensive line. This, Yahara contended while being interrogated by American intelligence officers, would have replaced the slow, methodical, and costly reduction of the Japanese defenses on Okinawa with a rapid collapse of organized resistance. Even though they were employed in a less than optimal fashion, Yahara added, tanks were the single most important factor in the eventual American victory.[24]

Given the way that they were employed, American tank units in the Pacific Theater would probably have been better off if they had been equipped with variants of the Churchill tank rather than Shermans. The great deficiencies of the Churchill—its slow speed and lack of operational mobility—would rarely have had a chance to display themselves on the many island battlefields of that theater. At the same time, the great virtue of the Churchill—its heavy armor—would have greatly reduced the vulnerability of American tank crews to the fire of the obsolescent Japanese antitank guns. (The principal Japanese antitank gun of World War II was a 47mm piece with relatively low muzzle velocity. It could penetrate the hull of a Sherman tank, but not that of a Churchill.) Had the American tank units been provided with a variety of funnies (Churchill AVREs, Crocodiles, and Kangaroos), they would have been even better prepared to deal with the Japanese defenders of bunkers and caves.

In the aftermath of World War II, senior American officers shared Yahara's high opinion of the value of tanks, but not his belief in the importance of concentrating them to achieve decisive effects. This non sequitur can be seen in the various reorganizations that the U.S. Army underwent in the decade that passed between the end of World War II and the high watermark of the U.S. Army's love affair with the atomic bomb. Tank units found a permanent home in the infantry divisions of both the Army and the Marine Corps.[25] At times, they even found their way into infantry regiments, replacing the infantry gun (cannon) and antitank companies that American commanders had found so difficult to integrate into the American way of war.[26] At the same time, the American armored division fell on hard times. Outside the Army, the armored division was under attack by the advocates of *push-button warfare*. (This was the idea that strategic air power, atomic weapons, and guided missiles had put conventional ground combat forces out of business.) Within the army, the American armored division had to compete with fully motorized infantry divisions that were often provided with more tanks than some Panzer divisions of the last three years of World War II.

11
GUNSLINGER

From the very start of armored warfare, a good proportion of armored fighting vehicles possessed the ability to destroy their opposite numbers. The small-caliber naval guns on the armored cars and trucks of 1914 and 1915, for example, were certainly capable of doing lethal harm to similar vehicles in enemy hands. The possibility of improving the ability of tanks to destroy other tanks informed British discussions of tank armament as early as the winter of 1917–1918.[1] Nonetheless, it was the mid-1930s before tanks and armored cars were routinely equipped with armor-piercing weapons. Even then, these weapons were often less powerful than the technology of the time permitted. Indeed, it was not until the latter years of World War II that tank designers made serious attempts to cram the biggest, most powerful tank-killing guns that they could into armored fighting vehicles. Once this trend started, it was hard to stop. As a result, the tank guns of the half-century following the end of World War II fired projectiles that were an order of magnitude larger than the typical tank-gun projectiles of the early 1940s. By the 1980s, the world's most advanced tanks had become little more than platforms for these guns, a means for bringing these guns into firing positions and protecting the crew as it located, identified, and "serviced" targets.

However capable of fighting other tanks some tanks of World War I and the 1920s may have been, the idea of optimizing tanks for the task of killing other tanks did not take hold until the mid-1930s. The first tanks to reflect this change of heart were the fast tanks intended for either mechanized cavalry formations or the rapid exploitation of breakthroughs. These tanks included British cruiser tanks, the French SOMUA (S-35), the Soviet BT-5, and the

German Panzer III, all of which were equipped with high-velocity antitank guns in the 37mm to 47mm range. Contemporary breakthrough tanks such as the Vickers Independent, the French Char B, and the Soviet T-35 were provided with both an antitank weapon of this type and a large-caliber, low-velocity gun. By the late 1930s, the new class of heavy infantry tanks (such as the British Matilda and its less-successful French and Soviet counterparts) were also being armed with high-velocity, small-caliber antitank guns. Indeed, by the eve of World War II, the only class of modern tanks that had yet to be provided with purpose-built antitank weapons were the French R-35 infantry tanks developed as one-for-one replacements for the venerable M1917 Renaults. Even then, plans were underway to replace the low-velocity 37mm guns on these tanks with the high-velocity weapons in the same caliber.[2]

Having high-velocity antitank guns and making full use of them were, however, two different things. The fast tanks of the late 1930s were, from the point of such things as weight and size of turret, usually capable of carrying much more powerful armament than they actually did. That they did not was usually a product of efforts by authorities to make tanks use the same sort of antitank ammunition as the antitank guns issued to the infantry, artillery, and antitank troops. (The most famous example of this phenomenon was the refusal of German ordnance authorities to conform to Hitler's desire to mount a 50mm gun in the early versions of the Panzer III. They opted to mount a 37mm gun instead, for the simple reason that the 37mm tank gun fired the same family of ammunition as the standard 37mm antitank gun.) The suboptimization of the guns carried by tanks was also a result of the widespread habit—born, perhaps, of the inherently improvised nature of the armored fighting vehicle—of treating tank armament as an afterthought. Most tank designers of the 1930s did not conceive of a tank with a particular gun in mind, but rather seem to have gone shopping for guns at a relatively late stage in the design process. The most powerful reason for keeping tank guns down below a certain size, however, had much less to do with the guns themselves than with the way that they found their targets.

Until the middle years of World War II, mechanical aids for tank gunners, such things as sophisticated sights and devices for range estimation, were either primitive or nonexistent. The chief means of finding the range to a target was to "walk" rounds towards it. As a smaller gun invariably fired smaller projectiles (and usually did so more quickly than larger guns) 37mm guns could use this technique with greater economy (as measured in percentage of rounds carried in the tank) and speed than 75mm guns or even 47mm guns. A semiautomatic

20mm gun was even better at this than a 37mm piece, while a machine gun was substantially better than either. Once the smaller gun got its range, it would also be able to fire a greater number of rounds at the targeted tank before the it was able to move out of the way. At a time when tanks tended to be knocked out by the cumulative effects of several hits rather than a single catastrophic impact, this was not an insignificant advantage.

The case for smaller guns being better able to hit tanks while inflicting greater total damage in a given amount of time was made towards the end of the 1930s by a German veteran of the Spanish Civil War. This officer was probably thinking in terms of antitank guns on ground mounts rather than those carried in tanks, but his reasoning clearly applies to both types of weapons.

It goes without saying," he wrote,

> that the heavier gun has a greater projectile, and that consequently the results of the individual hit will be comparatively greater. (The 20mm gun has a charge of 4 grams as opposed to 50 grams for the 47mm gun.) But the individual shot cannot be taken as a practical basis of comparison at all, as the larger gun will have far less chance of hitting the objective. Thus the decisive factor in anti-tank defense will be the question of which gun will prove quicker in finding the range and which one is capable of securing the greatest number of hits within a given time.[3]

The first tank-producing state to break away from the general tendency to provide tanks with smaller-than-necessary main armament was the Soviet Union. As early as 1931, Soviet designers were discussing the possibility of putting a low-velocity 76.2 mm gun on the BT tanks that were then developing. (76.2 mm had been the standard Russian field gun caliber since the introduction of the first Putilov quick-firing field gun in 1902.) The Russian ordnance factories of the early 1930s, however, were in no position to provide these weapons. In fact, the first 600 BT tanks to come off the production lines had to be built without any main gun at all. Modifying the BT so that it could deal with the extra weight and recoil of a 76.2mm gun, moreover, required considerable changes to the suspension, transmission, and chassis. The idea was thus shelved, and a 37mm high-velocity gun fitted instead.[4] The 76.2mm gun did, nonetheless, make its way onto the standard medium and heavy tanks of the Soviet Army of the mid-1930s, the T-28, and the T-35.[5]

The 76.2 mm gun would have to wait nearly a decade before finding its way onto large numbers of Soviet light tanks. As soon as sufficient numbers of 45mm guns became available, however, the Red Army began to put them on its light infantry and cavalry tanks. These 45mm guns were substantially more powerful than the high-velocity 37mm (1-pounder) and 40mm (2-pounder) guns then being built for contemporary French, German, and British tanks. The 45mm shell weighed more than twice as much as the 37mm or 40mm shells while possessing a significantly greater ability to penetrate armor plate.[6] Beginning in 1933, new tanks of the BT series were provided with a new (and larger) turret built around the 45mm gun. This same turret was also used for contemporary models of the T-26 light infantry tank.[7]

The Soviet BT and T-26 tanks first saw combat in the Spanish Civil War (1936–39). There, in a war that saw very few encounters between hostile tanks, they were used in situations where they had to engage targets such as antitank guns and machine gun nests. Thus, even though the Soviet 45mm gun was much better at this than the antitank weapons mounted on all other contemporary tanks, the Soviet military leadership concluded that their fast tanks needed an even larger gun.[8] Soviet authorities drew the same lesson from the experience of short wars that the Soviet Union fought against the Japanese in Mongolia (in 1938), the Poles in Poland (in 1939), and the Finns in Finland (1939–1940.) These, too, were wars in which Soviet tanks had rarely been called upon to fight other tanks, but were often engaged against infantry, field artillery, and antitank units.

As a result of the lessons drawn from the wars of the late 1930s, the next fast tank to go into large-scale production in the Soviet Union, the soon-to-be famous T-34, was equipped with a gun of unprecedented power. The caliber of the gun (76.2mm) was not, by itself, particularly impressive. Guns with bores of about that size had been fitted on tanks—including the Soviet T-28 medium and T-35 heavy tanks—for more than a decade. Contemporary British support tanks were already sporting 95mm (3.7-inch) howitzers. What distinguished the new 76.2mm gun from all other large tank guns was its length. It was some 50% longer than the 76.2mm guns mounted on the T-28 and T-35. As such, it enjoyed vastly superior characteristics where shooting at tanks was concerned—higher muzzle velocity, a flatter trajectory, greater inherent accuracy, and greatly improved ability to penetrate armored plate.[9]

The long 76.2mm gun was the first member of a class of tank guns that would, by the end of World War II, come to define the main battle tank. After the introduction of this piece, designers no longer had to choose between mounting a high-velocity antitank weapon or a large bore, general-purpose weapon in their smaller tanks. Neither did they have to try to fit both into their larger creations, such as multi-turreted monstrosities like the T-35, the Vickers Independent, and the *Neubaufahrzeuge*. They now had large bore, high-velocity weapons that did a much better job of killing tanks while serving just as well as a delivery mechanism for high explosive, canister, and smoke rounds.

The KV heavy tanks and T-34 fast tanks were originally intended to be part of a troika of Soviet tanks that would replace the existing fleet of BT fast tanks, T-28 medium tanks, and T-35 heavy tanks. The third member of this troika was the T-50, a heavy infantry tank that, in conception and characteristics, had much in common with the British Matilda. The experience of the first year of the Russo-Soviet War of 1941–1945, however, made it very clear that this troika was not going to meet the needs of the Soviet army. For reasons that were mostly related to its engine, the T-50 proved impossible to produce in sufficient numbers. The KV could be mass-produced by the Soviet techniques of the time, but was mechanically unreliable.[10] (A vastly improved model became available in 1943.) As a result, the Soviet armaments industry took advantage of the relocation of most tank factories to locations east of the Urals to concentrate its efforts on the T-34. In 1942, for example, 51% of Soviet tanks produced were T-34s. In 1943 and 1944 T-34s represented 79% of the total number of tanks rolling off Soviet production lines.[11]

In the case of the Soviet Union during World War II, production and possession were two entirely different things. In particular, they fail to address the issues of longevity—the degree to which the battlefield survivability or mechanical reliability influenced the role played by a given tank type in the Soviet tank fleet—and the thousands of tanks provided by Great Britain, Canada, and the United States. Nonetheless, the T-34 ended up providing the same service to the Soviet army as the Sherman performed for the English-speaking armies on the Western Front. It firmly established the idea that a single type of tank could both serve as the main weapon of armored divisions and provide close support to infantry.

The first postwar employment of the T-34 took place on the 25 June 1950, when a small North Korean armored division joined other North Korean forces in the invasion of South Korea. Known as the 105th Armored Brigade, this formation attacked along the main axis of the North Korean offensive with eighty T-34 tanks and a regiment of 2,500 truck-borne infantrymen. A unit of forty tanks detached from this formation supported a secondary attack by two North Korean infantry divisions. As the South

Korean infantry divisions that stood in the path of these tanks had neither antitank mines nor antitank guns, the impact of this relative handful of tanks was enormous. Tank terror took hold of much of the South Korean army, government, and population, contributing greatly to the collapse of South Korean resistance.[12]

The American forces flown in from Japan in response to the North Korean surprise attack were no better equipped to deal with tanks than their South Korean allies. In keeping with the theory that the best way to fight a tank was with another tank, the U.S. infantry regiments of 1950 were bereft of heavy antitank weapons. Unfortunately, the tanks that were supposed to replace them had yet to be provided to the U.S. forces stationed in the Far East. As a result, the first waves of Americans sent into combat against the North Koreans had to make do with 2.36-inch rocket launchers and 75mm recoilless rifles. As neither of these weapons was capable of inflicting any significant damage upon the heavily armored T-34, the first Americans to fight in the Korean War were all but defenseless in the face of North Korean armor.

From the point of view of Western armies, the North Korean armor was handled rather clumsily. The techniques for making the most of such things as speed and mass were conspicuous by their absence. Nonetheless, the basic tactic of sending tanks down a road to attack the attention of the defending infantry while the North Korean infantry worked around their flanks was an effective one.[13] If the defenders panicked, they ran into ambushes set by the enveloping infantry. If, as was the case with the famous Task Force Smith, the defenders attempted to fight the tanks, the North Korean infantry attacked them from the rear.

Once word of this uneven contest reached the appropriate authorities, the U.S. Armed Forces responded by flying out a better model of bazooka (the 3.5-inch), sending tanks by sea, and developing an improved recoilless rifle (the 106mm.) The immediate solution to the problem of North Korean armor lay not in the realm of weapons, however, but that of the operational art. The rampage of the 105th Armored Brigade was only stopped when the landing of the 1st Marine Division at Inchon effectively severed the fragile lines of communication of the invading North Koreans. Deprived of nearly all supplies, and faced with a hard fighting, well equipped, and very large American force in their rear, the North Korean army collapsed. Though they managed their retreat with somewhat more decorum than their cousins in the South Korean forces had a few weeks before, the North Korean army soon ceased to exist as a modern fighting organization. When, in the spring of 1951, it took to the field again, it was as the lightly armed auxiliary of a Chinese Communist expeditionary force fighting in the guerilla style.[14]

What little tank against tank fighting there was in Korea took place in the period between August and November of 1950. In those four months, the United States shipped 1,326 tanks—679 Shermans (M4A3E8), 309 Pershings (M26), 200 Pattons (M46) and 138 Chaffees (M24)—to Korea. This was a sufficient number of tanks to fill the tank battalions of four or five armored divisions. (About 2,100 substantially less-powerful tanks had been used by the ten German armored divisions that had invaded the Low Countries on 10 May 1940.) Instead of being assembled into divisions, however, these tanks were distributed to the tank battalions of U.S. infantry and the tank companies of infantry regiments, there to compensate for the fact that no other suitable antitank weapons were available to U.S. ground forces.[15]

One reason for the American policy of distributing tanks throughout the United Nations ground force in Korea was matched by a similar tendency on the part of North Korean forces. Fighting under skies that were increasingly dominated by U.S. and other United Nations aircraft, the North Koreans of the autumn of 1950 found it impossible to mass their armor as they had in the early days of summer. Instead, they resorted to their own version of the German technique of armored guerilla warfare. In addition to dispersing their tanks over a wide area in groups of two, three, or four, they became masters of the art of camouflage. This earned them the grudging praise of the pilots of American observation aircraft, who compared North Korean skill at hiding tanks in haystacks and villages to that of the Germans they had fought in the last year of World War II. At times, this camouflage was so good that American forces only discovered the presence of North Korean armor when their own tanks, firing at North Korean infantry in villages, tore the thatch off roofs.[16]

The tendency of both sides in the Korean War to deploy their tanks not merely in "penny packets" but in what might be called "farthing packets" made the tank against tank struggle of the autumn of 1950 very much a platoon commander's war. A study conducted immediately after the war by the Operations Research Office at Johns Hopkins University came to the conclusion that, of 101 tank-on-tank engagements fought between August and November of 1950, 94% involved fewer than five tanks on either side. The average number of tanks on each side of these 101 combats was roughly two. (More precisely, the average engagement involved 2.2 American tanks and 1.9 North Korean tanks.)[17]

In the summer of 1951, the war of movement gave way to position warfare. That the forces of the American-led coalition declined to use armor to break this stalemate was largely a matter of policy. Fighting under the flag of the United Nations for a negotiated peace, fearful of the political consequences of escalation, and eager to keep as much armor as possible in Western Europe, the United States and its allies refrained from conducting any offensive action on a large scale. They thus limited their use of tanks to the immediate support of infantry battalions, regiments, and divisions. The employment of tanks as complete companies was thus a relatively rare event. Attempts to break into the depth of the enemy position were never made.

The fact that the Communist forces in Korea declined to attempt to repeat their earlier success with armor was less a matter of policy than of the operational environment. American control of the air made it nearly impossible for the Communists to effectively concentrate, let alone employ, armored formations. As a result, the tanks made available to the North Korean forces by their Soviet patrons were kept well away from the front. The 105th Armored Brigade was expanded into an armored division that, along with a motorized infantry division, was held in reserve against the possibility of American landings along North Korea's exposed western coastline.[18]

The Communist armored vehicle most frequently seen in the position warfare phase of the Korean War was the SU-76 assault gun. Though the Soviet Union had declared this weapon obsolete in 1944, it was well suited to the Korean environment, small enough to be easily hidden but with a gun that was powerful enough to deal with a Sherman tank at close quarters. Fortunately for United Nations forces, the North Koreans rarely made the most of these advantages. Rather than employing the German technique of the *Lauerstellung*, which would have permitted the SU-76 to make the most of its small size, the North Koreans tended to put their assault guns in fixed positions. Though these positions were well camouflaged, they were rarely chosen with much imagination. Thus, it became relatively easy for American and British Commonwealth tank crews to "reverse engineer" a North Korean antitank ambush. This, in turn, allowed the United Nations tanks to use their superior guns and gunnery to knock out the assault guns from the relative safety of a distant hill.[19]

The experience of United Nations and North Korean armor in the Korean War confirmed a trend that had been very noticeable since the summer of 1944.[20] The use of a large caliber (75mm to 125mm), high-velocity gun as the main armament of tanks had turned combat between hostile tanks—combat which had once resembled a boxing match—into a species of pistol duel. Prior to the last year of World War II, the destruction of an enemy tank had been a matter of landing a series of good blows or, in rare circumstances, a knockout blow against the military equivalent of a glass jaw. Starting with 1944, the key to destroying hostile tanks in the second half of the twentieth century was the firing of the first accurate shot. Thanks to the vastly increased destructive power of the shells fired by the larger, more powerful tank guns, this shot was capable of doing so much damage that the target tank was rarely in a position to reply. This, in turn, put a premium on such things as the inherent ballistic accuracy of the gun, the quality of the sights and other aiming devices, and, most important of all, the marksmanship skills of the crew.

This phenomenon was best understood in the West, where the veterans of tank battles in North Africa and Western Europe dominated tank design for several decades after the end of World War II. With each successive generation of main battle tank, the guns got larger, with the 90mm standard of the 1950s becoming the 105mm standard of the 1960s and 1970s and the 120mm standard of the 1980s and 1990s. As the guns got larger, the ranges at which they could reliably destroy enemy tanks grew, from less than 1,000 meters in the immediate postwar period to over 3,000 meters by the 1980s. This, in turn, put a great premium on various aids to marksmanship—improved optic sights, thermal sights, night vision devices, range-finding machine guns, laser range finders, and ballistics computers of increasing sophistication. During this period, the weight of tanks crept slowly upwards, as power plants became more efficient and additional armor was added. At the heart of each new generation of tank introduced in the period between 1945 and 2000 was a more powerful gun and the increasingly sophisticated panoply of devices designed to make the most of the new weapon's increased range.

The most notable example of the predominance of the large-caliber, high-velocity tank gun in the second half of the twentieth century comes from the experience of the Israeli Defense Force. Before the mid-1960s, the armored elements of this army lacked the capability to effectively engage enemy tanks at the ranges that Western armies had come to accept as normal. One reason for this was the hand-me-down equipment available to Israeli tank units. Another was the nature of the threat. For most of the first twenty years (from 1948 to 1967) of Israel's existence, the armored elements of the armies of the front-line Arab states were poorly trained, poorly led, and equipped with weapons left over from the early days of World War II.[21] Because of this, Israeli tank units could usually accomplish what they needed without paying too much attention to the revolution in tank gunnery that had taken place.

This all changed in the mid-1960s. One reason was the widespread introduction of the British L7 105mm tank gun.[22] Whether provided as original equipment on American M60 main battle tanks or retrofitted onto Israel's motley collection of Shermans and Centurions, this excellent gun gave Israeli tank crews the capability to reliably knock out any tank in the Arab inventory at ranges in excess of 1,500 meters. Another reason was a massive increase in both the quantity and quality of tanks available to the front-line Arab states during this period. As early as the late 1950s, the more radical Arab states had begun to replace Renaults, Matildas and Panzer IV tanks that had been built in the late 1930s or early 1940s with large numbers of armored fighting vehicles of Soviet design. While some of these were T-34/85 tanks dating from the last year of World War II, most were of more recent manufacture. These included the same T-54 and T-55 main battle tanks that armed the Soviet armies facing NATO across the inter-German border.

The third reason for the tank gunnery revolution that took place in the Israeli Defense Force in the mid-1960s was a product of the definitive characteristics of the geography of the Middle East —the difficulty of finding enough water to support either intensive agriculture or modern standards of hygiene. In the case of Israel, the general shortage of ground water meant that the country was highly dependent upon water from the Sea of Galilee—water that flowed, via the Jordan River, from tributaries in Syria and Jordan. In September of 1964, a number of Arab states undertook a massive engineering project to control these tributaries, thus placing Arab governments in the position of controlling much of Israel's water supply. Fortunately for the Israelis, most of the construction work necessary to the success of this enterprise, which began in earnest in March of 1965, had to take place within a few thousand meters of Israeli territory.[23]

In what were to become known as the Water Battles, Israelis deployed tanks to positions from which they could fire upon the construction sites. Rather than engaging in harassing fire, which would have had the effect of causing large numbers of civilian casualties, the Israeli tanks developed the gunnery techniques needed to destroy specific pieces of Arab heavy equipment. In particular, they became adept at hitting individual Arab bulldozers and, when the latter arrived to protect the bulldozers, Arab tanks. Unable to respond in kind, the Arabs reacted to this large-caliber sniping in various ways—by moving the construction sites to more distant locations and by using field artillery to shell Israeli villages. When, however, both of these reactions were countered with attacks by Israeli aircraft, the Arabs agreed to both a cease fire and the cessation of their attempts to divert the Jordan.[24]

At the time of the Water Battles, the Israelis had experience with three types of modern main battle tanks—the British Centurion, the American Patton (M47, M48, and M60), and the Soviet T-54/55. The first of these had much in common with its direct ancestor, the Churchill tank of World War II. It was both the heaviest and the most heavily armored tank in the Israeli inventory. The second was lighter and faster, and thus well suited to the type of fast-moving operations that the Israelis conducted in the Sinai desert during the Six Day War of 1967. The Soviet tanks were considerably smaller than each of the Western tanks were. This greatly reduced their weight, thereby enhancing their capability to do all those things associated with operational maneuver. It was, in other words, much less dependent upon modern bridges, refueler trucks, and sophisticated maintenance than either the Centurion or the Patton. The experience of the Water Wars, however, convinced many Israelis that they needed a fourth type of main battle tank—one that was optimized for long-range sniping.

The Israeli desire for a "sniper tank" was confirmed by the fighting that took place on the Golan Heights during the Yom Kippur War of 1973. In this contest, a handful of Israeli tank battalions found themselves sitting in good firing positions while hundreds of Syrian tanks advanced against them across a wide expanse of open ground. Making use of their new skills, Israeli tank gunners were, on average, able to destroy several Syrian tanks before the latter got close enough to fire their own main armament. When this did happen, the heavy armor of the Israeli Centurions ensured that most of the Syrian main gun rounds that struck failed to cause catastrophic damage. Indeed, while nearly every Israeli tank on the Golan Heights during this war suffered some sort of serious combat damage, the vast majority of tanks were repaired and returned to battle within hours of being hit.[25]

Unfortunately for the Israelis, the men who fought in the tanks were not as easily repaired as the tanks themselves. Of the 2,500 Israelis who died in the Yom Kippur War, 1,500 were from the armored corps. More than anything else, this sobering fact ensured that the engineers working on the first entirely indigenous Israeli tank placed an extraordinarily high value on crew survivability. This is most easily seen in the decision to place the tank engine in the front of the hull and the extensive use of sloped armor. These obvious life-preserving features of this tank—which was unveiled as the *Merkava* ("chariot") in 1979—were complemented by a number of more subtle elements. The mechanism that drove the turret, for example was electric rather than hydraulic. (This eliminated the danger that flammable hydraulic fluid would catch fire inside the turret.)[26]

The crew survivability features of the Merkava were very much in keeping with its role as a "long-range sniper." The front mounting of the engine, for example, made possible a special ammunition compartment in the back of the tank. This was primarily a result of one of the chief observations made by Israeli observers of the Golan Heights battles of 1973—the fact that Israeli tanks quickly used up their onboard supplies of 105mm main gun ammunition. This compartment also allowed the Merkava to carry a four-man team of infantrymen, combat engineers, or commandos. Thus, for the first time since the invention of the tank, explicit provision had been made for the under-armor transport of escort troops.

Appreciation for the need to give escort troops the same degree of protection as tank crews also led the Israeli Defense Forces to resurrect the Kangaroo concept of World War II. This took the form of the *Achzarit*, a heavily armored personnel carrier based on the hull of a Soviet T-54/55 main battle tank. (The Israelis had captured large numbers of these from Arab armies.) In addition to benefiting from the heavy armor of a tank hull, the soldiers traveling inside the Achzarit are further protected by blocks of reactive armor. When struck by a high explosive round (such as that fired by a tank gun, recoilless rifle, or rocket propelled grenade), these blocks explode, thereby disrupting the penetrating effect of the initial explosion. When detonated by command of someone inside the Achzarit, this same armor serves as a Claymore mine, sending hundreds of lethal pellets in the direction of hostile infantrymen.[27]

The Merkava was the most successful of the sniper tank designs to come out of second half of the twentieth century. It was not, however, the only one. Starting in the 1950s, European tank designers have often explored the possibility of turretless tanks armed with full-size tank guns. Inspired by the more heavily armed of the German and Soviet assault guns of World War II, these would combine the advantage of the firepower of a weapon like the

Merkava with substantially reduced weight. The only one of these weapons to be produced in series and adopted by a major army, however, was the Swedish *Stridsvagen 105*. Others, including the Anglo-German *Jagdchieftan* project and a German attempt to build a turretless tank armed with two 105mm guns, never got beyond the prototype stage.

In the Soviet Union and the United States, the sniper tank concept took the form of tanks armed with antitank guided missiles. In the case of the Soviet Union, a number of missile tanks were under development during the late 1950s. These benefited from the heavy-handed patronage of Nikita Khrushchev, who had come to believe that gun-armed tanks would be rendered obsolete by antitank guided missiles. None of these projects, however, survived Khrushchev's fall from power.[28] Where the Soviet missile tanks were turretless, the two American tanks to be armed primarily with missiles had conventional turrets. The first of these was a Sheridan, a light tank officially classified as an "armored reconnaissance vehicle." The other was the M60A2, a modified version of the standard Patton tank. Both of these vehicles carried a short 152mm gun that could fire either unguided high explosive rounds or *Shillelagh* antitank guided missiles.

The inherent deficiency of both turretless gun-armed tanks and tanks armed with antitank guided missiles was that they were just too specialized. They were optimized for the task of killing other tanks, but largely unable to do all the other things that tanks have traditionally done on the battlefield. This deficiency is underscored by the fact that, despite having been designed for long-range sniping on the Golan Heights, the Merkava has never been used for that purpose. Rather, it has been used primarily in operations against guerillas of one sort or another, either the classic guerillas of southern Lebanon or the "post-modern" Palestinian fighters of the West Bank and Gaza. In those operations, the features designed to protect tank crews against rounds fired by hostile tanks or long-range antitank guided missiles have served instead to protect them from rocket-propelled grenades and suicide bombers.

Tanks armed with antitank guided missiles are even more specialized than turretless gun tanks. Where the latter can fire high-explosive rounds, smoke rounds, and other ordnance, the missile tank can only fire missiles with specialized antitank warheads. Indeed, as the latter were more thoroughly optimized for the task of penetrating tank armor, they became less useful for other battlefield purposes. In 1982, for example, British infantrymen fighting in the Falkland Islands used man-portable Milan antitank guided missiles to destroy Argentine machine gun positions.[29] By the 1990s, many top-of-the-line antitank guided missiles (such as the US TOW2B) were no longer suitable for such purposes. This was because they had been designed to function in the "fly over shoot down" mode.[30] (This is also known as "overfly top attack.") That is to say, their fusing mechanisms were built to set off the warhead while it was flying a few inches over the target tank rather than just in front of it. The warhead itself, moreover, was designed to explode downward (through the relatively thin roof armor of a tank) rather than the traditional forward direction.

In the course of the 1990s, engineers tackled the problem of overspecialization in antitank guided missiles by building various mechanisms that allow the gunner to choose different firing modes. This was a relatively easy thing to do and bore fruit in such designs as the Swedish Bill2.[31] An even simpler solution was to design a variety of different warheads. Thus, while the antitank version of the Russian Kornet antitank guided missile is optimized for use against tanks protected by reactive armor, the same missile can also carry a thermobaric warhead.[32] (Thermobaric warheads make use of refined versions of the fuel-air explosives developed by the U.S. Armed Forces in the 1950s. Upon activation, the warhead releases a fine mist of highly volatile fuel and, a fraction of a second later, ignites the mist to produce an extraordinarily powerful overpressure. As might be expected, Russian interest in these weapons is a direct outgrowth of the bitter urban combat that took place in Chechnya in the 1990s.)[33]

A much thornier problem faced by the designers of antitank guided missiles was that of speed, or, more precisely, time of flight. A 120mm tank gun of the types introduced in the 1980s and 1990s fired its projectile with a muzzle velocity that is well in excess 1,000 meters per second. (The 120mm gun on the French Leclerc tank, for example, fires its high-explosive rounds at 1,100 meters per second and its discarding sabot rounds at 1,790 meters per second.)[34] Typical antitank guided missiles of the same period flew at speeds that ranged from 100 meters per second to 420 meters per second. (Larger antitank guided missiles, which could only be fired from vehicles, tended to be faster than those which were small enough to be used by dismounted infantry units.) Put another way, in the last two decades of the twentieth century, a round fired from a tank gun was likely to be a minimum of three times faster than an antitank guided missile and might even be ten times as fast.[35]

The fact that a round fired from a tank gun was several times faster than an antitank guided missile put the latter at a considerable disadvantage in anything that resembled a fair fight. That is to say, a tank could fire several aimed tank rounds in the time that it took to launch an antitank guided missile and fly it to its target. By the mid-1970s, several Western armies were teaching their tank crews to exploit this phenomenon with an immediate action drill. The moment that they detected the launching of an antitank guided missile, the tank crews were to react by firing their main gun in the general direction of the telltale flash. While this was unlikely to score a direct hit upon the offending missile launcher, there was a good chance that the man operating the missile would be sufficiently unnerved (or at least distracted) to cause him to lose control of the missile. This bought the tank crew the time that it needed to bring more destructive fire to bear.

Ironically, antitank guided missiles of the first generation (introduced in the 1950s and 1960s) were much less vulnerable to this technique than the second generation (introduced in the 1970s and 1980s). The earlier weapons were launched into the air at a relatively high angle, gathered by the controller as they flew through the air, and then guided down to the target by means of joystick. This meant that, while the controller had to see the target, the missile itself could be kept in defilade. Second-generation antitank guided missiles, on the other hand, were fired along a path that was parallel to the ground. This meant that neither missile nor controller could make use of much in the way of cover. Indeed, the tendency of second-generation antitank guided missiles to dip slightly after leaving their launch tubes often limited them to particularly exposed firing positions. Thus, even though they were significantly faster than first-generation antitank guided missiles and much easier for a controller to master, second-generation antitank guided missiles were sometimes even more vulnerable to return fire from their intended targets.

Antitank guided missiles of the third generation, which started to appear in the 1990s, solved this problem using small television cameras and fiber-optic cable. The combination of these two civilian technologies allows both the missile launcher and the controller to remain in a place of comparative safety while the missile finds its way towards its target. The same combination also provides third-generation antitank guided missiles with both extraordinary accuracy and, in the moments before impact, the ability to provide the controller with a very close view of the intended target. This latter virtue allows the missile to be aimed at particular vulnerabilities of the targeted vehicle, makes it easier for the controller to avoid hitting friendly forces or noncombatants, and reduces the chances that a missile will be wasted on a target that has already been destroyed.

The ability of fiber-optic guided missiles to gather important target information until the moment of impact was demonstrated on 25 August 1998. On that day, an Israeli helicopter fired a fiber-optic guided missile at a civilian car driven by Hussam al-Amin,[36] a young guerilla leader fighting against the Israelis in southern Lebanon.[37] From the point of view of antitank technology, the remarkable thing about this incident was not that the Israelis undertook the attack or that Amin was killed. After all, the Israelis had been using laser-guided Hellfire missiles fired from helicopters to carry out similar assassinations since 1992.[38] The phenomenon worth noting was the fact that the missile controller in the Israeli helicopter was able to read the license plate of the car that the missiles were about to fly into and thus increase the chances of hitting the person they intended to kill.[39]

The advent of each generation of antitank guided missiles has led observers of military affairs to predict the demise of the gun-armed tank. On 14 September 1964, just one month before he was deposed in a bloodless coup, Soviet premier Nikita Khrushchev witnessed a firing demonstration in which first-generation antitank guided missiles quickly destroyed three moving tank targets. The next day he stood before a conference of the Soviet Communist Party and announced the impending obsolescence of the tank.[40] In the aftermath of the Arab-Israeli October War of 1973, a number of Western commentators made the same observation. Some of these were impressed by the success that first-generation antitank guided missiles in the hands of Egyptian forces had enjoyed against Israeli tanks. Others pointed to engagements (such as the well-documented Battle of Chinese Farm) in which the Israelis made good use of second-generation antitank guided missiles that had recently arrived from the United States. In the late 1980s and early 1990s, a somewhat smaller number of European and American writers saw great promise in the third generation of antitank guided missiles. Sobered, perhaps, by the failure of preceding predictions to come to pass, these authors did not go so far as to predict the complete elimination of the main battle tank, only its displacement as the principal means by which ground combat units destroyed hostile tanks.[41]

12
THE FUTURE OF ARMOR

Reduced to a simple diagram, the history of armored warfare in the twentieth century takes the form of the letter *x*. One of the two slanted lines that form the *x* is the tale of operational mobility—the ability to move rapidly when not in contact with the enemy. The other line depicts the development of combat power—the ability to inflict damage on the enemy while avoiding damage to one's own forces. At the beginning of the story, these two characteristics are embodied in very different classes of vehicles. Light armored vehicles (initially armored cars and trucks) had operational mobility while tanks had combat power. In the 1920s and 1930s, the light armored vehicles got better armor and more-powerful weapons, while the tanks became faster. In the middle of the story, which also coincides with the middle of the twentieth century, the two principal virtues of the armored vehicle are embodied in a single class of vehicle: an all-purpose tank such as the German Panzer III, the Soviet T-34, or the American Sherman. It was not long, however, before the two lines began to diverge again. By the end of the twentieth century, it was no longer possible to combine both operational mobility and first-class combat power in a single vehicle.

As might be expected, the armies that did the best job of exploiting the way that armored vehicles were evolving in the first half of the twentieth century, those of Germany and the Soviet Union, were also those that had the greatest interest in operational mobility. Similarly, the major army with the least interest in operational mobility, that of France reacted poorly to the impending arrival of the all-purpose tank. In the second half of the twentieth century, however, this relationship between understanding and effective response was reversed. The armies that did the best job of responding to the trend away from the all-purpose tank, those of the United States and the United Kingdom, did so at a time when they were entirely bereft of the concept of operational mobility. The army that had displayed the best understanding of operational mobility, that of the Soviet Union, held on the longest to the concept of the all-purpose tank. Indeed, the idea that an armored force with adequate operational mobility and adequate combat power was better than one with poor operational mobility and excellent combat power survived the collapse of the Soviet Union to find a home in the army of the Russian Republic.

For tank designers in the United States and United Kingdom, the eventual demise of the all-purpose tank was made clear by the fighting that took place on the Golan Heights during the Arab-Israeli October War of 1973. That contest, which resulted in the loss of six Soviet-made Syrian tanks to every one Western-made Israeli tank, confirmed the preexisting Anglo-American prejudice in favor of heavy armor and long-range gunnery. Indeed, it emboldened British and American tank designers to make enormous sacrifices in operational mobility (particularly a quantum leap in fuel consumption and a considerable increase in both size and weight). The result was the two tanks—the U.S. M1 Abrams and British Challenger—that so thoroughly dominated the battlefields of Iraq in 1991 and 2003.

The degree to which the heavy tank overmatched its all-purpose counterpart at the end of the last century is well illustrated by an anecdote from the Gulf War of 1991. At one point in the very short ground campaign, an Abrams tank of the U.S. 24th Mechanized Infantry Division became stuck in some mud. While it was waiting for a recovery vehicle, this tank was attacked by three Iraqi T-72 tanks of Soviet manufacture. The first two T-72s fired their 125mm main guns at ranges of about 1,000 meters, striking the American tank with shaped-charge rounds. These exploded harmlessly, resulting only in return fire that destroyed both tanks with the first two rounds fired. The third T-72 advanced to a range of 400 meters and fired a sabot round. This bounced off the turret of the Abrams, leaving a deep gouge in the armor. The Abrams returned the compliment with a sabot round of its own that penetrated a small dune that the Iraqi tank had been using for cover before causing catastrophic damage to the offending vehicle.

The tactical virtuosity of the Abrams tank, however, was not without cost. In particular, the heavy tank had a voracious appetite for fuel. Where the M60 Patton tank could move three miles for each gallon of fuel consumed, the Abrams required somewhere in the vicinity of two gallons of gasoline for each mile traveled and ten to twelve gallons for each hour spent sitting still with its combat systems turned on.[1] Put another way, each of the nearly 2,000 Abrams tanks involved in the ground war needed to fill its 500-gallon fuel tank about once per day. Among other things, this greatly complicated the effort to complete the victory of coalition forces by preventing the escape of all of the Republican Guard divisions that were retreating out of Kuwait. In simpler terms, U.S. forces could not complete the planned encirclement of the Republican Guard because many American units had (quite literally) run out of gas.[2] This happened, moreover, despite a Herculean effort to make an adequate supply of fuel available to coalition ground forces. (This effort began with the accumulation of a stockpile of some 39,000,000 gallons of gasoline and diesel fuel during the six months prior to the start of the ground war.)[3]

If the wars in Iraq in 1991 and 2003 contrasted the tactical virtues with the operational vices of Western heavy tanks, the Chechen Wars that began in 1994 highlighted the tactical deficiencies of the all-purpose tanks fielded by the armed forces of the Russian Republic. In particular, the design features needed to preserve the operational mobility of Russian tanks made them extremely vulnerable to the rocket propelled grenades wielded by Chechen fighters. (Those design features included relatively light armor, the lack of measures to inhibit internal explosions, the cramped crew compartments, and a limited ability to elevate and depress the main armament.) This vulnerability to rocket propelled grenades was particularly marked in urban areas, where the Chechens made extensive use of firing positions in basements and on the upper floors of multistory buildings.[4] Given this experience, it is not surprising that a good deal of Russian tank design work in the 1990s involved attempts to greatly improve the armored protection of combat vehicles. Of particular note was the design of a heavily armored personnel carrier that, like the Israeli Achzarit, made use of the hull and chassis of a main battle tank.

While lack of interest in operational mobility did much to facilitate the fielding of both the Abrams and the Challenger, it greatly hampered the development of the logical complement to the Western heavy tank. Indeed, during the time (the 1970s and 1980s) that the British and U.S. armies were most committed to the development of the heavy tank, they had completely abandoned the concept of the wheeled armored car. The light armored vehicles designed during this period—the most notable of which were the British

Warrior and the American Bradley infantry/cavalry fighting vehicles—were all provided with tracks. This, among other things, underscored their role as auxiliaries to the heavy tanks. Though they were capable of going much further on the same amount of fuel and crossing bridges that would collapse under the weight of a seventy-ton vehicle, the light tracked vehicles were supposed to remain in close proximity to the heavy tanks. What interest there was in wheeled armored vehicles was displayed by the French, who built upon their longstanding armored car tradition to field an impressive force of wheeled combat and reconnaissance vehicles. The larger varieties of these were designed to serve the needs of *couverture*—to make use of the excellent French network of superhighways to move forces from the interior of the country to its frontiers. The smaller varieties were tools for rapid intervention in the many client states that had emerged from the dissolution of the French overseas empire. As such, they were often found in the hands of the French Foreign Legion and the *Troupes de Marine.*

In the late 1970s, problems similar to that faced by Legionnaires and Marines in the service of France led the U.S. Marine Corps to raise three battalions of Light Armored Infantry. These were equipped with a variety of wheeled armored vehicles, some of which carried small infantry squads and others of which were armed with 81mm mortars or antitank guided missiles. In the course of the 1990s, companies from these battalions often took the place of the tank platoons that had traditionally formed part of Marine Expeditionary Units. (These are heavily reinforced infantry battalions loaded on amphibious ships that float near the world's trouble spots for several months at a time.) When so equipped, Marine Expeditionary Units were not only able to move larger forces ashore in a shorter period of time but also were able to move further inland than would otherwise be the case. The classic example of this took place in June of 1999 when the 26th Marine Expeditionary Unit—which included thirteen wheeled armored vehicles but no Abrams tanks—conducted a 200-mile (320-kilometer) road march from the Greek port of Thessaloniki to the southeastern corner of Kosovo.[5]

The success that the Marine Corps achieved with wheeled armored vehicles took place at a time when the U.S. Army was rediscovering its latent interest in rapid intervention. The Cold War was over and, apart from such anachronisms as North Korea and Iraq, there were few Soviet-style enemies left to fight. An even more pressing problem had been created by the lack of suitable infrastructure in many of the areas where the U.S. Army had been called to intervene in the 1990s. Without such infrastructure—modern roads, first-class bridges, and permanent bases—many of the Army's flagship systems, whether Apache helicopters or Abrams tanks, took a long time to deploy. Once deployed, they were often very difficult to keep in operation. Once this latter fact had been established by a handful of embarrassing incidents, much of the army's senior leadership began to display interest in the possibilities offered by wheeled armored vehicles.

The starting point for U.S. Army thinking about wheeled armored vehicles was the armored car—known to Marines as the Light Armored Vehicle (LAV)—adopted by the Marine Corps in the late 1970s. A few U.S. Army thinkers looked at this vehicle and quickly came to the conclusion that a combat unit based on it would have to fight in a way that was very different from that of units built around heavy tanks. In particular, they realized that such a unit had no business getting involved in a direct-fire contest with any but the weakest of opponents. Put another way, they understood that a combat unit that went to war in lightly armored vehicles could only fight if it made extensive use of indirect fire of one sort or another. Unfortunately, this view did not prevail. Instead, the Stryker Brigades that the U.S. Army created in 2002 were formed on a more traditional pattern. At the heart of each of these brigades is mechanized infantry of a conventional type. A bit of additional firepower is available in the form of self-propelled 105mm tank guns, vehicles that must be exposed in the manner of a tank in order to employ their weapons.

A far better solution would be to arm the wheeled armored vehicles with a variety of indirect fire weapons, such as turret-mounted mortars, fiber-optic guided missiles, small-caliber automatic cannon, and modest-sized bombardment rockets. The turret-mounted mortars (probably in the ubiquitous 120mm caliber) would be capable of firing unguided mortar bombs against infantry and guided projectiles against hostile tanks. The mortars would work in concert with fiber-optic guided missiles of various sizes. These would both find targets for the mortars and destroy particularly important point targets of their own. The automatic cannon, in a caliber in the range between 25mm and 35mm, would serve a variety of purposes. They would contribute to the indirect-fire capability of the unit while also dealing with low-flying aircraft and close-in targets. A pod of unguided bombardment rockets, probably in the well-supported 2.75-inch size, would provide each vehicle with a means of dealing with an ambush. It would also provide the unit as a whole with a means of delivering a short burst of high-volume area fire.[6]

Because effective indirect fire is dependent upon observers of various sorts, the wheeled armored vehicle unit would both incorporate and cooperate with a variety of reconnaissance assets. Organic assets would include short-range unmanned aerial vehicles, human forward observers, and small scout squads. These would be used in concert with manned aircraft, the larger sort of unmanned aerial vehicles, satellites, and liaison teams working with other friendly units. The manned aircraft should, if possible, be of the cooperative armed reconnaissance variety tested by the Marine Corps "Capable Warrior" experiments of the late 1990s. Also known as "Hunter Air" and "Aviation from the Sea," this type of aviation is based on the idea that aviators should do far more than "service" targets in response to formal requests. What they should do is form an integral part of an air-ground team, scouting ahead of fast-moving units while attacking enemy columns in ways that force the latter to either slow down or stop moving altogether.

The infantry that traveled with the indirect fire wheeled armored vehicle unit would represent a much smaller proportion of the whole than the infantry of a U.S. Army Stryker Brigade of 2002. Rather than providing the main combat power of the unit, it would serve the traditional functions of the small parties of infantry that have often accompanied mobile troops. It would seize and hold defiles, provide security at night and during such actions as the crossing of rivers, and it would deal with small woods, clusters of buildings, and other similar features. The unit would also have a relatively high proportion of combat engineers. In the advance, these would be located near the head of the column to deal with mines, rivers, and other obstacles. In retreat, they would be at the very end of the column, creating obstacles of their own. In all cases, they would form, with the organic infantry, the dismountable escort troops of the unit.[7]

With fiber optic guided missiles capable of flying out to ranges of fifteen kilometers or more and turret-mounted mortars with ranges in the vicinity of half that, an indirect fire wheeled armored vehicle unit would have little to fear from a similar-sized unit of first-class heavy tanks. As long as it identified the tank unit before the latter was able to engage with direct fire, it would be able to take a terrible toll of the tanks with little loss to itself. An ambush or other small-scale encounter would be a different story. Even after they had bought themselves a few precious seconds with their bombardment rockets, the wheeled armored vehicles at the head of an ambushed column would be at a considerable disadvantage. In any terrain where such an ambush would be possible, however, the wheeled armored vehicle unit, as a whole, would have the ability to quickly hide itself, gain the upper hand, and wreak a terrible revenge upon the miscreant tanks.

If this were the case, the days of the heavy tank as the premium long-range killer would be numbered. While a heavy tank would be too powerful for the simple task of overpowering wheeled armored vehicles in a direct fire contest, it would be largely impotent against the kind of precision indirect fire produced by the right sort of wheeled vehicle unit. This is not to say that the heavy tank would go the way of the dinosaur. On the contrary, the lessons learned in the Chechen Wars, as well as Israeli experience in the occupied territories, suggests that there is a role for heavy tanks in close combat. These would, however, be more like the funnies of the 79th Armoured Division than the Centurions of the Golan Heights. Some would carry powerful close-range weapons—the twenty-first century answer to the 290mm Dustbin spigot mortar of 1944. Others would be armored personnel carriers on the model of the Israeli Achzarit or the Heavy Infantry Fighting Vehicle proposed by Gregory Pickell. A number would possess the means of entering buildings in various ways, whereas a few might carry some sort of combat robots.

In the case of both light armored vehicles and heavy tanks, the variety of desired capabilities is likely to combine with their specialized application to create demand for modular designs. Turrets, weapons stations, and other similar features will be designed so that they can be swapped out in the field. This will not only allow a commander to customize his weapons mix, but will also facilitate the repair of combat damage. In the longer term, the proper use of modular design will extend the life of a given vehicle beyond the point where a change in technology or tactics makes a specific configuration obsolete. For expeditionary forces, the ability to quickly change key components of a fighting vehicle will allow a force to be prepared for a wide variety of problems without deploying a complete vehicle for each capability desired.

The exact form that armored vehicles of the near future is impossible to predict. There are too many variables; thus, there are too many possibilities. What is certain, however, is that the tendency towards uniformity that marked the story of the armored fighting vehicle in the middle years of the twentieth century has been reversed. The dominance of a single type of vehicle mounting a single type of weapon has ended. The great variety that characterized the early days of the armored fighting vehicle has returned. Indeed, it is fair to say that this level of variety may even be exceeded. The age of the tank is over. The age of tanks has begun.

Notes

Chapter 1:   Diverging Paths

1. For the purposes of this discussion, "small-caliber cannon" were quick-firing ("recoil-absorbing") cannon firing shells smaller than those that were fired by the standard field guns (with calibers between 75mm to 90mm) of the time. Common calibers included 37mm, 47mm, and 57mm. The "minor operations of war" include colonial warfare and the skirmishes between cavalry formations (in the plains) and light troops (in the mountains) that usually preceded the clash of the main bodies of civilized armies in eighteenth and nineteenth century European warfare.

2. Descriptions and pictures of the armored cars of the two decades before the outbreak of World War I abound, but comprehensive accounts of the early days of the armored car are rare. Exceptions include B. H. Liddell-Hart, *The Tanks* (London: Cassell, 1959), Vol. I, p. 13, and Walther Albrecht, *Gunther Burstyn und die Entwickelung der Panzerwaffe* (Osnabrück: Biblioverlag, 1973), pp. 46–47.

3. Alain Gougaud, *L'Aube de la Gloire, Les Autos-Mitrailleuses et les Chars Français Pendant la Grande Guerre* (Issy les Moulineaux: Société OCEBUR, c. 1987), pp. 44–46.

4. The first machine gun to be placed on one of the touring cars had been intended for antiaircraft work. Charles Rumney Samson, *Fights and Flights* (London: Ernest Benn Ltd., 1930), pp. 6 and 31.

5. The date of Commander Samson's first patrol was 29 August 1914. Samson, *Fights and Flights*, pp. 6–33.

6. More information about these vehicles can be found in B. T. White, *British Tanks and Fighting Vehicles, 1914–1945* (London: Ian Allan, 1970), pp. 99–101.

7. Gougaud, *L'Aube de la Gloire,* pp. 36–53.

8. Ibid.

9. Albrecht, *Gunther Burstyn und die Entwickelung der Panzerwaffe*, p. 49. On 27 September 1914, the British journalist F. Tennyson Jesse saw two of these "new steel-domed mitrailleuses" racing down the road near Ostend. "A Woman in Battle at Belgium's Last Stand," *Collier's Magazine*, 14 November 1914.

10. Gougaud, *L'Aube de la Gloire*, p. 70.

11. The Royal Navy Armoured Car Division had reached a strength of fifteen twelve-car squadrons when, in the summer of 1915, it was disbanded, and all but the squadrons that had been sent to Russia were handed over to the British army. These, in the guise of armored car "batteries" of the Machine Gun Corps, took part in internal security duties (in Egypt, India, and Ireland). They also supported horse cavalry formations taking part in the suppression of the Senussi Revolt (in Libya, in 1916) and the campaigns of Allenby in Palestine and Syria. David Fletcher, *War Cars: British Armoured Cars in the First World War* (London: H.M.S.O., 1987), p. 22.

12. Gougaud, *L'Aube de la Gloire,* pp. 61–64.

13. Ibid., pp. 63–64.

14. Semet, "Quelques aspects de la Campagne belge des Autos-Canons Mitrailleuses en Russie," *Bulletin Belge des Sciences Militaires*, June 1929, p. 473.

15. Gougaud, *L'Aube de la Gloire,* p. 71.

16. Résumés of the actions of each French armored car unit in 1918 can be found in Gougaud, *L'Aube de la Gloire,* pp. 88–97.

17. British armored cars returned to the Western Front in April of 1918, when the Seventeenth Battalion of the Tank Corps was converted from a tank unit into an armored car unit. This conversion, the only one that took place, was a response to the valuable work being performed by French armored car units and the Canadian Motor Machine Gun Brigade in the wake of the (still ongoing) German spring offensives. J. F. C. Fuller, *Tanks in the Great War, 1914–1918* (New York: E. P. Dutton, 1920), p. 289.

18. Bill Rawling, *Surviving Trench Warfare, Technology and the Canadian Corps, 1914–1918* (Toronto: University of Toronto Press, 1992), pp. 12–13.

19. John F. Wallace, *Dragons of Steel, Canadian Armour in Two World Wars* (Burnstown, Ontario: General Store Publishing House, 1995), pp. 17–24.

20. Raymond Brutinel was commissioned a major in 1914. By early 1918, he had risen to the rank of brigadier general and the command of the Canadian Machine Gun Corps, a post he held concurrently with command of the Canadian Independent Force. It is tempting to see the term "motor machine gun" as a direct translation of the French *"auto-mitrailleuse."* I have not, however, been able to find documentary evidence of this.

21. The exact role played by Raymond Brutinel in the development of machine gun tactics is a matter of some controversy. For views, see Graham Seaton Hutchinson, *Machine Guns: Their History and Tactical Employment* (London: MacMillan, 1938); Paddy Griffith, *Battle Tactics of the Western Front: The British Army's Art of the Attack 1916–1918* (New Haven: Yale University Press, 1994), and Wallace, *Dragons of Steel.*

22. Wallace, *Dragons of Steel*, pp. 50–58.

23. Ibid., pp. 60–63.

24. An overall description of the British plan for the Battle of Amiens can be found in the British official history: James E. Edmonds, editor, *Military Operations in France and Flanders, 1918* (London: H. M. S. O., 1947), Volume IV, pp. 16–39. The development of the defensive tactics of the sort used by the Germans at Amiens can be found in Graham Chamley Wynne, *If Germany Attacks, The Battle in Depth in the West* (London: Faber and Faber, 1940.)

25. Wallace, *Dragons of Steel*, pp. 60–63, and Shane B. Schreiber, *Shock Army of the British Empire: The Canadian Corps in the Last 100 Days of the Great War* (Westport, CT: Praeger, 1997), p. 36.

26. Wallace, *Dragons of Steel*, pp. 64–65.

27. W. Arthur Steele, "Wireless Telegraphy in the Canadian Corps in France," *Canadian Defence Quarterly*, October 1930, p. 87.

28. The four German infantry battalions blocking Canadian access to the Amiens-Roye highway were from the 225th Infantry Division. Of the other five infantry battalions of the division, two were well south of Amiens-Roye Highway, facing the French Forty-Second Infantry Division, and three were resting well behind the main defensive position. Two of these "resting battalions" should have come to the aid of the four battalions facing the Canadian onslaught, but they were caught up in a different engagement several kilometers northeast of the Amiens-Roye Highway. The third resting battalion, which belonged to the regiment facing the French Forty-second Infantry Division, was located near the village of Beaucourt, just north of the Amiens-Roye Highway and eight or so kilometers east of the point where the Canadians began their attack. Thilo von Bose, *Die Katastrophe des 8. August, 1918* (Berlin: Stalling, 1930), pp. 23–39 (for an analysis of the strength of German units involved in the battle) and pp. 147–53 (for the fight between elements of the Third Canadian Infantry Division and the German 225th Infantry Division.)

29. Wallace, *Dragons of Steel*, pp. 64–65.

30. This was the First Reserve Division, of nine infantry battalions. Bose, *Die Katastrophe des 8. August 1918*, p. 132.

31. The four German infantry battalions encountered by the armored cars near Beaucourt were the three resting battalions of the 192d Infantry Division and the resting battalion of the Eighteenth Infantry Regiment (which was then being attacked by the French Forty-second Infantry Division) of the 225th Infantry Division. As were nearly all the German infantry units at Amiens (save those of the recently refurbished 117th Infantry Division), these battalions were at full strength where heavy weapons were concerned, but were desperately short of riflemen. Bose, *Die Katastrophe des 8. August 1918*, pp. 154 and 172.

32. Steele, "Wireless Telegraphy in the Canadian Corps in France," pp. 90–91 and Wallace, *Dragons of Steel*, p. 69.

33. The story of the British Seventeenth Armored Car Battalion at Amiens is briefly told in John Monash, *Australian Victories in France in 1918* (London:

Hutchinson, 1920), pp. 106–12 and Clough Williams-Ellis and A. Williams-Ellis, *The Tank Corps* (New York: George H. Doran, 1919), pp. 290–91. It is important to note that the Seventeenth Armored Car Battalion was not, as the number might indicate, one of seventeen or more armored car battalions of the British army of the time. Rather, it was the Seventeenth Battalion of the Tank Corps, a unit that, alone among Tank Corps Battalions then serving in France and Flanders, was equipped with heavy armored cars.

34. Edmunds, *Military Operations in France and Flanders, 1918*, Volume IV, pp. 59–60 and André Laffargue, *Foch et la Bataille de 1918* (Paris: Arthaud, 1967), pp. 279–82.

35. Wallace, *Dragons of Steel*, pp. 68–69

36. The name used by the Canadian Independent Force for the last three months of World War I was "Brutinel's Brigade." Attachments during this same period included heavy armored cars from the same Seventeenth Armored Car Battalion that had been employed in the sector of the Australian Corps at Amiens, a British bicycle battalion (the XVIII Corps Bicycle Battalion) and horse cavalrymen from British and Canadian regiments. Wallace, *Dragons of Steel*, pp. 69–75.

37. Ibid.

38. Delaying resistance became a core technique for the German army of the 1920s. For a detailed description, see Friedrich von Cochenhausen, *Die Truppenführung, Ein Handbuch für den Truppenführer und seine Gehilfen* (Berlin: E. S. Mittler und Sohn, 1928).

39. Wallace, *Dragons of Steel*, pp. 76–83.

40. Fuller, *Tanks in the Great War*, pp. 293–4.

CHAPTER 2: Open Flanks

1. Gougaud, *L'Aube de la Gloire*, p. 36 and Friedrich von Merkatz, *Geschichte der Maschinen-Gewehr Abteilung Nr. 1* (Zeulenroda, Thüringen: B. Sporn, 1936).

2. The most accessible account of this operation is the first chapter of Bryan Perrett, *Seize and Hold: Master Strokes on the Battlefield* (London: Arms and Armor, 1994). The definitive account is Bernhard Bellin, *Sturmgruppe Picht: Ein Erinnerungsblatt aus dem Kriege Gegen die Rumänen im Jahre 1916* (Berlin: Verlag Tradition Wilhelm Kolk, 1929).

3. Captain Picht's battalion was not the first German infantry unit to be transported in motor vehicles. Shortly before the outbreak of war, there were experiments in which the Jäger/elite light infantry battalions attached to cavalry divisions were mounted in trucks. In the course of the mobile campaign of 1914, these experiments bore fruit when trucks were used to move Jäger battalions from one point to another within the zone of operations of cavalry divisions.

4. The three cavalry squadrons that took part in the expedition had, exclusive of officers' servants and wagon drivers, about eighty troopers each. Given that a

standard cavalry division of the time had twenty-four squadrons, it is reasonable to assume that a complete cavalry division assembled for the Baltic Islands operation would have slightly fewer than 2,000 troopers. In a firefight, however, about a quarter of these would be occupied as horse-holders. Thus, the horse cavalry division would have had foxhole strength of 1,500 men. With a platoon of three machine guns for every four squadrons, the number of machine guns in a cavalry division would have been eighteen. Figures for these calculations are taken from the embarkation tables in XXIII R. K., Anlage zur Kriegstagbuch, Erfahrungen v. 17.10.16-1.7.18., translated as Germany. Reichsarchiv. Capture of Oesel, Moon, and Dago, XXIII. Reserve Corps, Annexes to War Diary, currently filed with German WWI Military Records in Record Group 165, U.S. National Archives.

5. The truck figures are from 42. I.D., Anlage zur Kriegstagbuch, v. 1.9.17-21.10.17, translated as Germany. Reichsarchiv. Capture of Oesel, Moon, and Dago, 42. I.D., Annexes to War Diary, currently filed with German WWI Military Records in Record Group 165, Records of the War Department General and Special Staffs, U.S. National Archives, Washington, D.C.

6. The description of the course of the capture of the Baltic Islands is taken from Erich von Tschischwitz, *Armee und Marine bei Eroberung der Baltischen Inseln im Oktober 1917* (Berlin: Eisenschmidt, 1931). At least two English language translations of this work have been made. One of these, by Major Samuel Cummings, USMC, is available as a manuscript at the Marine Corps Research Center in Quantico, Virginia.

7. George C. Mitchell, "The Rout of the Turks by Allenby's Cavalry, Palestine Campaign," *The Cavalry Journal*, Volume XXIX, Number 119 (April 1920), pp. 28–43 and Volume XXIX, Number 120 (May 1920), pp. 174–206. Colonel Mitchell was a regular officer of the U.S. Army.

8. One of the earliest and most eloquent spokesmen for this point of view was the Canadian engineer, Captain E. L. M. Burns. E. L. M. Burns, "The Mechanicalization of Cavalry," *Canadian Defense Quarterly*, Volume I, Number 3, April 1924, pp. 3–7.

9. Captain Burns calculated that each cavalry horse required eight gallons (sixteen pounds) of water and twenty pounds of forage each day. Ibid., p. 3. Given a "saber" strength of 18,000 mounted men, this meant that the daily tonnage of supplies needed to keep the cavalry horses of the Desert Mounted Corps in fighting trim would have amounted to 324 tons a day. This figure does not include the spare horses, pack animals, or the draft animals used to pull the wagons and guns of artillery, machine gun, supply, headquarters, and communications units.

10. Raymond Savage, *Allenby of Armageddon* (Indianapolis: Bobbs-Merrill, 1926), pp. 209–210.

11. Mitchell, op. cit., p. 35.

12. Savage, op. cit., p. 247.

13. A troop of British Empire cavalry might be able to field as many as sixty horsemen. When the troop dismounted, however, one man in four was left behind as a horse-holder. Mitchell, op. cit., p. 203.

14. Mitchell, op. cit., pp. 189 and 202–203.

15. For more on Stosstrupp tactics, see Bruce Gudmundsson, *Storm Troop Tactics: Innovation in the German Army, 1914–1918* (New York: Praeger, 1989) and John English and Bruce Gudmundsson, *On Infantry* (Westport, CT: Praeger, 1995).

16. Alfred Higgins Burne, "Notes on the Palestine Campaign, No. 5—The Land of Moab," *Fighting Forces*, Volume IX, No. 5, December 1932, pp. 540–41.

17. U.S. Army G-2 Report, "Army Maneuvers, September 21st to 25th, 1925," U.S. National Archives, Record Group 165, Box 641.

18. Erwin Hermann, "Die Friedensarmeen der Sieger und der Besiegten des Weltkrieges," *Wissen und Wehr*, 1922, pp 332–34.

19. Volker R. Berghahn, *Imperial Germany, 1871–1914* (Providence, RI: Berghahn Books, 1994), p. 43.

20. For purposes of comparison, independent squadrons and battalions have been grouped into standard regiments and divisions. (Prior to 1919, German cavalry divisions were not permanently organized, but assembled for maneuvers and at mobilization. The numbers are thus derived by giving one cavalry regiment to each infantry division and then dividing the number of remaining cavalry regiments by six, which was the usual allocation of cavalry regiments to cavalry divisions in this period.) Allowance has also been made for the presence, particularly in 1899, of nonstandard regiments. The numbers of "sabers" and "rifles" refer to the units of the active army at war strength. The mobilization of 1914, which created hundreds of new infantry regiments but only a few cavalry regiments, greatly increased the ratio of arms in favor of the infantry. The source for 1899 is Specht, "Supplement to the Organization, Composition, and Strength of the German Army," in Gustav Sigel, editor, *German Military Forces of the 19th Century* (Chicago: Werner, 1900), p. 97. For 1911, "Le Nouveau Quinquennat Militaire Allemand," *Revue Militaire des Armées Étrangéres*, April 1911, p. 257. For 1920–1933, von Cochenhausen, *Die Truppenführung*, p. 5.

21. Albert Benary, *Der Kavallerist* (Charlottenburg: Verlag Offene Worte, ca. 1923), p. 23.

22. Hasso von Manteuffel, *Reiter-ABC für Schützen- und Felddienst* (Berlin: E.S. Mittler, 1934), p. 155.

23. The German "infantry" and "cavalry" guns of the late 1920s, 1930s, and World War II were of two types, light and heavy. The light guns, which fired 75mm shells, were the direct descendents of the direct-fire version of the 76mm light trench mortar of World War I. Both the design of the weapon and its concept of employment were also influenced by the various cut-down field pieces and mountain howitzers used by German assault battalions in that war.

24. In manuals and war games, German soldiers often described the units whose structure conformed to the requirements of clandestine rearmament plans as "modern" or "of a modern army." In doing this, they made no secret of the fact that these were the type of units Germany would deploy in case of war. Descriptions of the structures of such "modern" cavalry divisions can be found in various sources. These include James Corum, *The Roots of Blitzkrieg: Hans von*

Seeckt and German Military Reform (Lawrence, KS: University Press of Kansas, 1992), p. 209 and von Cochenhausen, *Die Truppenführung: Ein Handbuch für den Truppenführer und Seine Gehilfen,* p. 7, as well as the records of German high-level maneuvers and staff rides held during the 1920s. (Some of the latter can be found in the microfilmed collection of captured German records of the U.S. National Archives, Microfilm Series T-78, "Records of Headquarters, Army High Command." Others are located in voluminous files of attaché and observer reports filed in Record Group 165.)

CHAPTER 3: Broken Ground

1. A handful of caterpillar tractors belonging to farmers in Tunisia were requisitioned by the French Army soon after the outbreak of war. These found their way to the Vosges Mountains, where they were used to haul heavy artillery pieces over difficult terrain. Pierre Estienne, *Vehicules à Chenille, Leur Rôle Sur le Champ de Bataille, Leur Utilisation dans les Travaux de Paix* (Coulommiers: Paul Brodard, 1920), p. 7.

2. Ernest D. Swinton, *Eyewitness* (New York: Arno, 1972), pp. 60 and 75–79.

3. Fuller, *Tanks in the Great War*, pp. 22–28 and minutes of meetings of the Landship Committee held on 24 March 1915, 11 June 1915, and 14 June 1915. These are pasted in a bound volume called *Confidential Memoranda*, Stern 1/1/1 1915 Feb–1915 Dec, Papers of Lieutenant Colonel Sir Albert Gerald Stern, KBE, CMG (1878–1966), Liddell-Hart Centre for Military Archives, King's College London. As some of the memoranda are undated and the pages of the bound volume are numbered, material from this collection is hereafter referred to as "Stern, *Confidential Memoranda*" and identified with a page number.

4. Stern, *Confidential Memoranda,* pp. 7 and 13–14.

5. "Low, flat, and wet as is the rest of Flanders, the maritime belt is lower, flatter, and wetter." Douglas W. Johnson, *Battlefields of the World War* (New York: Oxford University Press, 1921), pp. 42–44.

6. Marc Sorrentino, "Le siècle des chars: Petite Histoire d'une Machine qui Changea la Guerre," *X-Passion, La Revue des Élèves de l'École Polytechnique,* Volume 30 (3rd Trimester, 2001), pp. 54–55 and Michel Pesqueur, "L'evolution du Concept Français d'Emploi des Chars Entre 1917 et 1924," *Revue Internationale d'Histoire Militaire*, No. 81 (2001), (internet version at http://www.stratisc.org/partenaires/cfhm/rihm/81/RIHM_81_PESQUEUR.html).

7. Jean Baptiste Estienne graduated from the prestigious *École Polytechnique* (which might well be described as a combination of West Point and the Massachusetts Institute of Technology) in 1880. In the years between 1880 and 1914, he commanded a variety of field artillery units, invented surveying instruments for the use of field artillery officers, and formally organized French military aviation. Jules M. Challeat, *Histoire Technique de L'Artillerie de Terre en France Pendant un Siècle (1816–1910)* (Paris: Imprimerie Nationale, 1935), p. 429.

8. Ferdinand Joseph Deygas, *Les Chars d'assaut, leur passé, leur avenir* (Paris: Charles-Lavauzelle, 1937), p. 91.

9. Early production models of the Saint Chamond were armed with the Schneider 75mm field gun—a privately developed weapon that was marginally lighter than the standard M1897 75mm field gun. Later production models carried the somewhat heavier M1897. John Sayen, "French Tanks 1916–1918," *Tactical Notebook*, November 1992.

10. Percin's own ideas about artillery are explained in the many books that he wrote (or coauthored) during the decade before the outbreak of World War I. These include *La Manœuvre de Lorlanges Exécutée par le 13° Corps le 12 Septembre 1908* (Paris: Berger-Levrault, 1909); *La Liaison des Armes* (Paris: Chapelot, 1909); and *L'artillerie aux manoeuveres de Picardie en 1910* (Paris: Berger-Levrault, 1911). Arguments against Percin's ideas are very prominent in the issues of the *Revue d'Artillerie* appearing in the years between 1911 and 1914.

11. P. M. H. Lucas, *L'Evolution des Idées Tacticques en France et Allemagne Pendant la Guerre de 1914–1918* (Paris: Berger-Levrault, 1932), pp. 177–78.

12. *Journal des Marches et Operations de la Groupe AS 3, Journal des Marches et Operations de la 5éme Groupe AS,* and *Journal des Marches et Operations du Groupement II d'AS*, SHAT, Carton 26N1244, entries for 16 April 1917.

13. Bruno Destour, "Berry-au-Bac," (on the website "Histoire Dans Tous Ses Etats," http://www.chronicus.com/pgm/dossiers/bdberrybac.htm).

14. Lucas, *L'Evolution des Idées Tacticques en France et Allemagne*, pp. 175 and 191–93.

15. 10eme Corps d'Armée, 3ème Bureau, No. U/280 dated 13 August 1918, "Extrait de l'Ordre Général d'Operation Pour l'Attaque de 15 Août," SHAT, 24N3150.

16. U.S. Army, Historical Branch, War Plans Division, General Staff, *A Study in Battle Formation* (Washington, DC: Government Printing Office, 1920), pp. 10–17 and Mark E. Grotelueschen, *Doctrine Under Trial: American Artillery Employment in World War I* (Westport, CT: Greenwood Press, 2001), pp. 78–79.

17. C. E. Hudson, "Flanking Machine-Gun Fire," *Infantry Journal*, February 1925, pp. 17–21.

18. The decline in the number of tanks available to British forces on the Western Front in the last months of 1918 is well documented in David Childs, *A Peripheral Weapon? The Production and Employment of British Tanks in the First World War* (Westport, CT: Greenwood Press, 1999), pp. 171–195 and Paddy Griffith, *Battle Tactics of the Western Front: The British Army's Art of the Attack 1916–1918* (New Haven, CT: Yale University Press, 1994), pp. 166–69.

19. The history of the conception and production of French light tanks is given in Dutil, *Les Chars d'Assaut, Leur Création et Leur Rôle Pendant la Guerre 1915–1918* (Paris: Berger-Levrault, 1919), Chapter V.

20. France, Armée, Ière Armée, État-Major, 3ème Bureau, N° 3-159/3, "Ordre Général d'Operations N° 617," 12 Août 1918, SHAT, carton 24N3150 and France, Armée, 10éme Corps d'Armée, État-Major, 3ème Bureau, N° U/280, "Etrait de lOr-

dre Général d'Operations pour l'attaque de 15 Août," 13 Août, 1918, SHAT, carton 24N3150.

21. For a description of the role played by the automatic rifle in the French tactics of 1916–1918, see Gerard Demaison and Yves Buffetaut, *Honour Bound: The Chauchat Machine Rifle* (Cobourg, Ontario: Collector Grade Publications, 1995), pp. 58–65.

22. By the end of World War I, as well as throughout 1920s, French light tanks were organized in a way that paralleled the triangular organization of the infantry. A tank regiment of three tank battalions would thus be attached to an infantry division of three infantry regiments. Each tank battalion would, in turn, attach one of its three tank companies to an infantry battalion. This left a platoon of five tanks (three armed with 37mm guns and two with machine guns) for each infantry company. Wilhelm Balck, *Entwickelung der Taktik im Weltkriege* (Berlin: R. Eisenschmidt, 1922), pp. 398–99 and Ramspacher, *Le Général Estienne*, p. 70.

23. In the attack on Montdidier, for example, each infantry division of the X Army Corps set aside a battalion of twelve 75mm guns exclusively for the job of combating enemy antitank guns. Directed by an observer flying in a specially designated airplane, this battalion was to fire smoke shells on the edges of woods, villages, and other places where antitank guns or the observation posts of antitank gun units might be located. France, Armée, 10éme Corps d'Armée, État-Major, 3ème Bureau, N° U/280, "Etrait de l'Ordre Général d'Operations pour l'attaque de 15 Août," 13 Août, 1918, SHAT, carton 24N3150.

24. From about 1901 through 1943, the standard French field piece was the M1897 75mm field gun. Most shells (except those with older models of timed fuse) fired by this piece had a range of about 8,000 meters. This, combined with the need to find suitable firing positions, resulted in placement of artillery batteries well behind the front lines. Because of this, the requirement that attacking forces stay within the range of the supporting artillery translated into an effective limit of five kilometers or less for an attacking force.

25. Robert Doughty, *The Seeds of Disaster: The Development of French Army Doctrine, 1919–1939* (Hamden, CT: Archon, 1985), pp. 82–87. It is interesting to note that the interwar French Army paid relatively sparse attention to the tank attack at Soissons (Villers-Cotterêts) in July of 1918. This attack, which was one of the larger French tank attacks of the entire war, made a much larger impression on the interwar German theorists such as Ludwig Ritter von Eimansberger and the often-anonymous writers of articles in the *Militärwochenblatt*.

26. For a description of the battle of Reims in 1918, see Bruce Gudmundsson, *On Artillery* (Westport, CT: Praeger, 1993).

27. Ramspacher, *Le Général Estienne*, pp. 93 and 96.

28. Doughty, *Seeds of Disaster*, pp. 87–88; C.A. Willoughby, "The French in Morocco," *Infantry Journal*, January, 1926, pp. 7–19 and C. B. Stone, Jr., "The Moroccan Campaign of 1925," *Infantry Journal*, January, 1926, pp. 20–23.

29. Jean Estienne, *Conférence faite le 15 février 1920 sur les chars d'assaut* (Paris: Librarie de l'enseignement technique, 1920), pp. 42–43.

30. Ramspacher, *Le Général Estienne*, pp. 96–97.

31. For a description of the effect the lack of operational mobility of the Char B had on French units in 1940, see Robert Doughty, *The Breaking Point: Sedan and the Fall of France, 1940* (Hamden, CT: Archon, 1990), pp. 285–87.

32. Doughty, *The Seeds of Disaster*, p. 152.

33. France. Ministére de la Guerre, *Instruction sur L'Emploi Tactique des Grandes Unités* (Paris: Charles Lavauzelle & Cie., 1940), p. 166.

34. Hoffmann, "Doctrine, Tank Technology, and Execution," pp. 304–5 and R. F. K. B., "Tank Tactics in the Russian Army," pp. 37–41.

35. Hoffmann, "Doctrine, Tank Technology, and Execution," pp. 304–5 and R. F. K. B., "Tank Tactics in the Russian Army," pp. 37–41.

36. Giffard Martel, *An Outspoken Soldier* (London: Sifton Praed, 1949), pp. 136–37. An almost identical account of the Soviet Maneuvers of 1936 is given in Giffard Martel, *The Russian Outlook* (London: Michael Joseph, 1947), pp. 13–20.

37. Martel, *An Outspoken Soldier*, p. 136.

38. The roles played by the members of this troika are the subject of considerable debate. Richard Simpkin saw Tukhachevsky as the prophet, with Triandafillov and Isserson as his disciples. The Russian author (a former Soviet officer) who writes under the pen name of "Viktor Suvorov" views Triandafillov as the visionary and Tukhachevsky as a heartless butcher who favored "battering ram" tactics. Simpkin, *Deep Battle*, pp. 3–13 and Viktor Suvorov, *Icebreaker: Who Started the Second World War?* (London: Hamish Hamilton, 1990), pp. 47–50.

39. *PU-36*, translated and quoted in Simpkin, *Deep Battle*, p. 182.

40. Ibid., pp. 179–80 and 221.

41. Estimates of just how large the Soviet tank fleet of 1940 might have been vary considerably, but tend to fall in the range between 20,000 and 30,000. Edwin Bacon, "Soviet Military Losses in World War II," *The Journal of Slavic Military Studies*, Vol. 6, No. 4 (December 1993), pp. 619–20. The Soviet tank fleet at the beginning of World War II was thus at least six times the size of the second and third largest tank fleets of the day—those of France and Germany.

CHAPTER 4: Iron Steed

1. In 1929, the number of armored car squadrons was reduced from twenty to nineteen. Report of the U.S. Military Attaché in Paris, dated 15 November 1929, US National Archives, Record Group 165. In 1932, an organizational snapshot provided by the *Bulletin Officiel des Ministéres de la Guerre, des Pension, et de l'Air* (1932, Numero 30, p. 2209) showed that there were but eighteen armored car squadrons authorized that year. After 1932, however, the formation of new armored car regiments for cavalry formations greatly increased the number of armored cars in French service.

2. In 1923, provision was made to assemble the armored car squadrons of each division's three horse cavalry brigades into a battalion—a *groupe d'autos-mitrailleuses* of three squadrons of twelve combat vehicles each. M. Richard Morati, *France : Composition des Divisions de Cavalerie 1918–1940,* http://orbat.com/site/data/historical/france/cavalry1918-1940.html.

3. "France, Cavalry Organization and Armament," unsigned report in the files of the U.S. Army War College, US National Archives, Record Group 165, Entry 77, Box 868. The document is undated, but is clearly from the period between the end of World War I and the French evacuation of the Rhineland in June of 1930.

4. The company-size *groupe mixte d'autos-canons et autos-mitrailleuses* became the *escadron d'autos-mitrailleuses,* thereby allowing the creation of battalion-sized *groupes d'escadrons d'autos-mitrailleuses.* At the same time, the fact that the White armored cars (with which the French armored car units were exclusively equipped) were provided with both machine guns and 37mm guns made it possible to convert the three *groupes d'autos-canons* (equipped with 47mm guns mounted in armored trucks) into regular armored car units.

5. Because they were based on the chassis of trucks made by the White Motor Company of Cleveland, Ohio, these vehicles were generally referred to as the "White armored cars." Production of this new model started during the latter months of World War I, just in time to re-equip one squadron six weeks before the armistice of 11 November 1918. Gougaud, *L'Aube de Gloire,* p. 78.

6. The decline in the number of French European horse cavalry units, as well as the staying power of those horsed regiments serving in North Africa and the Levant, can be seen in the many reports on the subject made by the U.S. military attachés in Paris. These can be found in the U.S. National Archives, Record Group 165, Entry 77, Box 864.

7. Maurice Wiktorin, "Cavalry in European Armies," *The Cavalry Journal,* May-June 1931, p. 35.

8. In the case of both Great Britain and France, the loss of horse cavalry recruited from the native populations of overseas possessions, particularly those of India and North Africa, was much less than that of horse cavalry recruited in the home country.

9. Harold R. Winton, *To Change an Army: General Sir John Burnett-Stuart and British Armored Doctrine, 1927–1938* (Lawrence, KS: University Press of Kansas, 1988), p. 26 and Shelford Bidwell and Dominick Graham, *Fire-power: British Army Weapons and Theories of War, 1904–1945* (London: Allen and Unwin, 1982), p. 173.

10. G. N. Macready, "The Trend of Organization in the Army," *Journal of the Royal United Services Institution,* February 1935.

11. W. K.," "Die Pferdebestand Deutschlands am 1. Dezember 1928," *Artilleristische Rundschau,* Heft. 2, January 1929, pp. 104–6.

12. Nancy R. Deuel, *A Historical Time Line of North American Horses,* http://www.cavalry.org/Horse_History.htm

13. Roger R. Reese, *Stalin's Reluctant Soldiers: A Social History of the Red Army, 1925–1941* (Lawrence, KS: University Press of Kansas, 1996), p. 35.

14. Cochenhausen, *Die Truppenführung, Ein Handbuch für den Truppenführer und seine Gehilfen*, pp. 1–7. The two types of infantry divisions presented by Cochenhausen are analyzed in Bruce Gudmundsson, "Two German Infantry Divisions of 1928," *Tactical Notebook*, February 1994.

15. The "silent motorization" of the support elements of horse cavalry units, like many things that pertain to the less glamorous aspects of military life, is rather poorly documented. Indeed, one can usually only see that it took place by comparing the table of organization or equipment list for a given unit from a particular time with similar documents from a few years earlier or later. One of the few explicit descriptions of this problem can be found in the statement made by the British secretary of state for war to Parliament in the late winter of 1927. U.S. Army G-2 Report, "England (Military): Changes in Organization and Equipment," dated 9 March 1927, U.S. National Archives, RG165, Entry 77, Box 641.

16. At the end of World War I, eight cavalry regiments ("Yeomanry Regiments") of the part-time Territorial Army were converted into armored car companies of the Royal Tank Corps. Expanded to battalion size in 1937, these units were activated in World War II as complete regiments. David Hughes, James Broshot, and Alan Philson, *The British Armies in World War Two: An Organizational History, Volume I, British Armoured and Cavalry Divisions* (West Chester, OH: George Nafziger, 1999), pp. 14–15, hereafter referred to as Hughes, et al., *British Armoured and Cavalry Divisions*.

17. H. V. S. Charrington, "Experiences of a Mechanized Cavalryman," *Canadian Defence Quarterly*, July 1931, pp. 498–503.

18. Morati, *France : Composition des Divisions de Cavalerie 1918–1940*. Each of the five battalions of *dragons portés* inherited the battle honors of both the converted dragoon regiment and the bicycle battalion of the division to which it was assigned. This suggests that at least some of the personnel of the *dragons portés* were former bicycle troopers. Serge Andolenko, *Receueil Historique de l'Arme Blindé et de la Cavalerie* (Paris, Eurimprim, 1968), pp. 44–48.

19. Report of the U.S. Military Attaché, Paris, dated 15 November 1929, U.S. National Archives, Record Group 165, Entry 77, Box 864.

20. A French horse cavalry brigade of the 1920s and early 1930s had sixteen heavy machine guns and sixty-four automatic rifles. Wiktorin, "Cavalry in European Armies," p. 35. The precise organization of a *bataillon de dragons portés* varied greatly in the 1930s, with the small three-squadron battalions of 1929 and 1930 growing into the five-squadron battalions of the late 1930s. Most varieties of this type of unit, however, had sixteen to twenty heavy machine guns, fifty-four automatic rifles, and a small number of infantry heavy weapons (some combination of 60mm mortars, 81mm mortars, 37mm guns and 25mm antitank guns). Germany, Generalstab des Heeres, *Merkblatt über französische Truppenführung und Taktik* (Berlin: Reichsdruckerei, 1936), organizational diagrams, and France, Ministère de la Guerre, *Instruction Provisoire Pour les Unités de Dragons Portés* (Paris: Imprimerie Nationale, 1938).

21. *Instruction Provisoire Pour les Unités de Dragons Portés*, p. 9.

22. "Aufklärung in die Ferne, Aufklärung einer französischen Kavalleriedivision, Type Armée Moderne 1932," *Militärwochenblatt*, 1935, Nr. 47, p. 1622. The "Type Armée Moderne 1932" cavalry division never went beyond the stage of experimental unit. It did, however, mark the beginning of an era in which the motor-powered elements (including artillery, engineers, services, and an increasingly larger complement of armored cars) of the horse cavalry division were larger than the animal-powered ones.

23. Arguments for and against complete motorization of infantry and cavalry divisions filled the French military press of the early and middle 1930s. Many of the articles (and even one of the books) on this subject were translated by U.S. Army officers serving in France and are on file at the U.S. National Archives, Record Group 165, Entry 77, Boxes 868–873.

24. In contrast to other "fast" divisions, which were built upon the framework of existing horse cavalry divisions, the Austrian *Schnelle Division* and its Czechoslovak counterpart were built from the ground up. (Prior to forming their fast divisions, neither country had maintained a cavalry division of any sort.) Bundesministerium für Landesverteidigung, *Österreichs Wehrmacht, 1937 (*Vienna: Wiener Stadt-Stimmen, 1937), pp. 17–20; Austria, Heeresgeschichtliches Museum, 1918–1968, *Die Streitkräfte der Republik Österreich, Katalog zur Sonderaufstellung im Heeresgeschichtlichen Museum Wien*, 1968 (Vienna, 1968); Henrik Krog, *European armed forces from 1920 to 1950*, http://www.geocities.com/kumbayaaa; and the rather extensive collection of translations and reports prepared by U.S. military attachés in the interwar period, U.S. National Archives, Record Group 165, Entry 77.

25. For the "mixed" divisions called for in the Polish mobilization plans of 1930 to 1934, see Krog, *European armed forces from 1920 to 1950*. For discussions of possible hybrid cavalry formations of the U.S. Army, see the many articles on the subject in the *U.S. Cavalry Journal* for the years 1931 to 1935. For German discussions, see the many articles in the *Militärwochenblatt* for the same period.

26. Brigadier General W. H. Harts, "The Reorganization of the French Army," dated 17 June 1927, U.S. National Archives, Record Group 165, Entry 77, Box 864.

27. Official French concern about the strength and composition of the covering force begins almost immediately after the end of World War I. See, *inter alia*, M. Jean Fabry, *Rapport Fait au nom de la Commission de l'Armée Chargée d'Examiner le Projet de Loi sur L'Organisation Générale de l'Armée* (Paris: Martinet, 1922), pp. 54–56.

28. For examples of the many proposals centered on the use of professional soldiers to protect the mobilization of a mass army, see, *inter alia*, General Antoine Targe, *La Garde de nos Frontières; Constitution et Organisation des Forces de Couverture* (Paris: Charles-Lavauzelle, 1930) and the many articles published on the subject in *La France Militaire* during the late 1920s and early 1930s.

29. Advocates for the use of conscripts and selected reservists to man the "covering force" included General Marie Eugene Debeney, who devoted a whole chapter of his *La Guerre et les Hommes: Reflexions d'Aprés Guerre* (Paris: Librarie Plon, 1937) to the subject.

30. In many of the discussions of the covering force, French commentators were quite open about the possible need to occupy forward positions in a "neutral country that had asked for assistance." See, among many others, the article by General M. E. Debeney in the *Revue des Deux Mondes*, March 1936. (This article was translated by the assistant military attaché in Paris, Report #22, 624W, 11 July 1936, U.S. National Archives, Record Group 77, Box 868.) While it is possible that this may have been Switzerland or even Spain, the most likely candidates for occupation by the covering force would be Belgium, the Netherlands, and Luxembourg. Because of this, it is fair to say that the covering force plan prefigures the disastrous Dyle Maneuver of May 1940 (an attempt to take up positions in Belgium and the Netherlands that accomplished little more than the delivery of some of France's best divisions into a position where they were swept up by the German "cut of the scythe").

31. The key figure in the rise in official French interest in motorization may well have been General Louis Maurin, an artilleryman who had been closely associated with motorization for nearly two decades (to the point where one retired French general described him as "an apostle of motorization"). In 1918, Maurin commanded the General Reserve of Artillery, which made extensive use of motor transport to move artillery units, particularly those armed with heavy guns and howitzers, from one part of the western front to another. From 1922 to 1934, he was Inspector General of Artillery, holding, from 1927 onwards, the additional office of Inspector General for Motorization of the Army. In 1934, he became minister of war. U.S. Military Attaché Paris, Report #20,950, 12 November 1934, U.S. National Archives, Record Group 165, Entry 77, Box 868. General Maurin's views on motorization are laid out in detail in *L'armée Moderne*, (Paris, E. Flammarion,1938).

32. P. Chapelle, "Les Routes," *Revue de Cavalerie*, Volume 47, May-June 1937, pp. 272–4.

33. One of the three infantry regiments of the infantry division at the Mailly maneuvers of 1932 was only partially motorized. The heavy weapons and unit trains had trucks assigned, but the infantrymen were moved in trucks or busses kept in a general pool. In keeping with French doctrine of the time, the infantry division was reinforced with a battalion of light infantry tanks. Braun, "Heeresmotorisierung und Erfahrungen mit Kampfwagen in Frankreich," *Militärwochenblatt*, 1933, Nr. 45, pp. 1540–41.

34. The organization of the battalions of *dragons portés* varied greatly during the 1930s, with the chief difference between different types of battalions being the presence or absence of an armored car squadron, the number and types of heavy weapons, and whether the two non-motorcycle rifle squadrons were equipped with cross-country vehicles or road-bound trucks.

35. John Sayen, "The Organization of French Armor (Part II)," *Tactical Notebook*, August 1993.

36. In 1933, students conducting map studies at the *Ecole de Guerre* employed a cavalry division with, among other units, two squadrons of *autos-mitrailleuses de combat* and three battalions of *dragons-portés*. U.S. Military Attaché Paris, Report

#19,901, 17 November, 1933, U.S. National Archives, Record Group 165, Entry 77, Box 868.

37. Descriptions of the various types of French light mechanized division can be found in the contemporary reports of U.S. military attachés as well as Morati, *France: Composition des Divisions de Cavalerie 1918–1940*; John Sayen, "The Organization of French Armor (Part IV)," *Tactical Notebook*, April 1994; both the 1936 and 1939 editions of Germany, Generalstab des Heeres, *Merkblatt über französische Truppenführung und Taktik;* and Stephane Commans, *Order of Battle, Division Légère Mécanique (1940)*, http://enpointe.chez.tiscali.fr/dlm.html.

38. The possibility of attaching independent battalions from a general reserve of spare units, including tanks and additional units of *dragons portés*, explains a curious feature of most versions of the light mechanized division—the fact that three battalions of *dragons portés* were assembled into a regiment that, in turn, was the only combat unit subordinate to a brigade headquarters.

39. The average tank strength of the German tank battalion of May 1940 was derived by taking the average tank strength of the German tank brigade of that time and dividing it by four. Figures for each tank brigade come from Leo W. G. Niehorster, *German World War II Organizational Series, Volume 2/I, Mechanized Army and Divisions, (10th May, 1940)* (Hanover: Niehorster, 1990.)

40. Information on the inability of the guns of all German tanks but the 75mm gun on the Panzer IV to penetrate the armor of the SOMUA can be found in many places. A very powerful confirmation of this fact, however, comes from the lessons-learned report of the Third Panzer Brigade of the Third Panzer Division: *Bericht über Kampferfahrungen bei den bisherigen Kämpfen im Westen*, 4 June 1940, U.S. National Archives, Microfilm Series T-314, Roll 569.

41. Third Panzer Brigade, *Bericht über Kampferfahrungen bei den bisherigen Kämpfen im Westen*.

42. The phenomenon of French tanks failing to take advantage of German soldiers who were both nearby and vulnerable is well documented in the popular literature of the battle for France that emerged in Germany soon after the end of the campaign. See, for examples, the two articles published in the U.S. *Field Artillery Journal* in October of 1941: Ferdinand Schneider-Kostalski, "Tank Battle" (from *Die Panzertruppe* of December 1940) and Ernst von Jungenfeld, "German Panzers vs. French Light Mechanized Divisions" (from the *Berliner Illustrierte Zeitung*).

CHAPTER 5: The Third Way

1. For an argument that the German Army of the 1920s was as well prepared for war against the French as it was for a conflict with the Poles, see Corum, *The Roots of Blitzkrieg*, p.197.

2. Germany. Reichswehrministerium. *Richtlinien für die Führung des hinhaltenden Kampfes* (Berlin: Reichswehrministerium, 1931), pp. 2–16.

3. This outside force could be diplomatic pressure from powers such as Great Britain, the Soviet Union, or the United States; the raising of new German forces from veterans, paramilitary organizations, and the police; or even large-scale military intervention by a friendly power such as Italy.

4. This proportion is arrived at by comparing the number of infantry battalions (sixty-three) and cavalry regiments (eighteen battalion equivalents) in the German Army of the 1920s with the carrying ability of the motor transport detachments (*Kraftfahrabteilungen*) of all seven infantry divisions (fourteen battalions.)

5. Friedrich von Cochenhausen, *Die Truppenführung: Ein Handbuch für den Truppenführer und seine Gehilfen* (Berlin: E. S. Mittler und Sohn, 1928), pp. 2–7, 82–84, 91, and 199–207. This book, a commercially published handbook for officers, should not be confused with the famous German field service regulations of 1933, which were also called *Truppenführung*.

6. The belief that tanks would become operationally significant when their rate of movement and reliability approached that of armored cars was expressed as early as 1925 by the author of an encyclopedic treatise on position warfare. Friedrich Seeßelberg, *Der Stellungskrieg* (Berlin: E. S. Mittler, 1926), p. 371.

7. Ernst Volckheim, *Der Kampfwagen in der Heutigen Kriegführung* (Berlin, E. S. Mittler, 1924).

8. Though the *Kraftfahrabteilungen* were not divided into companies until after their conversion into combat units, the German army of the interwar period did possess three *Kraftfahr* companies. These were the independent motorized companies that were assigned, at the rate of one per division, to the three cavalry divisions of the *Reichswehr*. Bruce Gudmundsson, "Two German Infantry Divisions of 1928," *Tactical Notebook*, February 1924. This article relies heavily upon Cochenhausen, *Die Truppenführung*.

9. Carl Dirks and Karl-Heinz Jansen, *Der Krieg der Generäle: Hitler als Werkzeug der Wehrmacht*, (Berlin: Propyläen Verlag, 1999), p. 75 and Georg Tessin, *Deutsche Verbände und Truppen, 1918–1939*, (Osnabrück: Biblio Verlag, 1974), pp. 262–3.

10. Balsi (pseudonym), *3,7 cm PAK*, http://balsi.de/37pak.htm.

11. Robert Citino, *The Evolution of Blitzkrieg Tactics: Germany Defends Itself Against Poland* (Westport, CT: Greenwood Press, 1987), pp. 184–7.

12. Each of the motorized combat brigades consisted of six antitank battalions and three motorized reconnaissance battalions. The two antitank battalions and one motorized reconnaissance battalion not assigned to brigades were formed into the independent First Motorized Combat Regiment (*1. Kraftfahrkampfregiment*) for service in the detached province of East Prussia. Tessin, *Deutsche Verbände und Truppen, 1918–1939*, pp. 262–4.

13. Sometime after its complete motorization, the Third Cavalry Division was renamed the "Light Division" (*leichte Division*). It should not be confused with the entirely separate First Light Brigade formed in 1935 or the First, Second, and Third Light Divisions formed in 1938. Tessin, *Deutsche Verbände und Truppen, 1918–1939*, pp. 262–4 and 398–400.

14. Nicholas Reynolds, *Treason Was No Crime: Ludwig Beck, Chief of the German General Staff* (London: William Kimber, 1976), pp. 104–105. Until the spring of 1935, the German General Staff was still thinly disguised as the *Truppenamt* (the 'Formation Office'). Beck was thus officially designated as "Chief of the Truppenamt" rather than "Chief of the General Staff." After the accession of Hitler in January of 1933, however, very few Germans bothered to keep up the charade with anyone but the most naïve of foreign visitors.

15. For examples of these brigades and battle-groups in action, see Ludwig Maercker, *Vom Kaiserheer zur Reichswehr* (Leipzig: R. F. Koehler, 1921).

16. Often mistranslated as "troop leadership," *Truppenführung* refers to the leading of *Truppenverbände* (combined-arms formations such as mixed brigades, large battle groups, divisions, and corps) by a *Truppenführer* (an officer, usually of the rank of colonel or higher) commanding a force of more than one arm.

17. Ludwig Ritter von Eimannsberger, *Der Kampfwagenkrieg* (München: J. F. Lehmanns Verlag, 1934).

18. The term *Jäger* seems to have had a double meaning for Eimannsberger. On the one hand, it linked the infantry battalions of his Jäger brigades to the traditions of many German and Austrian elite, light infantry units. On the other, it evoked an image of the "hunting" of hostile tanks—particularly tanks that had been driven into a killing zone (*Jagdkessel*) where large numbers of antitank guns were lying in ambush.

19. Eimannsberger's Kampfwagen division consisted of two tank brigades, one Jäger brigade, two engineer battalions (one of which was dedicated to the employment and clearing of land mines), one armored car battalion, and three artillery battalions. The artillery battalions were to be equipped with "triple-purpose" guns—weapons that could serve as traditional field guns, antitank guns, or antiaircraft guns. One of the three artillery battalions was to have self-propelled carriages for its guns. For a diagram of this division and Eimannsberger's plan for a motorized infantry division, see Bruce Gudmundsson, "The Unknown Prophet: General von Eimannsberger and the Panzer Division," *Tactical Notebook*, July 1992.

20. Not to be confused with the on-site history lessons called staff rides in the U.S. Army of the late twentieth century, a staff ride in the German army of the period 1859 through 1939 was a "tactical exercise without troops" in which likely scenarios were examined out on the actual terrain. For examples of the classic German staff rides of the elder Helmuth von Moltke, see "Moltke's Staff Rides," *Tactical Notebook*, April 1993 and September 1993. For those of Alfred Count Schlieffen, see Robert Foley, *Alfred von Schlieffen's Military Writings* (London: Frank Cass, 2002).

21. The Germans of the time distinguished between the "subordination" (*unterstellung*) of one unit or formation to another and the relationship that directed two units or formations to cooperate (*Anweisung auf Zusammenarbeit*). In the former case, the commander of the subordinated (*unterstellt*) unit obeyed the orders of the commander of the unit designated as superior. In the latter case, the two units were directed to cooperate with each other as peers. It is

worth noting that a unit or formation could be subordinated to a unit of the same echelon, a unit commanded by an officer with the same rank, or, in exceptional cases, even a unit of a lower echelon or an officer with a lower rank. Thus, in this case, the armored corps could be subordinated to the infantry corps or even one of the infantry divisions. For an analogy in the German elastic defense doctrine of the latter two years of World War I, see G. C. Wynne, *If Germany Attacks* (Westport, CT: Greenwood Press, 1976).

22. Generalstab des Heeres, Nr. 1695/35 geh, dated 25.7.1935, "Nachträgliche Betrachtungen zu dem Einsatz des Panzerkorps in der Lage der Truppenamtsreise vom 13.6.1935," reprinted as Appendix 35 to Müller, *General Ludwig Beck,* pp. 460–65.

23. For a balanced overview of Moltke's operational plans during the period from 1857 to 1869, see Captain Schäfer, "Moltke's Staff Rides", *Journal of the Royal United Service Institution,* August 1913, pp. 1089–1100. For the Austrian (German-language) original see Schäfer, "Moltkes Generalstabsreisen," *Streffleurs,* June 1912, pp. 933–58.) For a revision of the British translation, with maps and explanatory notes, see the series "Moltke's Staff Rides" in Volume III of *Tactical Notebook.*

24. Tessin, *Deutsche Verbände und Truppen, 1918–1939,* pp. 262–64 and 398–400.

25. Generalstab des Heeres, O. Qu. I/2. Abt. Nr. 2655/35 g. Kdos. IIa, dated 30.12.1935, "Erwägungen über die Erhöhung der Angriffskraft des Heeres," reprinted as Appendix 37 to Klaus-Jürgen Müller, *General Ludwig Beck: Studien und Dokument zur poltitisch-militarischen Vorstellungswelt und Tätigkeit des Generalstablschefs des deutschen Heeres 1933–1938* (Boppard am Rhein: H. Boldt, 1980), pp. 470–72, hereafter referred to Beck "Erwägungen."

26. The antitank capabilities of these antitank tanks led Beck to consider the eventual replacement of the towed antitank guns of corps level antitank battalions with standard-type tank battalions. Generalstab des Heeres, O. Qu. I/2. Abt. Nr. 162/36 g. Kdos. IIa, dated 30.1.1936, "Erhöhung der Angriffskraft des Heeres," reprinted as Appendix 39 to Müller, *General Ludwig Beck,* pp. 486–88, hereafter referred to as Beck, "Erhöhung." Beck uses the term "*Tak*" (*Tankabwehrkannone,* antitank gun) to describe the 37mm gun. This implies a weapon far more powerful than the low-velocity 37mm infantry guns mounted on many then-contemporary French and American tanks.

27. These three armored divisions were officially established on 15 October 1935, three months after the field tests of the 1st Panzer Division on the Munster training grounds and four months after his staff ride. Guderian, *Erinnerungen,* p. 29 and Tessin, *Deutsche Verband und Truppen, 1918–1939,* p. 230.

28. In his memoirs, Guderian wrote that these tank brigades were to be used *only* for cooperation with infantry formations. Guderian, *Erinnerungen,* p. 30. That statement fits better with Guderian's postwar attempt to portray himself as a progressive beset by reactionary forces than it does with the memoranda Beck wrote at this time.

29. Beck, *Erwägungen*, pp. 472 and 474.

30. The term *direct cooperation* is a tricky one. If the method of employment contemplated in Beck's staff ride of 1935 is any indication, it did not involve any mixing below the level of the regiment or brigade. That is to say, there was no provision for motorized rifle battalions or companies to work with tank battalions or companies.

31. Beck uses the term *reinforced regiment* to describe these units, which he assumes will consist of three battalions. Beck, *Erwägerung*, pp. 475–76. In the period from 1935 to 1939, most German *Schützen* regiments consisted of two battalions. In the light divisions, two of these regiments were joined to form a *Kavallerie Schützen* brigade. In the armored divisions, one of these regiments and an independent motorcycle battalion formed the Schützen brigade.

32. Beck "Erwägungen," p. 474.

33. This reconnaissance brigade (*Aufklärungsregiment*) was made up of three of the nine motorized reconnaissance battalions existing in the German army of 1936. The commander of this brigade was simultaneously the Higher Cavalry Commander for Motorized Reconnaissance and reported directly to the commanding general for Armored Troops. Tessin, *Deutsche Verband und Truppen, 1918–1939*, p. 233.

34. The Germans may have borrowed the idea of calling their armored cooperation infantry *Schützen* from von Eimannsberger. The terms *Jäger* and *Schützen* were, in nineteenth century German armies, nearly synonymous. In 1845, for example, all but one of the Schützen battalions of the Prussian army were redesignated as *Jäger*. The remaining Schützen battalion, which belonged to the Guard Corps, used the weapons, uniforms, rank structure, terminology, and traditions of a Jäger battalion, and, with the Jäger battalions, was supervised by the Inspector of Jäger and Schützen. Curt Jany, *Geschichte der Preußischen Armee vom 15. Jahrhundert bis 1914* (Osnabruck: Biblio Verlag, 1967), p. 197.

35. Kommando der Panzertruppen, Ia Üb Nr. 3670/35 geh., 24. Dezember 1935, "Erfahrungsbericht über die Versuchsübungen einer Panzerdivision auf dem Truppenübungsplatz Munster im August 1935," p. 22 and Anlage 1., U.S. National Archives, Captured German Records, Series T-79, Roll 52.

36. In 1935, Lutz was simultaneously the corps-level Commander of Armored Troops (*Kommandierende General der Panzertruppen*) and the Inspector of Motorized Combat Troops (*Inspektor der Kraftfahrkampftruppen.*) The former position gave Lutz direct command over the existing armored divisions and any more that might be raised. The latter position gave Lutz supervisory authority (to include design of tables of organization and equipment, the writing of manuals, and the running of training schools) over all tank, Schützen, antitank, and motorized reconnaissance units. Guderian, *Erinnerungen*, p. 24. These were the exact counterpart of the status and powers enjoyed by Lutz's contemporary, the Inspector of Cavalry and Commanding General of the Cavalry Corps. Tessin, *Deutsche Verband und Truppen, 1918–1939*, p. 227–28.

37. Beck "Erwägungen." p. 473 and "Erhöhung," pp. 488–90.

Chapter 6: Beyond Theory

1. All information on the German order of battle in the Polish campaign that is used in this chapter is drawn from a reconciliation of information drawn from Leo W. G. Niehorster, *German World War II Organizational Series, Volume 1/I, Mechanized Army and Waffen-SS Units, (1 September 1939)* (Hanover: Niehorster, 1990) and Georg Tessin, *Formationsgeschichte der Wehrmacht, 1933–1939* (Boppard am Rhein: Harald Boldt Verlag, 1959), pp. 11–15, 20–26, and 54–62.

2. Commanded by Ewald von Kleist, the XXIICorps was formed upon mobilization. Apart from the Third Mountain Division, which was part of the corps for the first week of the campaign, all of its elements were fully motorized. XXII. Armee Korps, *Kriegtagbuch Nr. 1*, U.S. National Archives, Captured German Records, Microfilm Series T-314, Roll 665.

3. Robert M. Kennedy, *The German Campaign in Poland (1939)* (Washington, D.C.: U.S. Government Printing Office, 1956), Map opposite p. 71.

4. The vulnerability of tanks in the Polish woods is underscored by the ambush of tanks of the Fourth Panzer Division by a brigade of Polish horse cavalry. Armed with some of the best light antitank weapons of the period– (37mm guns of Swedish design and the indigenous "Ur" antitank rifles), the Polish troopers knocked out over fifty German tanks. This same Polish cavalry brigade, with less than one-third of the riflemen and one-fifteenth of the artillery, would have been no match for the German infantry division that had spent the day of that battle inching its way forward on secondary routes. Steven Zaloga and Victor Madej, *The Polish Campaign, 1939* (New York: Hippocrene Books, 1985), p. 114.

5. The Second Panzer and Fourth Light were also Austrian divisions. This greatly facilitated their mobilization, as well as transport to their jumping-off positions in Slovakia. The XVIII Army Corps, one of the "territorial" corps formed when the Austrian and German Armies were merged in 1938, would later become famous as the XVIII Mountain Corps.

6. Purists will note that the Second Panzer Division and Fourth Light Division joined the XXII Corps on the 2 September, while both divisions were still in the Carpathians. For the next week, however, the Third Mountain Division was attached to the XXII Corps for the purpose of facilitating the move over the mountains. This muscle-powered division was returned to its parent XVIII Corps on 8 September, making the XXII Corps a purely gasoline-powered formation for the rest of the campaign. XXII. Armee Korps, *Kriegtagbuch Nr. 1*, U.S. National Archives, Captured German Records, Microfilm Series 314, Roll 665.

7. 31. Division, "Erfahrungsbericht über die Kämpfe in Polen," dated 3 October 1939, U.S. National Archives, Captured German Records, Microfilm Series T-78, Roll 861, and Kennedy, *The German Campaign in Poland*, Map 9.

8. Kennedy, *The German Campaign in Poland*, pp. 80–81.

9. Liddell-Hart, *The German Generals Talk*, p. 93.

10. Letter from Heinz Guderian to Sir Basil H. Liddell-Hart, 20 December 1949, preserved in the Liddell-Hart Papers and quoted by Cooper, *The German Army*, p. 174.

11. Guderian, *Panzer Leader*, pp. 82–83.

12. Zaloga and Madej, *The Polish Campaign, 1939*, pp. 138–39.

13. Kennedy, *The German Campaign in Poland*, Map 10.

14. All organizational data relating to the 1940 campaign in France and the Low Countries is from Leo W. G. Niehorster, *German World War II Organizational Series, Volume 2/I, Mechanized Army and Divisions, (10th May, 1940)* and *Volume 2/II, Mechanized GHQ Units and Waffen-SS Divisions, (10th May, 1940)* (Hanover: Niehorster, 1990).

15. Nehring, *Die Geschichte der deutschen Panzerwaffe*, p. 154.

16. The fate of the bulk of German horse cavalry is explained in Chapter 3. Richter, *Die Geschichte der deutschen Kavallerie*, p. 101.

17. Friedrich von Cochenhausen, *Taktisches Handbuch für den Truppenführer und seine Gehilfen* (Berlin: E. S. Mittler und Sohn, 1940), pp. 38–68.

18. In German military parlance, a *Gruppe* is a formation commanded by a corps commander. Though the headquarters of *Panzergruppe von Kleist* was nothing more than the re-christened headquarters of the XXII Army Corps and, though the Panzergruppe was subordinated to the Twelfth Army, it is reasonable to call it a small army. After all, what else does one call a formation of eight divisions and scores of non-divisional units organized into three corps?

19. Ulrich List, *Westfront 1939/40, Erinnerungen des Feindarbeiters im OKH* (Neckargemünd: Kurt Vowinkel Verlag, 1959), Map 10.

20. At a time when most German armored divisions had to make do with twenty-four light (105mm) field howitzers, the motorized infantry brigade forming the main effort of Panzergruppe von Kleist was supported by the fire of 236 artillery pieces, eight of which were the monstrous 210mm heavy field mortars. Florian Rothbrust, *Guderian's XIXth Panzer Corps and the Battle of France, Breakthrough in the Ardennes, May, 1940* (New York: Praeger, 1990), pp. 146–47. This account of the breakthrough at Sedan, written by a serving officer of the United States Army, is the best single source for the military-technical details of the operation.

21. Lewis, *Forgotten Legions*, pp. 54–55.

22. For more details on the role of the infantry in the German crossing of the Meuse, see English and Gudmundsson, *On Infantry*, Chapter 4.

23. The Germans took 61,238 casualties (dead, missing, or seriously wounded) between 10 May and 4 June. Between 5 June and the end of hostilities on 25 June, they lost half again as much—95,254 dead, missing, or seriously wounded. "Abschlußbericht des OKW über den Feldzug in Frankreich (5.6.–25.6.1940)," in Hans-Adolf Jacobsen, ed., *Dokumente zum Westfeldzug 1940.* (Berlin: Musterschmidt Verlag, 1960), pp. 286–87. When broken down to a daily average, the difference between the losses of the first and second phases of the German campaign is even greater. In the twenty-five days that passed between 10 May and 4 June, the

Germans lost an average of 2,450 men a day. In the twenty days between 5 June and 25 June, the Germans lost nearly twice as many men, an average of 4,763, each day.

24. The chief casualty of the creation of standard motorized divisions was the motorized corps made up entirely of motorized infantry divisions.

25. For a detailed description of the fighting south of Amiens, see English and Gudmundsson, *On Infantry*, pp. 68–77.

26. Gen. Kdo. XVI. A.K. Ia 210/40 geh.and appendices, U.S. National Archives, Captured German Records, Microfilm Series T-314, Roll 569; Guy Chapman, *Why France Fell* (New York: Holt, Rhinehart, and Winston, 1968), p. 242; and "Die 1. Kompanie Schützenregiment 12 durchstößt die feindlichen Befestigungslinien südlich Peronne am 5. Juni," *Militärwissenschaftliche Rundschau, 1940*, Heft 4, pp. 382–85.

27. For a detailed description of the role Rommel's Seventh Panzer Division played in this part of the operation, see R. H. S. Stolfi, *A Bias for Action: The German 7th Panzer Division in France and Russia, 1940–41* (Quantico, VA, Marine Corps Association, 1991).

28. Guy Chapman, *Why France Fell*, p. 250–54.

29. For detailed examples of these combats, see A. Golaz, "Vandy, 9 Juin, 1940," *Revue Historique de l'Armée*, 1961, Numero 1.

30. Guderian, *Panzer Leader*, p. 124.

31. Chapman, *Why France Fell*, p. 276.

CHAPTER 7: Mixing It Up

1. Heinz Guderian's opinion is recorded in his *Panzer Leader*, p. 139, that of General von Thoma in Liddell-Hart's, *The German Generals Talk*, pp. 96–97.

2. In addition to the twenty armored divisions, the Germans had formed the "Obstacle Formation Libya" (*Sperr Verband Libyen*), a custom-tailored organization designed to provide "corset stays" to the Italians. This formation, which was subsequently known as the Fifth Light Division and would eventually evolve into the Twenty-first Panzer Division, included an armored regiment of 116 tanks. As one of the twenty armored divisions was also sent to Libya before Barbarossa, the Germans had nineteen armored divisions, with some 2,895 tanks, available for that operation. Niehorster, *German World War II Organizational Series, Volume 2/I, Mechanized Army Divisions, (10th May, 1940)*, pp. 32–33.

3. The statistics used in this paragraph were derived from Niehorster, *German World War II Organizational Series, Volume 2/I, Mechanized Army Divisions, (10th May, 1940)* and *German World War II Organizational Series, Volume 3/I, Mechanized Army Divisions, (22nd June, 1941)* The figures refer to official allowances for tanks serving as part of tank regiments. The numbers include neither the tank reserve detachment of each battalion nor specialized vehicles (e.g., command tanks lacking main armament, signal vehicles, and engineer vehicles.) The official allowances,

which were custom-tailored to each division, accurately reflect the numbers and types of tanks available. The one exception was the substitution of about ninety Mark I tanks for the more capable Mark II tanks. Erick Grove, *Panzerkampfwagen I and II, German Light Tanks, 1935–1945* (London: Almark, 1979), p.13.

    4. See Chapter 5 of this work for a discussion of Beck's ideas.

    5. Niehorster, *Volume 3/I, Mechanized Army Divisions, (22nd June, 1941)*, p. 42.

    6. Ibid., p. 49.

    7. The exception was the Seventh Panzer Division, which had five battalions of motorized infantry, four in trucks and one on motorcycles. Niehorster, *Volume 3/I, Mechanized Army Divisions, (22nd June, 1941)*, p.18.

    8. Niehorster, *Volume 3/I, Mechanized Army Divisions, (22nd June, 1941)*, pp. 12–31 and 41–43. The artillery of the armored division was also increased, from two to three battalions. This increase was, however, usually little more than the official recognition of the common practice of providing each armored division with a "spare" artillery battalion from the general headquarters reserve.

    9. For the details of these engagements, see Chapter 5 of this work.

    10. Albert Seaton , *The Battle for Moscow* (London: Rupert Hart Davis, 1971), p. 109

    11. Felix Steiner, *Die Armee der Geächteten* (Göttingen, 1963), quoted by Jehuda Wallach, *The Dogma of the Battle of Annihilation*, p. 277.

    12. General Frido von Senger und Etterlin, *Neither Fear nor Hope: The Wartime Memoirs of the German Defender of Cassino* (Novato, CA: Presidio Press, 1989), pp. 22–23.

    13. Klaus Christian Richter, *Die Geschichte der deutschen Kavallerie, 1919–1945* (Stuttgart: Motorbuch Verlag, 1978), p. 165.

    14. A popular cavalry slogan during the interwar years was "The cavalry rides in order to shoot, and shoots in order to ride again." Richter, *Die Geschichte der deutschen Kavallerie*, p. 31.

    15. Ibid., appendix d. 14.

    16. Of all the men who had a great influence on the shaping of the German army, Guderian may have been closest to appreciating the potential of horse cavalry. In 1938, while Inspector of Quick Troops, he had advocated the formation of additional cavalry divisions that, in contrast to the existing cavalry divisions, would go to war as complete formations. (The two cavalry divisions then serving in the German army were, on mobilization in 1939, broken up to provide reconnaissance units for infantry divisions.) This proposal was rejected by higher authorities because of the difficulty of providing suitable horses. Richter, *Die Geschichte der deutschen Kavallerie*, p. 29.

    17. As with the campaign in Poland, the distribution of German divisions among the various corps is somewhat misleading. While motorized divisions were initially assigned to nonmotorized corps and muscle-powered divisions were assigned to corps that were otherwise fully motorized, this was an expedient for purposes of assembly and the crossing of the frontier. Once the fully motorized divisions

began to outpace the others, the motorized corps shed their muscle-powered escorts and the nonmotorized corps launched their gasoline-powered divisions.

18. The new corps headquarters had numbers over twenty-four, e.g. XXXXVI. Panzer Korps and XXXXVII Panzer Korps. This reorganization was thus the cause of the jumble of Roman numerals that often appears in accounts of the 1941 campaign.

19. Rudolf Steiger, *Armored Tactics as Reflected in 1939–1941 German War Diaries* (Washington, D.C.: U.S. Army, 1975), pp. 107–108.

20. Steiger, *Armored Tactics,* pp. 40–42. The 88mm and 100mm guns rarely formed a part of armored or motorized divisions at this time. Apart from the one four-gun battery of 100mm guns in the division artillery regiment of seven armored divisions, the guns employed in this role came from independent heavy artillery battalions, antiaircraft battalions, and heavy antitank companies attached to the motorized corps. Niehorster, *Volume 3/I,* pp. 12–31 *and 3/II*, pp. 19, 31, and 40.

21. Eric Grove, *Panzerkampfwagen I & II, German Light Tanks, 1935–45* (London: Altmark, 1979), p. 13.

22. Horst Scheibert, *Panzergrenadier Motorcycle and Panzer Reconnaissance Units* (West Chester, PA: Schiffer, 1991), pp. 80–81; August Schmidt, *Geschichte der 10. Division* (Bad Nauheim, Podzun-Verlag, 1963), pp. 300–301; 3. Panzer Division, Anlage zu 3.Pz.Div. Ia Nr. 700/43g II. Ang von 22.4.43, "Erfahrungen und Vorschläge zur Gliederung eines Kradschützen-Bataillons," U.S. National Archives, Captured German Records, Microfilm Series T-78, Roll 620.

23. Of the thirty armored divisions in the German army in April 1942, thirteen had only one tank battalion, ten had two, and seven had three. Five of these divisions were being formed or converted in France and six more were elsewhere than the Russian Front. Thus, while the absolute number of German armored divisions had increased by more than 50%, the number of armored divisions present for duty on the Eastern Front remained the same. Nehring, *Die Geschichte der deutschen Panzerwaffe,* pp. 253–54.

24. Cooper, *The German Army,* pp. 408–409.

25. For more on the subject of mission tactics, see Dirk Oetting, *Auftragstaktik, Geschichte und Gegenwart einer Führungskonzeption* (Frankfurt am Main: Report Verlag, 1994).

26. A "square" German infantry division of the period from 1890 to 1914 could be easily broken down into four detachments of one infantry regiment, one artillery battalion, and one cavalry squadron each. For more on the square division, see English and Gudmundsson, *On Infantry,* Chapter 1. For examples of German war games featuring detachments, see the series "Moltke's Tactical Decision Games" in Volume I (October 1991 through September 1992) of *Tactical Notebook.*

27. Julius von Verdy du Vernois, (Sir H. J. T. Hildyard, trans.), *Studies in Troop Leading* (London, Henry S. King, 1872), p. 7.

28. Not all of the armored divisions of 1939 and 1940 had full tank brigades. Four had a single regiment that was directly subordinated to the division commander.

In 1941, all of the German armored divisions had been reorganized around a single tank regiment and were thus able to eliminate the tank brigade as an echelon. For the purposes of this paragraph, the term *brigade* refers to the element of tanks or motorized infantry directly subordinate to the division.

29. Liddell-Hart, *The German Generals Talk*, p. 93.

30. Steiger, *Armored Tactics,* pp.33–38.

31. 4. Leichte Division, "Übersicht über Gefechte, beteiligte Truppen, Beute, und Verluste," and Ia Nr. 61 k/39 g. Kdos. "Erfahrungsbericht" 22.10.1939, Captured German Records, U. S. National Archives, Series T-315, Roll 230.

32. Balck, *Battelle Interviews*, July 1979, p. 13.

33. Günter Fraschka, *Der Panzer-Graf, General Graf Strachwitz—ein Leben für Deutschland* (Rastatt in Baden, Erich Pabel Verlag, 1962), p. 164.

34. 17. Panzerdivision, Ia Nr. 412/43 g. K., Captured German Records, U. S. National Archives, Series T-78, Roll 620. A translation of this document has been published as "The New Tank Tactics," *Tactical Notebook*, June 1992.

35. In keeping with longstanding German tradition, the all arms commander was to lead from the front. He was to be sufficiently far forward to observe the battle but not so far forward that he got too involved in the actions of the tank group. For once the tank group became engaged in combat, the chief means by which the all arms commander could influence the battle became, as at the beginning of the fight, the infantry group. "The New Tank Tactics," pp. 1–2.

36. Ibid.

37. Ibid.

38. It's important to note that German artillery commanders—from battery commanders to the generals commanding artillery task forces containing hundreds of pieces—insisted on personally observing the battlefield. For details, see Gudmundsson, *On Artillery.*

39. "Zusammenwirken von Panzern und Artillerie," *Nachrichtenblatt der Panzertruppen*, Nr. 11, May 1944, pp. 11–12. The *Nachrichtenblatt der Panzertruppen* was an official circular of the *Inspectorate of Armored Troops* that was classified as Secret.

40. Sigfried Henrici, "Die Artillerie der Panzerdivision," *Wehrkunde*, Volume 8, 1958, pp. 439–41.

41. "Hermann Balck's Proposed Reorganization for the Großdeutschland Division, 14 April, 1943," *Tactical Notebook*, November 1993, p. 3.

42. Balck did not specify exactly what these might be, but the *Raupenschlepper Ost,* a vehicle designed to carry infantry ammunition, seems to have been the type of vehicle about which he was thinking. U.S. National Archives, Captured German Records, Microfilm Series T-78, Roll 620.

43. "Hermann Balck's Proposed Reorganization for the Großdeutschland Division, 14 April, 1943," pp. 1–4.

44. Ibid.

45. Von Senger und Etterlin, *Panzergrenadiere*, pp. 203–204 and 215–16.

46. Ibid., pp. 203–204 and 216–18. For more on the various self-propelled weapons, see Chapter 8 of this work.

47. Nehring, *Die Geschichte der deutschen Panzerwaffe*, appendix, pp. 2–3.

48. The third experiment was the formation of permanent armored corps. These consisted of two small armored divisions whose service units had been consolidated at corps level. Nehring, *Die Geschichte der deutschen Panzerwaffe*, appendix pp.2–3.

CHAPTER 8:   The Armored Guerilla

1. For a brief treatment the role played by artillery in these offensives, see Gudmundsson, *Storm Troop Tactics*, Chapter 9, and *On Artillery*, Chapter 6. For a more detailed look, see David T. Zabicki, *Steel Wind* (Wesport: Praeger, 1994).

2. Erich von Manstein, *Aus Einem Soldatenleben, 1887–1939* (Bonn: Athenäum Verlag, 1958), pp. 243–44.

3. Manstein, *Aus Einem Soldatenleben*, pp. 244–45. For detailed examples of how a German infantry battalion commander employed his infantry guns, see the series of tactical decision games published in Volume I of *Tactical Notebook*. Whether infantry guns were assigned to infantry battalions or regiments was a function of the degree to which battalions were expected to operate independently. The battalions of mountain infantry, light (Jäger) infantry, motorcycle infantry, and certain types of motorized infantry were provided with their own infantry guns. The battalions of ordinary infantry units, which were expected to operate within range of the regimental infantry guns, had no infantry guns of their own.

4. Manstein, *Aus Einem Soldatenleben*, pp. 244–45.

5. J. Walter Spielberger (James C. Cable, trans.), *Sturmgeschütz and Its Variants* (Atglen, PA: Schiffer Publishing, 1993), pp. 10–11.

6. Manstein, *Aus Einem Soldatenleben*, pp. 246–47.

7. It is interesting to note that three batteries of four guns each was the traditional organization of a German horse artillery battalion.

8. In 1940, thirty-eight 150mm infantry guns were mounted on light tank chassis were used to equip six independent "self-propelled infantry gun" companies that were attached to some armored divisions. Top heavy and poorly protected, these weapons nonetheless performed yeoman service until sufficient numbers of "real" assault guns became available. Leo W. G. Niehorster, *German World War II Organizational Series. Volume 2/II, Mechanized Army and Waffen-SS Units (10th May, 1940)* (Hanover: Niehorster, 1990), pp. 32 and 36.

9. Leo W. G. Niehorster, *German World War II Organizational Series. Volume 3/II, Mechanized Army and Waffen-SS Units (22nd June, 1941)* (Hanover: Niehorster, 1990), p. 34.

10. Adolph von Schell (A. E. Turner, trans.), *The Tactics of Field Artillery* (London: Harrison and Son, 1889), p. 121.

11. A. Seeger (Edmund Gruber, trans.), "Our Baptism of Fire," *The Field Artillery Journal*, Volume V, Number 4, October-December, 1915, pp. 659–65.

12. For more on how horse artillery fit into the organizational structure of the German army of World War I, see "The 1st Cavalry Corps," *Tactical Notebook*, April 1992.

13. This was reflected in the terminology used to describe the two types of artillery. Horse artillery was *Reitende Artillerie* (literally "riding artillery"). Ordinary field artillery was *Fahrende Artillerie* (literally "driving artillery").

14. Günther Blumentritt, *The German Armies of 1914 and 1939*, U.S. Army Foreign Military Studies, MS B-296, pp. 26–27. The Foreign Military Studies were reports written by former Axis officers at the behest of the U.S. Army. They are on file at the U.S. National Archives. An index has been published by the Garland Publishing Company.

15. The word *Lauerstellung* might be translated as "ambush position." The German word *Lauer* is a cognate of the English word "lair" and has the same connotation of a beast of prey waiting to pounce on his victim.

16. Kurt Bischoff, *Im Trommelfeuer, Die Herbstschlacht in der Champagne, 1915* (Leipzig: Gebrüder Fändrich, 1939), pp. 39–63.

17. Ibid.

18. "Lessons Drawn from the Combats of Infantry Division 'Großdeutschland,' 28 June to 25 December, 1942," *Tactical Notebook*, June 1993.

19. The German technique of adjusting artillery fire by bracketing greatly surprised their French opponents of 1870 and 1871. For a description of what it was like to be bracketed during the Franco-Prussian War, see "Counter-Battery Fire," *Tactical Notebook*, February 1992.

20. The production figures are from a report of the "Adolf Hitler Panzerprogramm," produced around May of 1944, U.S. National Archives, Captured German Records, Series T-78, Roll 619. (The document identification markings are illegible.) The figures for vehicles available on the Eastern Front are from *Panzeroffizier beim Chef Generalstab des Heeres, Nr. 561/44 GK*, Captured German Records, Series T-78, Roll 620. The information on tank and antitank units equipped with assault guns is from *Der Generalinspektor der Panzertruppen, "Übersicht der Heeres-Armee- und Korps-Panzetruppen,"* Captured German Records, Series T-78, Roll 623, frames 477–495.

21. "The Invisible Assault Gun," *Tactical Notebook*, June 1993.

22. The number of the tank hunter companies was created by adding 1,000 to the number of the division in which the company served. Tank Hunter Company 1045 was thus part of the antitank battalion of the Forty-fifth Infantry Division.

23. *Nachrichtenblatt der Panzertruppen*, No. 18, December 1944. Copies of most issues of the *Nachrichtenblatt der Panzertruppen* have been preserved in U.S. National Archives, Captured German Documents, Series T-78, Roll 623.

24. The battalion consisted of forty-nine Panzer IV tanks and forty-four assault guns (both equipped with long-barreled 75mm guns) *Nachrichtenblatt der Panzertruppen*, No. 8, February 1944.

25. 78. Sturmdivision, Ia, *"Sturmgeschütz-Begleitkompanie,"* 22/4/43. U.S. National Archives, Captured German Documents, Series T-315, Roll 1100, Frames 164–165.

26. The German description was *"auf dem Kommandowege gestellt,"* which corresponds to the popular American military expression "out of hide."

27. To ensure this expertise, the pathfinder was to have the rank of *Gefreiter* (Lance Corporal) or *Unteroffizier* (Sergeant). 78. Sturmdivision, Ia, *"Sturmgeschütz-Begleitkompanie,"* 22/4/43.

28. A second type of escort battery, one equipped with 14 Panzer II tanks, was "official" from February through November 1944. However, only four of these units were raised. Spielberger, *Sturmgeschütz*, p. 239.

29. "Assault Gun and Assault Artillery Brigades of 1944," *Tactical Notebook*, June 1993 and Gottfried Tornau and Franz Kurowski, *Sturmartillerie: Fels in der Brandung* (Herford: Maximilian Verlag, 1965), pp. 278–85.

30. Tornau and Kurowski, *Sturmartillerie*, pp. 293–94.

31. By way of contrast, the one platoon of combat engineers was normally attached, as an intact unit, to a single assault gun battery. Assigning the engineers to particular vehicles was forbidden. Ibid., p. 294.

32. "Bezeichnung der Panzerjäger-Waffen," *Nachrichtenblatt der Panzertruppen*, Nr. 16, October 1944, pp. 16–17.

33. "Die Kanonengruppe in der Pz. Gren.Komp.c. (gp),"*Nachrichtenblatt der Panzertruppen*, Nr. 4, October 1943, p. 7.

34. Ibid.

35. An extensive treatment of these vehicles can be found in the March, 1945 edition of the official U.S. Army guide to the German army. U.S. War Department, *Handbook on the German Military Forces* (Baton Rouge: Louisiana State University Press, 1995).

36. Rudolf Berdach and Erich Dethleffsen, *Der Artillerie gewidmet* (Vienna: Berdach, 1975), pp. 14–16 and appendix III.B.1. and Roger Bruge, *Faites Sauter La Ligne Maginot* (Paris: Fayard, 1973), pp. 211–69. The latter work contains the definitive account of the fall of the *ouvrage* at La Ferté. For a popular account, see Bruce Gudmundsson, "After Dunkirk," *MHQ*, Spring, 1996.

37. A technical description, as well as a table of organization and a list of which companies were assigned to which divisions can be found in Niehorster, *2/II*, p. 36.

38. Appendices to 9. Panzerdivision, Ib, "Kriegstagbuch," U.S. National Archives, Captured German Records, Microfilm Series T315, Roll 532, frames 39, 83, and 10. Panzerdivision, Ia, "Kriegstagbuch," Microfilm Series T-315, role 559; also consulted were a variety of partially burned orders and reports from the Ninth Infantry Division, Microfilm Series T-315, Roll 508.

39. "Chart for the "Adolf Hitler Panzerprogramm," U.S. National Archives, Captured German Documents, Microfilm Series T-78, Roll 619. The term *first-class antitank gun* refers to German built 75mm antitank guns and Soviet 76.2mm antitank guns.

40. Ibid.

41. Von Senger und Etterlin, *Panzergrenadiere*, pp. 203–204 and 216–18.

42. General der Infanterie b Chef Gen St d H IV. Nr. 6886/43 geh., dated 20 October 1943, U.S. National Archives, Captured German Records, Microfilm Series T-78, Roll 759.

43. The best document on German antitank warfare during this period is the film *Männer Gegen Panzer*. Published under the title *Men against Tanks*, it is available on videotape from International Historic Films, P.O. Box 29035, Chicago, IL 60629.

44. Der Chef des Generalstabes des Heeres, "Übersicht über Panzerabschüsse aufgeschlüsselt auf die verschiedenen Waffen (Ostfront)," U.S. National Archives, Captured German Records, Microfilm Series T-78, Roll 619.

45. For a discussion of Soviet infantry tactics during this period, see English and Gudmundsson, *On Infantry*, Chapter 5.

46. "Hermann Balck's Proposed Organization for the Großdeutschland Division, 14 April, 1943," *Tactical Notebook*, November 1993, p. 1.

47. Burkhart Mueller-Hillebrand, *Small Unit Tactics, Tactics of Individual Arms (Russian Armored Command) Examples from World War II,* Part I, U.S. Army Foreign Military Studies MS P-060f, pp. 35–37.

CHAPTER 9: A Family Resemblance

1. Adolf von Schell, who would soon play an important role in the expansion of German armored forces, attended the U.S. Army infantry school in 1930 and 1931 and visited the First Mechanized Cavalry Brigade at Fort Knox in 1936. Adolf von Schell, *Battle Leadership* (Quantico, VA: Marine Corps Association, 1982), pp. 5–6 and Mildred H. Gillie, *Forging the Thunderbolt* (Harrisburg: Military Service Publishing, 1947), p. 89.

2. For a brief synopsis of U.S. Army perceptions of the Blitzkrieg in the months immediately following the fall of France, see Christopher R. Gabel, *Seek, Strike, and Destroy: U.S. Army Tank Destroyer Doctrine in World War II* (Fort Leavenworth, KS: U.S. Army Command and General Staff College, 1985), pp. 9–10. For examples, see the various U.S. Army service journals of the time (e.g., the *Infantry Journal*, the *Field Artillery Journal*, the *Coast Artillery Journal*) as well as popular magazines such as *Time*.

3. Like many myths coming out of 1940, the story of multitudes of well-armed German tanks is still alive. As late as 1986, an otherwise well-informed Pentagon journalist could write. "In 1940, the U.S. Army had 464 tanks in all, armed mostly with machine guns. The Germans had over 5,000, armed mostly with 75mm cannon." Arthur Hadley, *The Straw Giant: Triumph and Failure of America's Armed Forces* (New York: Random House, 1986), p. 37.

4. For more on U.S. Army tank destroyers, see Gabel, *Seek, Strike, and Destroy* and Charles M. Baily, *Faint Praise: American Tanks and Tank Destroyers During*

World War II (Hamden, CT: Archon, 1983). Ironically, the inspiration for the tank destroyer concept seems to have been a French proposal, made in May of 1940, to create units of *chasseurs de chars* equipped, like the early American tank destroyer units, with anti-tank guns mounted on the backs of cross-country trucks. "Mobile Units for Operation against Tanks and Mechanized Forces," Military Attaché Paris, Report No. 25,729-W, 1 June 1940, U.S. National Archives, Record Group 165.

5. Raymond E. Lee, "The Mobile Division, Present Status of Mobile Division and Army Mechanization," Military Attaché London, Report No. 38916. G. Bryan Conrad, "The Armored Division, January, 1940," Military Attaché London, Report No. 40811 and "The Armored Division, April, 1940," Military Attaché London, Report No. 41106. All of these attaché reports can be found in the U.S. National Archives, Record Group 165. Giffard Le Q. Martel, *Our Armored Forces* (London: Faber & Faber, 1947), Appendix D.

6. "R. A. C. Lizard Exercise, R. A. C. Training Instruction No. 1," enclosed with V. E. Pritchard, "Tactical Employment of Armored Units," Military Attaché London, Report No. 42258, January, 30, 1941, U.S. National Archives, Record Group 165.

7. There were no separate antitank battalions in the American armored division of 1940. The division's 37mm antitank guns were spread among the various artillery and infantry battalions. John Sayen, "The Armored Division, 1940–1942," *Tactical Notebook*, Volume II, May 1993. If heavier antitank guns were needed, they were to be provided by the tank destroyer battalions of the general headquarters reserve.

8. The British "Field Regiment, Royal Artillery" had eighteen 25-pounder gun-howitzers. The U.S. "Field Artillery Battalion" had twelve 105mm howitzers and eight 75mm field guns. "The Armored Division, 1940–1942," *Tactical Notebook*.

9. Gillie, *Forging the Thunderbolt*, p. 215.

10. "General Note on Armored Forces," enclosed with V. E. Pritchard, "Tactical Employment of Armored Units," Military Attaché London, Report No. 42258, January, 30, 1941, U.S. National Archives, Record Group 165.

11. U.S. Army, Historical Branch, War Plans Division, General Staff, *A Study in Battle Formation* (Washington, DC: U.S. Government Printing Office, 1920), p. 30.

12. J. P. Harris, *Men, Ideas and Tanks* (Manchester: Manchester University Press, 1995) p. 93.

13. The fourth "tank battalion" was initially an armored car regiment, but, beginning in 1943, was more likely to be an armored reconnaissance regiment equipped with light tanks. As larger and more powerful tanks became available, these tended to displace the light tanks to the point where the armored reconnaissance regiment began to resemble the other tank battalions in the division. Hughes, et al., *British Armoured and Cavalry Divisions* and Wallace, *Dragons of Steel*, pp. 166–69.

14. Combat commands had actually been introduced as part of the 1942 reform of the American armored division. This created a somewhat unwieldy situation in which combat command headquarters competed with regimental headquarters.

15. Wayne D. Smart, "Armored Divisions' Combat Commands," *The Cavalry Journal*, March-April, 1946, pp. 42–44.

16. Hughes, et al., *British Armoured and Cavalry Divisions*, p. 33.

17. Ibid., p. 77.

18. W. V. E. Prichard, "Infantry with an Armored Division," Military Attaché London, Report No. 42250, January 29, 1941. U.S. National Archives, Record Group 165.

19. Hughes, et al., *British Armoured and Cavalry Divisions*, p. 19.

20. Great Britain, *21 Army Group, The Armoured Division in Battle* (Holland: December, 1944), p. 14. The author wishes to thank Lieutenant Colonel John A. English, CD (Ret.) for locating and photocopying this document.

21. Hughes, et al., *British Armoured and Cavalry Divisions*, p. 19.

22. Ibid., pp. 91–93.

23. Smart, "Armored Divisions' Combat Commands," p. 43.

24. Emerson A. Hurley, "Tank Infantry Teamwork at its Peak in the Armored Division," *Armored Cavalry Journal*, May-June, 1947, pp. 27–28.

25. Half of the artillery battalions assigned to the task forces, as well as the tank destroyer platoons, came from General Headquarters Reserve units attached to the Fifth Armored Division. The self-propelled 105mm cannon came from the assault gun platoons of the armored and armored infantry battalions. The 81mm mortar platoon, which was only assigned to the smaller of the two task forces, came from the armored infantry battalion.

26. The extent to which the German army was fighting in this fashion has not been emphasized or even acknowledged in most English-language histories dealing with the last year of the war in Northwest Europe. The semi-guerilla character of most of the German forces facing the Western Allies in 1944 and 1945 is, however, evident in the order of battle maps prepared by the Historical Section of the Army High Command (O.K.H.) and preserved at the U.S. National Archives (Captured German Documents, Series T-78, Roll 136). German unit histories dealing with this period paint a similar picture. See, among others, Gustav W. Schrodek, *Ihr Glaube Galt dem Vaterland* (Munich: Schild Verlag, 1976) and Friedrich Bruns, ed., *Die Panzerbrigade 106 FHH* (Celle: F. Bruns, 1982).

27. See, for observations on cross-attachment and tactical examples, U.S. Army, Forces in the European Theater, General Board, *Organization, Equipment and Tactical Employment of the Armored Division*, on file in the library of the Army War College, Carlisle, PA, pp. 7–22.

CHAPTER 10: Breakthrough

1. Giffard Martel, *Our Armoured Forces* (London: Faber and Faber, 1945), pp. 47–48.

2. Ibid., p. 47. The 3-inch (77mm) howitzer was not provided with high-explosive shells until after the start of World War II.

3. Ibid., p. 49.

4. Ibid., pp. 151–53.

5. Ibid., pp. 359–61.

6. Peter Chamberlain and Chris Ellis, *The Churchill Tank* (London: Arms and Armour, 1971), p. 19.

7. Ibid., pp. 21–22.

8. In preparation for the Normandy landings, the Seventy-ninth Armoured Division also facilitated the employment of DD (Duplex Drive) tanks. These were standard Sherman tanks that had been provided with a floatation device that allowed them to swim, albeit very slowly. Large numbers of DD tanks were assembled for use in the Normandy landings. Bad weather, however, ensured that only eighty of the 130 DD tanks launched on 6 June 1944 reached dry land. The handful that did reach the beach, however, performed yeoman service during the early hours of the landing. Great Britain, *79th Armoured Division, Final Report* (n.p., 1945), pp. 63–64. A copy of this report is on file at the U.S. Army Military History Institute, Carlisle, Pennsylvania.

9. Known to the British as Buffaloes, the amphibious tractors were of the type developed by the United States Marine Corps for the Pacific island-hopping campaign. Though they would have been useful during the Normandy landings, they did not become available until the autumn of 1944. Anonymous, *The Story of the 79th Armoured Division* (Location Unknown: 79th Armoured Division, 1945), p. 142.

10. General Eisenhower's official report for the Normandy landing contains the following tribute to the specialized armor used on 6 June 1944. "Apart from the factor of tactical surprise, the comparatively light casualties which we sustained on all beaches, except Omaha, were in large measure due to the success of the novel mechanical contrivances which we employed and to the staggering moral and material effect of the mass of armor landed in the leading waves of the assault. It is doubtful if the assault forces could have firmly established themselves without the assistance of these weapons." Quoted in Basil Liddell-Hart, *The Tanks* (London: Cassell, 1959), p. 332.

11. 79th Armoured Division, *Final Report*, p. 66.

12. Ibid., p. 24.

13. Ibid.

14. John English, *The Canadian Army in the Normandy Campaign* (Westport, CT: Praeger, 1991), has a complete account of the role played by infantry (armored and otherwise) in this campaign. For synopses, see White, *British Tanks and Fighting Vehicles, 1914–1945*, pp. 298–99 and Wallace, *Dragons of Steel*, p. 231.

15. Wallace, *Dragons of Steel*, pp. 231–32.

16. Bernard L. Montgomery, "The British Army Group in Europe, 1944–45, Conclusion," *The Cavalry Journal*, March-April 1946, p. 48. This article originally appeared in the *Journal of the Royal United Service Institution*.

17. Strictly speaking, the term *Kangaroo* applied only to the modified *Ram*, an under-gunned Canadian tank built on the chassis of the American M3 (Lee-Grant) tank. (The production models of the Ram had been sent to Europe with 57mm/ 6-pounder guns as main armament and were thus obsolete by the time of the Normandy landings.) However, as a number of distinguished experts, particularly Field Marshal Montgomery, B. H. Liddell-Hart, and Richard Simpkin, have used the term to cover all Anglo-Canadian armored personnel carriers built upon modified tank chassis and hulls, I am happy to do the same.

18. White, *British Tanks and Fighting Vehicles, 1914–1945*, pp. 298—99, Wallace, *Dragons of Steel*, p. 172, and Liddell-Hart, *The Tanks*, Volume II, pp. 329–30.

19. For examples, see Bryan Perrett, *Iron Fist: Classic Armoured Warfare Case Studies* (London: Arms and Armour, 1996), pp. 124 and Liddell-Hart, *The Tanks*, Volume II, Chapters 16 and 17.

20. Montgomery, *The Armored Division in Battle*, pp. 27–28.

21. For more on the absence of good heavy weapons tactics in the British and American military traditions, see English and Gudmundsson, *On Infantry*.

22. William R. Campbell, "Tanks With Infantry," *Armored Cavalry Journal*, September-October, 1947, pp. 50–51.

23. For a detailed, tank-crew level account of the role played by American armor in the war against Japan, see Oscar E. Gilbert, *Marine Tank Battles in the Pacific* (Conshohocken, PA: Combined Books, 2001).

24. U.S. Tenth Army, Prisoner of War Interrogation Report #22, p. 11, U.S. National Archives, Record Group 407, Entry 427, Box 2955.

25. "New Infantry and Armored Divisions," *The Field Artillery Journal*, January-February, 1947, pp. 33–35; and George McCutchen and John F. Staples, "Organization of the New Infantry Division," *The Field Artillery Journal*, September-October, 1949, pp. 199–201.

26. U.S. Army cannon companies tended to be used in the indirect fire role and, to that end, were often tied into the artillery fire control system. This undermined any rationale for keeping these weapons within the infantry regiment. U.S. Twelfth Army Group, "Battle Experiences," Numbers 5, 6 and 58, U.S. National Archives, Record Group 337, Entry 47, Box 90, Folder 319.1. For an overview of life in an American cannon company in World War II, see W. Stanford Smith, *The Cannoneers* (Manhattan, Kansas: Sunflower University, 1993).

CHAPTER 11: Gunslinger

1. Childs, *A Peripheral Weapon?*, pp. 77–79.

2. The last French light infantry tank to be produced before World War II (the R-40) was also the first to be provided with a high-velocity antitank gun. John Sayen, "The Organization of French Armor (Part II)," *Tactical Notebook*, July 1993.

3. Anonymous, "Tanks in the Spanish War," *The Royal Tank Corps Journal*, No. 5, January 1938, p. 23.

4. George T. Hoffmann, "Doctrine, Tank Technology, and Execution: I. A. Khalepskii and the Red Army Fulfillment of Deep Offensive Operations," *Journal of Slavic Military Studies*, Vol. 9, June 1996, pp. 296 and 301.

5. Most versions of the T-28 medium tank and T-35 heavy tanks were equipped with either the short-barreled version of the 76.2mm gun or the standard version of that piece. "The T-28 Medium Tank," *The Russian Battlefield*, http://www.battlefield.ru/t28.html and "the T-35 Heavy Tank," *The Russian Battlefield*, http://www.battlefield.ru/t35.html.

6. The shells for the Soviet 45mm gun (M1932, M1934, and M1938) weighed 2.15 kilograms (a little less than five pounds). Valeriy Potapov (Rodion Podorozhn, trans.), "45mm Tank Gun Model 1932/38," *The Russian Battlefield*, http://www.battlefield.ru/armaments/20k.html.

7. "The T-26 Light Tank," *The Russian Battlefield*, http://www.battlefield.ru/t26.html.

8. Steven J. Zaloga, "Soviet Tank Operations in the Spanish Civil War," *Journal of Slavic Military Studies*, Vol. 12, September 1999, made available at http://libraryautomation.com/nymas/ soviet_tank_operations_in_the_sp.htm.

9. "Specification and Armor Penetration Values for the Soviet Tank Cannons," *The Russian Battlefield*, http://www.battlefield.ru/guns/defin_4.html.

10. Stephen L. Sewell, "Red Star-White Elephant," *Armor*, July-August 2002.

11. Steven J. Zaloga and Jim Kinnear, *T-34-85 Medium Tank 1944-94* (Oxford: Osprey, 1996), p. 7.

12. Roy E. Appleman, *South to the Naktong, North to the Yalu* (Washington, D.C.: U.S. Army Center of Military History, 1992), pp. 10-13, 24-25, 31-32, and Map I.

13. Ibid., p. 146.

14. The extent of the "demodernization" of the North Korean army can be seen in Charles R. Shrader, *Communist Logistics in the Korean War* (Westport, CT: Greenwood, 1992), Chapter 7. For the effect of this transformation on the "sharp end" of the North Korean forces, see Headquarters, U.S. Far East Command, Military Intelligence Section, General Staff, "History of the North Korean Army," on file at the U.S. Army Military History Institute, Carlisle Barracks, Pennsylvania.

15. Vincent McRae and Alvin D. Coox, *Tank-vs-Tank Combat in Korea* (Chevy Chase, MD: The Johns Hopkins University, 1954), p. 12.

16. Ibid., p. 66.

17. Ibid., p. 15.

18. "History of the North Korean Army," pp. 47-48.

19. David Warner, "The Soviet SU-76 SP Gun in Korea," *AFV G-2*, Volume 6, Number 7, pp. 16-20.

20. For a detailed description of how the "first accurate shot" phenomenon played out in the Normandy campaign of 1944, see Roman J. Jarymowycz, *Tank Tactics from Normandy to Lorraine* (Boulder, CO: Lynne Rienner, 2002), Chapter 13.

21. For detailed descriptions of the armies of front-line Arab states during the first two decades of Israel's existence, see Kenneth Pollack, *Arabs at War, Military Effectiveness, 1948–1991* (Lincoln: University of Nebraska, 2003).

22. Martin van Creveld, *The Sword and the Olive: A Critical History of the Israeli Defense Force* (New York: Public Affairs, 1998), pp. 160–206.

23. Israel Tal, *National Security, The Israeli Experience* (Westport, CT: Praeger, 2000), p. 132.

24. Van Creveld, *The Sword and the Olive*, p. 171 and Tal, *National Security*, p. 133.

25. Van Creveld, ibid., 229–32 and Tal, ibid., pp. 178–79.

26. Samuel M. Katz, *Merkava Main Battle Tank* (Oxford: Osprey, 1997), pp. 17–21.

27. Gregory A. Pickell, "Designing the Next Infantry Fighting Vehicle," *Infantry*, July-August 1996 and Marsh Gelbard, "Achzarit: Israel's Assault Solution," *Jane's Intelligence Review*, July 1997, pp. 315–18.

28. United States Marine Corps Intelligence Activity, *Soviet/Russian Armor and Artillery Design Practices: 1945–1995* (Quantico, VA: United States Marine Corps, 1996), pp. I–75 and I–76.

29. David Bongard, "A TNDM Analysis of Goose Green-Darwin," 28 May 1982, *The International TNDM Newsletter*, Volume 1, Number 2, October 1996, p. 8.

30. "TOW2 Heavy Antitank Missile, USA," http://www.army-technology.com/projects/tow/.

31. The Swedish Bill2 antitank guided missile avoids the overspecialization caused by "flyover top attack" by means of a feature that allows the gunner to fire the missile in one of three modes. The first of these is flyover top attack. The second is the traditional forward attack for use against soft targets. The third is a special mode for firing at hovering helicopters. Bill2 Antitank Guided Weapon, Sweden," http://www.armytechnology.com/projects/bofors/.

32. A second exception to the general rule of the over-optimized antitank guided missile is provided by the case of the Russian Kornet missile, which can be provided with a thermobaric (fuel-air) warhead as well as a tandem antitank warhead. (A tandem warhead is one designed to defeat reactive armor by means of a small explosive charge that sets off the reactive armor before the main charge gets close enough to be significantly diminished.) "Two-Fisted Trouble? Russian Antitank Missile May Give Iraq Extra Punch," *ABCNews.com*, 27 March 2003.

33. Jonathan Marcus, "How Thermobaric Bombs Work," *BBC News*, 4 March 2002, http://news.bbc.co.uk/1/hi/world/south_asia/1854371.stm.

34. "French Main Battle Tank," *AFV Interiors Web Magazine*, Vol.5 No.1, 2003, http://www.kithobbyist.com/AFVInteriors/leclerc/leclerc2.html.

35. USMC, *Soviet/Russian Armor and Artillery Design Practices: 1945–1995*, pp. II-14 and II-15.

36. According to some sources, a second Israeli helicopter fired a second missile at the car. See, among others, Zeina Khodr, "Lebanon Braces for the Worst," *Al-Ahram Weekly On-line*, 3–9 September 1998, Issue No. 393.

37. United Nations, General Assembly, Fifty-third session, *Letter dated 25 September 1998 from the Permanent Representative of Lebanon to the United Nations.*

38. Tony Geraghty and David Leigh, "The Name of the Game is Assassination," *The Guardian*, Thursday, December 19, 2002.

39. It is interesting to note that the Israeli use of a third-generation antitank guided missile to kill Hussam al-Amin took place a few days before the state-owned Rafael armaments company signed an agreement with a German industrial consortium to build and market such weapons in Europe. Christopher Foss, "Israel Pitches AT Missiles at Europe," *Jane's Defence Weekly*, 2 September 1998, p. 12.

40. *Soviet/Russian Armor and Artillery Design Practices: 1945–1995*, p. I-76.

41. See, among others, Bruce I. Gudmundsson, "New Tanks for Old: How Marines Should Think about Armored Vehicles," *Marine Corps Gazette*, December 1988.

CHAPTER 12: The Future of Armor

1. The figure for fuel consumed by an Abrams tank while idling is from the U.S. Department of Defense, Office of the Under Secretary of Defense for Acquisition, Technology and Logistics/Defense Science Board, *More Capable Warfighting through Reduced Fuel Burden* (Washington, DC: U.S. Department of Defense, 2001), p. 44. The figure for the miles-per-gallon fuel efficiency of the Abrams tank is somewhat more controversial. Over the years, published estimates have varied considerably, from slightly less than two gallons per mile as many as six gallons per mile. The figure given in the text is taken from John Pike's excellent website, http://www.globalsecurity.org.

2. "Logistics units were hard-pressed to keep up with the rapid pace of maneuver units. Both logistics structure and doctrine were found wanting in the high tempo offensive operation. HET and off-road truck mobility were limited, and MSRs into Iraq few and constricted. Had the operation lasted longer, maneuver forces would have outrun their fuel and other support." United States Department of Defense, *Final Report to Congress: Conduct of the Persian Gulf Wa*r (Washington, DC: U.S. Government Printing Office, 1992), p. 297.

3. Ibid., p. 241.

4. After many disasters, the Russians responded to these tactics with a replay of the tactics used so successfully against German rocket propelled grenades in 1945. In particular, they kept their tanks and other armored vehicles beyond the reach of rocket propelled grenades. (In 1945, this had been 100 meters or so. In the 1990s, it was 300 meters.) Thus prevented from taking part in close combat, the Russian tanks were limited to providing preparatory and supporting fires for assault troops on foot. Lester Grau, "Technology and the Second Chechen Campaign: Not All New and Not All That Much," pp. 106–107. Michael Orr, "Better or Just Not as Bad? An Evaluation of Russian Combat Effectiveness in the Second Chechen War,"

pp. 94–96, gives examples of Russian techniques that involved using tanks to support infantry assault groups at much closer range. Both of these articles are published in Anne Aldis (ed.), *The Second Chechen War* (Camberly: Strategic and Combat Studies Institute, 2000).

5. *DoD News Briefing*, Saturday, June 5, 1999-12:20 P.M., http://www.fas.org/man/dod-101/ops/docs99/t06051999_t0605asd.htm.

6. Many of the ideas contained in this paragraph were inspired by the "Raider" proposal of Chris Yunker and Howard Feldmeyer. This very detailed proposal, which was privately published in several iterations during the 1990s, was written when Major Yunker and Major Feldmeyer were serving officers in the United States Marine Corps.

7. Those who remember Chapter 7 of this work will see the close affiliation between the concept of "dismountable escort troops" and the *Begleittruppen* ("escort troops") of German assault gun battalions of World War II.

Bibliographical Note

As is also the case with other books of this series, *On Armor* is based on an extremely eclectic collection of sources, most of which were used primarily in the writing of a single chapter. For this reason, a conventional bibliography is probably less useful to most readers than a chapter-by-chapter commentary. This commentary serves to provide a somewhat broader context for the specific references found in the notes at the end of every chapter. In addition, it is likely to be of greater assistance than an ordinary listing of books and other sources to those attempting further research.

The one indispensable source for the first chapter of *On Armor* was Alain Gougaud, *L'Aube de la Gloire: Les Autos-Mitrailleuses et les Chars Français Pendant la Grande Guerre* (Issy les Moulineaux: Société OCEBUR, ca. 1987). In addition to telling a story that is virtually unknown in the English-speaking world, *L'Aube de la Gloire* takes a unique angle on the relationship between armored cars and tanks in the French army of World War I. In particular, it portrays the French armored car organization as the immediate predecessor and, indeed, one of the most important progenitors of the French tank force. The British side of this story is much more likely to be familiar to English-speaking readers. One reason for this is the work of David Fletcher, particularly his *War Cars: British Armoured Cars in the First World War* (London: H.M.S.O., 1987). The same can be said of the tale of the Canadian Independent Forces, which is ably told by John F. Wallace in his *Dragons of Steel: Canadian Armour in Two World Wars* (Burnstown, Ontario: General Store Publishing House, 1995).

Two of the three major events described in the second chapter are the subject of comprehensive monographs. These are Bernhard Bellin, *Sturmgruppe Picht: Ein Erinnerungsblatt aus dem Kriege gegen die Rumänen im Jahre 1916* (Berlin: Verlag Tradition Wilhelm Kolk, 1929) and Erich von Tschischwitz, *Armee und Marine bei Eroberung der Baltischen Inseln im Oktober 1917* (Berlin: Eisenschmidt, 1931). The third event—the use of cavalry by Sir Edmund Allenby to help drive the Turks out of Palestine and Syria—is also well documented, with many works available in English. Because of its extensive treatment of military-technical issues, the most useful of these was the long article ("The Rout of the Turks by Allenby's Cavalry, Palestine Campaign") that Colonel George C. Mitchell published in the *The Cavalry Journal* in April and May 1920. Material on the German cavalry of the 1920s came from the many commercially published semiofficial works of the era as well as the many reports made by contemporary U.S. officers serving as military attachés and official observers at maneuvers. An excellent collection of the former is at the Library of Congress in Washington, D.C. The latter—which provide many opportunities to get fresh perspectives on the European armies of the first half of the twentieth century—are preserved at the U.S. National Archives in College Park, Maryland, in Record Group 165.

The third chapter makes extensive use of archival sources. The material on the early months of the British tank program are from the papers of Sir Albert Stern kept at Liddell Hart Centre for Military Archives at King's College of the University of London. (These are an indispensable source for anyone who wants to examine the various twists and turns needed to convert the gargantuan projects for "landships" into the tanks that were actually fielded.) The documents that allowed me to tell the tale of employment of French tanks on the battlefields of World War I are largely taken from the unit records on file at the Service Historique de l'Armée de Terre in the Château de Vincennes, just east of Paris. (These, like much of the French records of World War I, remain largely unexplored.)

As befits the broad scope of its subject, the fourth chapter exploits a wide variety of sources. Much of the information about French organization and strategic concepts during the interwar period comes either from published official sources or from the memoirs of French officers serving at this time. An important supplement to this material comes from a combination of the reports of U.S. military attachés and the contemporary military press. These two sources were also invaluable for the descriptions of what was going on outside of France at the time. Journals that proved useful include the

Militärwochenblatt, the *Revue de Cavalerie*, the U.S. *Cavalry Journal*, the *Journal of the Royal United Services Institution*, and the *Canadian Defense Quarterly*.

The fifth chapter was inspired by, and relies heavily upon, the work of the two scholars who have done the most to document the life and work of Ludwig Beck—Nicholas Reynolds and Klaus-Jürgen Müller. This material is reinforced by both contemporary German army documents preserved on microfilm at the U.S. National Archives and contemporary published works found at the Library of Congress. The tale of the evolution of the various units of the Reichswehr into units associated with mechanized warfare relies heavily upon the facts provided by Georg Tessin's *Deutsche Verbände und Truppen, 1918–1939* (Osnabrück: Biblio Verlag, 1974).

In the sixth, seventh, and eighth chapters, the same service that Tessin provides for the fifth chapter is provided by the many volumes of Leo Niehorster's extraordinary *German World War II Organizational Series*. These chapters are, however, primarily based on German records captured at the end of World War II and preserved on microfilm at the U.S. National Archives. (This collection, which runs into millions of pages on thousands of microfilm reels, is a treasure trove of documents that historians have only begun to exploit.)

Attaché reports—this time from the U.S. military attaché in London—play a key role in the ninth chapter. These are also on file at the U.S. National Archives in College Park. For the tenth chapter, a pair of histories written by the British 79th Armoured Division at the end of World War II—both of which were found by William Schneck at the U.S. Army Military History Institute at Carlisle, Pennsylvania, provided information that was not available anywhere else. The writing of the eleventh chapter began with insights gleaned from a study done soon after the end of the Korean War—Vincent McRae and Alvin D. Coox, *Tank-vs-Tank Combat in Korea* (Chevy Chase, MD: The Johns Hopkins University, 1954). A copy of this book, which was originally published as a classified document, can be found in the records of the U.S. Marine Corps on file at the U.S. National Archives in College Park.

INDEX

1st Armoured Division (British mechanized formation), 138
1st Assault Brigade (British mechanized unit), 151
1st Cavalry Division (German horse cavalry formation), 73
1st Infantry Division (U.S. formation), 155
1st Light Division (German mechanized formation), 88
1st Marine Division (U.S. formation), 162
1st Motorized Combat Brigade (German motorized unit), 71
1st Mountain Division (German formation), 99
1st Panzer Division (German mechanized formation), 94, 105
2nd Armoured Brigade (British armored unit), 138
2nd Light Division (German mechanized formation), 87
2nd Motorized Combat Brigade (German motorized unit), 71
2nd Motor Machine Gun Brigade (Canadian motorized unit), 10

2nd Panzer Division (German mechanized formation), 84, 94, 102
3rd Canadian Infantry Division, 15
3rd Cavalry Division (German motorized formation), 73
3rd Light Division (German mechanized formation), 87
4th Australian Light Horse Brigade (Australian cavalry formation), 27
4th Light Division (German mechanized formation), 84, 105
4th Panzer Brigade (German armored unit), 87
4th Panzer Division (German armored unit), 87, 97
5th Canadian Infantry Division, dissolution of (1918), 10
5th Panzer Division (German mechanized formation), 85, 89
7th Panzer Division (German mechanized formation), 89
10th Panzer Division (German mechanized formation), 84
11th Armoured Division (British mechanized formation), 138

11th Panzer Division (German mechanized formation), 109
15th Field Artillery Regiment (German unit), 117
17th Armoured Car Battalion (British armored car unit), 15, 18
17th Panzer Division (German mechanized formation), 106
21st Panzer Division (German mechanized formation), 127
24th Mechanized Infantry Division (U.S. formation), 174
26th Marine Expeditionary Unit (U.S. amphibious task force), 176
35th (Czech tank in German service), 96, 103
38th (Czech tank in German service), 96, 103
60th Infantry Division (British formation), 29
78th Assault Division (German formation), 123
79th Armoured Division (British mechanized formation), 151, 154
105th Armored Brigade (North Korean mechanized formation), 161
745th Tank Battalion (U.S. armored unit), 155

Aachen (European city), 155
Abbéville (French city), 93
Abd el Krim (Berber leader), 45, 54
Accompanying tanks, 44
Achtung Panzer! (Guderian), 91
Achzarit (Israeli heavy armored personnel carrier), 168, 175
Advanced detachments (Vorausabteilungen), 99
Aisne (river in France), 93
Aix-la-Chapelle (European city), 155
Allenby, Sir Edmund (British officer), 27
All tank school, 74
AMC (French armored car), 61
AMD (French armored car), 61
Amiens, Battle of
  (5–6 June 1940), 93
  (8 August 1918), 11
Al-Amin, Hussam (Arab guerilla leader), 172
Amman (town in Ottoman Empire), 29
Anglo-Boer War, Second (1899–1902), 1
Antitank formations (motorized formations designed to fight tanks), 73
Antitank guided missiles, 171
Antitank guns, self-propelled, 111
Antitank tank (German concept), 78
Antwerp (Belgian city), 4
Arab-Israeli Wars, 166
Arensburg (town on the island of Oesel), 26
Armored brigades (British armored units), 147
Armored division
  British armored formation, 135
  U.S. mechanized formation, 135
Armored personnel carriers, 58, 96
Armored plate, thickness of (for armored cars), 6
Armoured Division in Battle, The (British pamphlet), 154
Army Group Mackensen (German formation), 21
Artillerie d'assaut (French tactical concept), 39
Artillerie d'Assaut (French term for tanks), 40
Artillerie Speciale (French term for tanks), 40
Artillery, self-propelled, 109
Assault artillery
  French tactical concept, 39
  French term for tanks, 40

Assault engineer battalions (German unit), 90
Assault gun (German armored vehicle), 113
Assault Gun Battalion 189 (German armored unit), 123
Assault gun escort company (German motorized unit), 123
Atomic weapons, 156
Auftragstaktik (German philosophy of command and control), 104
Austria-Hungary, armed forces, 21
Auto-canon, 3, 4
Automatic cannon (25mm to 35mm), 177
Auto-mitrailleuse, 3, 4
Aviation from the Sea (U.S. concept), 178
AVRE (British engineer tank), 150

Baentsch, Alfred (German officer and theorist), 90
Balck, Herman (German officer), 109
Ballistics computers, 166
Baltic Fleet (Russian naval formation), 23
Barbarossa (German operation launched 22 June 1941), 83, 96
Bataille conduite (French tactical concept), 45
Bataillon des Autos-Canons Mitrailleuses (Belgian armored car unit), 5
Bayonet strength (military expression), 99
Bazooka (U.S. antitank rocket launcher), 149, 162
Beaucourt (French village near the city of Amiens), 15
Beck, Ludwig (German officer), 74, 115
Beersheba (town in Ottoman Empire), 27
Begleitkompagnie (German motorized unit), 123

BegleitPanzer (German escort tanks), 125
Benary, Albert (German military officer and author), 31
Berlin Reconnaissance Brigade (German motorized unit), 75
Berry-au-Bac
  French tank attack (16 April 1917), 40, 42
  town in France, 40
Bicycle Brigade von Quadt (German unit), 22
Big wheel (concept for early British tank), 36
Bill2 (Swedish antitank guided missile), 170
Blitzkrieg, 83
Bombardment rockets (2.75"), 177
Bracketing (technique for finding range), 120
Bradley (U.S. infantry fighting vehicle), 176
Breakthrough tanks, 46
Brennpunkt (German operational concept), 66
Brigade (as used by the German army), 74, 109, 111
Brigade de combat (French mechanized unit), 73
British Expeditionary Force, 91
Brutinel, Raymond (Canadian military officer), 9
BT (Soviet tank series), 49, 159
BT-5 (Soviet tank), 157
Bucharest, 21
Budapest, 21
Bumble Bee (German self-propelled howitzer), 128
Buses, urban omnibuses used to transport infantry, 20

Caen (French city), 153
Canadian Corps Cyclist Battalion, 12
Canadian Independent Force, 11

Canadian Machine Gun Corps, 10
Capable Warrior (U.S. field
    experiments), 178
Capital tank, 145
Carden-Lloyd (British armaments
    firm), 73
Casualties, among Israeli tank crews,
    167
Caterpillar tractors, 35
Cavalry divisions, 4, 5
    French army, 20, 31
    German army, 20, 31
Cavalry regiments of the German Army
    (1899), 31
    (1914), 30
    (1920–33), 31
Cavalry regiments of the Polish army
    (1922), 30
Centurion (British tank), 166
Chaffee (U.S. tank), 163
Challenger (British tank), 174
Champagne (French region), 119
Char B (French breakthrough tank),
    46, 101
Chars d'accompagnement (French
    accompanying tanks), 44
Chars de manoeuvre ensemble (French
    tactical concept), 47
Chasseur battalions (French light
    infantry units), 20
Chechen Wars, 175
Chemin des Dames (ridge in France),
    40
Chevauchée (attack through rear areas),
    51
Chinese Farm, Battle of, 172
Christie (family of tanks), 48, 68
Christie, J. Walter (American inventor),
    48
Churchill (British tank), 148, 156
Churchill, Winston S., 36
Claymore (antipersonnel mine), 168
Close support tanks
    British tactical concept, 74
    Soviet tactical concept, 48
Coast defense artillery, 25
Combat command (U.S. mechanized
    formation), 138
Coup de main (military operation), 86
Couverture (French operational
    concept), 59
Covering force, 59
Crabs (British mine-clearing tanks),
    151
Crocodile (British flame-thrower tank),
    151
Cross-country personnel arriers
    (unarmored), 58
Cruiser tanks, 147
Czestochowa (Polish city), 97

Dagoe (island in the Gulf of Riga), 23
Danube River, 21
Defilade (positions for antitank guided
    missiles), 171
Delaying resistance (hinhaltende
    Widerstand, German operational
    concept), 17, 66
Desert Mounted Corps, 27
Destremau, M.F.E. (French naval
    officer and builder of improvised
    armored cars), 2
Detachements (German task forces), 104
Dieppe (French city), 150
Distant action tanks (Soviet tactical
    concept), 48
Division légère méchanique (French
    mechanized formation), 60, 73,
    80, 91
Dragons portés (French motorized
    infantry), 57
Dragon's teeth (antitank obstacles),
    150
Dunkirk (French city), 4, 91

École Supérieure de Guerre (French war
    college), 45
Ehrhardt (German armaments firm), 2

Eisenhower, Dwight D. (U.S. officer), 151
Epsom (British operation in Normandy), 152
Escort troops
　carried in the Merkava tank, 168
　for close defense of assault guns or tanks, 123, 155
Estienne, Jean Baptiste (French military officer), 38

Falkland Islands, 169
Farthing packets, 163
Fascines, 38
Fast divisions (type of motorized formation), 58
Fiber-optic guided missiles, 171
Fifth Army (British formation), 9
Fire brigades (German operational reserves), 131
First Army (French formation), 44
Flamethrower tanks, 88, 151
Fly over shoot down mode, 170
Force de couverture (French covering force), 59
Fourth Army (French formation), 45
Frankfurt am Oder (German city), 71
French Foreign Legion, 176
Fritsch, Werner von (German officer), 115
Fuel-air explosives, 170
Fuel consumption (of tanks), 46, 174
Funnies (specialized armored vehicles), 154
Further support tanks (Soviet tactical concept), 48

Gallieni, Joseph Simon (French general), 5
Gap (operational problem), 99
German army, organization for the invasion of Poland, 84
German offensive (21 March 1918), 9
Gneisenau (German warship), 2, 3

Golan Heights, 167
Goodwood (British operation in Normandy), 138, 152
Gothic Line, 138
Grand operations, 65
Grenadier Guards (British regiment), 140
Grenadier Guards Battle Group (British mechanized task force), 140
Großdeutschland (German mechanized unit and formation), 88, 106, 109, 120, 131
Grosstraktor (German tank), 71
Groupe cycliste (French bicycle battalion), 32
Groupes d'Autos-Canons (French armored car units), 5
Groupes d'Autos-Canons de 47 (French armored car units), 6
Groupes Mixtes d'Autos-Mitrailleuses Autos-Canons (French armored car units), 6–8
Guards Armoured Division (British mechanized formation), 140
Guderian, Heinz (German military officer), 75, 84, 87, 91, 95, 108
"Guderian's Duck" (nickname for *Hetzer*), 121
Guerillas, German (in East Africa in World War I), 8
Gun
　7.62mm (Soviet dual purpose field and antitank gun), 127
　7.62mm (Soviet tank guns), 48, 159, 160
　20mm (generic antitank gun), 159
　20mm (German antiaircraft gun), 128
　20mm (German tank gun), 61
　37mm (French antitank gun), 160
　37mm (German antiaircraft gun), 128
　37mm (German antitank gun), 78, 104, 158, 160

37mm (Soviet tank gun), 48, 159
37mm, Model 1885 (French low-velocity canon), 2, 6
40mm (British antitank gun), 146, 160
45mm (Soviet tank gun), 48
47mm (antiaircraft gun, as armament for early British tanks), 37
47mm (British antitank gun), 146
47mm (British tank gun), 74
47mm (French antitank gun), 46, 61
47mm (French naval gun), 6
47mm (generic antitank gun), 159
47mm (Japanese antitank gun), 156
50mm (German antitank gun), 103, 149, 158
57mm (British antitank gun), 150
57mm (British naval gun, as armament for early British tanks), 37
75mm (as armament for early British tanks), 37
75mm (field gun, as armament for Schneider tanks), 38
75mm (French low-velocity tank gun), 46
75mm (German antitank gun), 103, 121, 123, 149
75mm (German infantry and cavalry gun), 32, 39, 69, 113, 127, 154
75mm (U.S. tank gun), 148, 152
75mm, Model 1897 (French field gun), 4, 39
76mm (U.S. tank gun), 149
76mm/37mm (German anti-tank/infantry gun), 69
88mm (German dual-purpose antiaircraft and antitank gun), 101, 127
90mm (generic tank gun), 165

100mm (German heavy field gun), 101
105mm (British tank gun), 166
105mm (generic tank gun), 165
105mm (U.S. gun for wheeled vehicles), 177
120mm (generic tank gun), 165
2-pounder (antiaircraft gun, as armament for early British tanks), 37
2-pounder (British antitank gun), 146, 160
3-pounder (British tank gun), 74
6-pounder (British antitank gun), 150
6-pounder (British naval gun, as armament for early British tanks), 37
18-pounder (British field gun), 43
25-pounder (British gun-howitzer), 153
Gunnery, tank, 159, 166
Guns, dummy, 71

H-35 (French tank), 62
Heavy armored personnel carrier, 151, 153, 168, 175
Heavy Infantry Fighting Vehicle, 179
Heavy infantry tank, 146
Hedgehog tactics, 93
Hellfire (U.S. guided missile), 172
Hetzer (German armored vehicle), 121
Hinhaltende Widerstand (delaying resistance, German operational concept), 17, 66
Hitler, Adolf (German dictator), 69, 98
Hollow-charge projectiles, 116
Holt tractor, 38
Hornet (German self-propelled antitank gun), 128
Hornisse (German self-propelled antitank gun), 128
Horse artillery, 117
Horses, shortage of, 55

INDEX 229

Hoth, Hermann (German officer), 92
Howitzer
  3-inch (British tank piece), 146
  3.7-inch (main armament for British support tank), 74, 146, 152, 160
  75mm (German low-velocity vehicle-mounted piece), 70, 101, 129
  77mm (British tank piece), 146
  95mm (main armament for British support tank), 74, 146, 152
  105mm (German field piece), 108, 119
  105mm (U.S. field piece), 135, 153
  150mm (German heavy field piece), 41, 99, 108
  150mm (German heavy infantry gun), 114, 127
  210mm (German heavy field piece), 41
Hughes, Sam (Canadian Minister of Militia), 9
Hummel (German self-propelled howitzer), 128
Hunter Air (U.S. concept), 178
Hybrid units (units using both horses and motor vehicles), 71

II Corps (Canadian formation), 153
Inchon, 162
Infantry accompanying guns (as substitute for tanks), 43
Infantry and cavalry guns, 39, 69, 113, 127, 154, 156
Infantry divisions (German foot-mobile formations), 98
Infantry tank, 146
Infantry units, tanks as part of, 156
Internal security, use of armored cars for, 10
Iron Gate (geographical feature in Romania), 21
Israeli Defense Force, 166

Isserson, G. (Soviet officer and theorist), 50
I tank (British category of tank), 146

Jablonka Pass (defile on the border between Poland and Slovakia), 86
Jäger battalions (German light infantry units), 20
Jäger Brigade (formation imagined by Ludwig von Eimannsberger), 75
Johns Hopkins University, 163
Jomini, Antoine (Swiss officer and theorist), 65
Jordan (river in Asia), 166

Kampfgrupe Strachwitz (German battle group), 106
Kampfgruppen (German task forces), 105
Kampfwagenabwehrabteilung (German motorized unit), 70
Kampfwagen Brigade (formation imagined by Ludwig von Eimannsberger), 75
Kampfwagenbrigade (German armored unit), 73
Kampfwagen Division (formation imagined by Ludwig von Eimannsberger), 75
Kangaroo (heavy armored personnel carrier), 151, 153
Kesselschlacht (German operational concept), 50
Khruschev, Nikita (Soviet premier), 172
Kleist, Ewald von (German officer), 85, 89
Korean War (1950–53), 161
Kornet (Russian antitank guided missile), 170
Kraftfahrabteilung (German motorized unit), 68

Kraftfahrkampftruppen (German branch of service), 69
Kraftfahrkampftruppenbrigaden (German motorized units), 71
Kraftfahrtruppen (German branch of service), 68
KV (Soviet tank), 122

Landesjäger Korps (German formation), 74
Landships (concept for early British tank), 36
Landships Committee, 36
Landsverk (Swedish tank), 71
Laser range finders, 166
Lauerstellung (German tactical technique), 119, 164
La Zelée (French warship), 2
Lebanon, 172
LeClerc (French tank), 170
Le Havre (French city), 93
Le Quesnel (French village near the city of Amiens), 15
Libya, tribal revolt, 8
Liddell Hart, Basil Henry (British journalist and historian), 83
Light Armored Infantry (U.S. mechanized units), 176
Light Armored Vehicle (U.S. wheeled armored vehicle), 176
Light division (German mechanized unit), 80
Light mechanized division (French mechanized formation), 60, 73, 80, 91
Lutz, Oswald (German officer), 80

M1 (U.S. tank), 174
M24 (U.S. tank), 163
M26 (U.S. tank), 163
M46 (U.S. tank), 163
M60 (U.S. tank), 166
M60A2 (U.S. missile tank), 168

Machine guns, as weapons of cavalry units, 32
Mackensen, August (German military officer), 21
Main battle tank, 160
Malmaison, French tank attack (23 October 1917), 42
Maneuvers
  British army (1925), 30
  German army (1932), 71
  Soviet army (1936), 49
Manstein, Erich von (German officer), 113
Manteuffel, Hasso von (German military officer), 32
Marine Expeditionary Units (U.S. amphibious task forces), 176
Marines, Royal, 3, 4
Maritime Belt (region of Flanders), 37
Marne, Battle of, 5
Matilda (British tank), 158
Mechanized brigade (Soviet mechanized unit), 79
Medium tank (German concept), 78
Mercia (fictional country portrayed in British maneuvers), 30
Merkava (Israeli tank), 168
Meuse (river in Northwest Europe), 90
Mézières (French village near the city of Amiens), 15
Milan (European antitank guided missile), 169
Minsk, Soviet army maneuvers at, 49
Mius (river in the Soviet Union), 131
Moltke, Hellmuth von (1800–1891, German officer and theorist), 78
Montdidier, French tank attack (8 August 1918), 44
Montgomery, Bernard Law (British officer), 139, 145
Monthermé (town in France), 90
Moon (island in the Gulf of Riga), 23
Morocco, 1, 45

Mortar
  3-inch (British infantry mortars), 138
  6-inch (British trench mortar), 12
  76mm (German trench mortar), 39, 69
  81mm, 154
  120mm, 154
  290mm (Petard), 150
Motor battalion (British motorized infantry unit), 138
Motorcycle infantry, 71, 80, 97
Motorcycles (as mounts for dispatch riders), 12
Motorization of cavalry units, 55
Motorized infantry division
  French motorized formation, 81
  German motorized formation, 81, 88, 98
Motorized reconnaissance, 71
Motor machine-gun batteries (Canadian motorized units), 9
Motor Machine Gun Brigade (Canadian motorized unit), 9
Mounted riflemen, Canadian, 9
Multi-turreted tanks, 160–61

Naval officers, role in early armored car units, 5
Neubaufahrzeuge (German tank), 71
Ninth Army (German formation), 21

Oesel, island in the Gulf of Riga, 23
Okinawa (Pacific island), 155
Oliver, Lunsford E. (U.S. officer), 142
Omaha Beach, 151
Operational art, 65, 173
Operational distance (military problem), 98
Operational mobility, 173
Operations Research Office (Johns Hopkins University), 163
Operativ (German adjective), 65

Organisationsabteilung (German military department), 69
Orrisar (village on the island of Oesel), 25
Overfly top attack mode, 170

Pakfront (Gernan name for Soviet antitank trap), 106
Palestine, 27
Palestinian fighters, 169
Pamerort (village on the island of Oesel), 25
Panther (German tank), 102
Panzer I (German tank), 48, 62, 73, 96, 103
Panzer II (German tank), 61, 96, 103, 125
Panzer III (German tank), 61, 96, 103, 120, 158
Panzer IV (German tank), 61, 96, 103, 120
Panzerabwehrabteilung (German motorized unit), 70
Panzerabwehrkanonen auf Selbstfahrlaffetten, 126
Panzer division (German mechanized formation), 70, 78
  reduction of tank strength of, 96
Panzerfaust (German rocket-propelled grenade), 149
Panzergrenadier division (German mechanized formation), 111
Panzergruppe (German mechanized formation), 92, 101
Panzergruppe Guderian (German mechanized formation), 92
Panzergruppe von Kleist (German mechanized formation), 89, 101
Panzerjäger (German antitank troops), 126
Panzerjäger Kompagnie 1045 (German armored unit), 121
Panzer Korps (German mechanized formation), 101

Panzerschreck (German antitank rocket launcher), 149
Panzerverband Kempf (German mechanized formation), 84, 88
Paris, defense of (1914), 5
Patton (U.S. tank), 163
Pedrails (type of wheel proposed for early British tanks), 36
Penny packets, 163
Pershing (U.S. tank), 163
Petard (British 290mm spigot mortar), 150
Phosgene (poison gas), 42
Pickell, Gregory (U.S. officer and theorist), 179
Pocket (operational phenomenon), 98
Poland, 66, 83
Preparatory fire (prior to tank attack), 42
Priest (self-propelled 105mm howitzer), 153
Propaganda, German, 134
PU-36 (Soviet field service regulations), 50
Push-button warfare, 156
Putilov (Russian field gun), 159

R-35 (French tank), 158
Radio communications (at the Battle of Amiens), 12
Range-finding machine guns, 166
Range of engagement (in tank battles), 165
Reactived armor, 168
Recoilless rifle (75mm and 106mm), 162
Refueler trucks, 167
Regimental system (British army), 140
Régiment de combat (French mechanized unit), 61
Régiment de découverte (French mechanized unit), 61
Regimentsgruppen (German task forces), 105
Reichswehr, 70
Reims, Battle of (15 July 1918), 45
Renault (French light infantry tanks), 43
Republican Guard (Iraqi military organization), 175
Reserve of firepower (French operational concept), 32
Riga, Gulf of, 23
River crossing (type of military operation), 90
Rocket launcher (U.S. antitank rocket launcher), 162
Rocket-propelled grenades, 149, 168, 175
Romania, 20
Rommel, Erwin (German officer), 93
Rouen (French city), 93
Royal Naval Air Service, 3
Royal Naval Armored Car Division, 6, 8
Royal Tank Corps, 56
Russian Civil War (1917–22), 30
Russo-Polish War (1920–21), 30

Salisbury Plain, 74
Samson, Charles Rumney (British naval officer and armored car pioneer), 3, 6
Scharnhorst (German warship), 2, 3
Schell, Adolph von (German officer), 117
Schlichting, Sigusmund von (German officer and theorist), 65
Schneider (early French tank), 38
Schneider (French armaments firm), 2
Schnelle Truppen, 88
Schützen
  German light infantry, 80
  German motorized infantry, 80, 85, 96
Schwerpunkt (German concept), 66, 70, 84, 114

Schwerpunktartig eingesezt (German military expression), 70
Schwerpunktwaffe (German concept), 114
Scout tank (German concept), 78
Sea of Galilee, 166
Section Technique de Chars (French design bureau), 46
Sedan (French city), 90
Seine (river in France), 93
Self-propelled antitank guns, 111, 121, 126
Self-propelled artillery, 109
Semi-automatic small caliber tank guns, 158
Senger und Etterlin, Frido von (German officer and author), 106
Sheridan (U.S. missile tank), 168
Sherman (U.S. tank), 142, 160, 163
Shillelagh (U.S. antitank guided missile), 168
Simonds, G.G. (Canadian officer), 153
Sinai Desert, 28
Six Day War (1967), 167
Sixth Army (German formation), 117
Slovakia, 84
Smoke shells, 96, 114
Sniper tank, 167
Soissons, Battle of (18 July 1918), 45
Solferino effect, 28
Somme (river in France), 93
SOMUA S-35 (French tank), 61, 157
Soviet invasions
  of Finland (1939–40), 160
  of Mongolia (1938), 160
  of Poland (1939), 160
Spanish Civil War, 159
Staff ride, German exercise without troops of 1935, 75
St. Chamond (early French tank), 39
Stosstrupps (German assault squads), 29
St. Petersburg (Russian city), 23

Strachwitz, Hyacinth Graf von (German officer), 106
Stridsvagen 105 (Swedish turretless tank), 168
Stryker brigades (U.S. mechanized units), 176
Stuart (American light tank), 137, 148
Stuart, J.E.B. (American cavalry officer), 137
Stuka (German aircraft), 93
Sturmgeschützbegleitkompagnie (German motorized unit), 123
Sturmgruppe Picht (German unit), 22
SU-76 (Soviet assault gun), 164
Submarines, Royal Navy, 23
Suez Canal, 28
Support Group (British unit), 135
Suppressive fire (during tank attack), 43
Swinger brigade (British organizational concept), 147
Sworbe Peninsula, 25
Syria, 27

T-26 (Soviet tank), 48
T-27 (Soviet tank), 48
T-28 (Soviet tank), 48, 159
T-34 (Soviet tank), 101, 122, 146
T-34/35 (Soviet tank), 166
T-35 (Soviet tank), 48, 159
T-50 (Soviet tank), 160
T-54 (Soviet tank), 166
T-55 (Soviet tank), 166
Tactics of separate brigades, 105, 138
Tagga (bay on the island of Oesel), 25
Tahiti, 2
Tank battalions, Ludwig Beck's concept for, 78
Tank Brigade (British armored unit), 74, 79
Tank brigades
  British armored units, 147
  German armored units, 75
  Soviet armored units, 75, 79

Tank destruction statistics, German, for Eastern Front in World War II, 130
Tankette, 73
Tank Hunter Company 1045 (German armored unit), 121
Task Force Smith (U.S. task force), 162
Telephone, use of civilian network for military communications and intelligence, 4
Television, as a guidance mechanism for missiles, 171
Tenth Army (French formation), 43
Thermobaric warheads, 170
Thessaloniki (Greek city), 176
Third Army (German formation), 86
Thoma, Wilhelm Ritter von, 105
Time-of-flight of antitank projectiles, 170
Tourelle monoplace, 146
TOW2B (U.S. antitank guided missile), 170
Triandafillov, Viktor (Soviet officer and theorist), 50
Troupes de Marine (French Marines), 176
Truppenamt (German military department), 69
Truppenführung (German field service regulations), 75
Tukhachevsky, Mikhail (Soviet officer), 50
Tunisia, 150
Turnu Sevarin (Romanian town), 22
Turret-mounted mortars, 177
Twelfth Army (German formation), 93
Type 45 Panzer division (German organizational concept), 111
Type Armée Moderne (French organizational concept), 58

United Nations Organization, 164

Verfolgungsgruppen (German task forces), 105

Versailles, Treaty of, 66
Vickers (British armaments firm), 2, 72
Vickers Independent (British tank), 160
Vickers Mark I (British tank), 71
Vickers medium (British tank), 74
VIII Corps (German formation), 85
Volckheim, Ernst (German officer and theorist), 67, 74
Vollmer LK (early German tank), 71
Vorausabteilungen (German forward detachments), 99
Vorausabteilung Lang (German detachment), 99

Waffen SS, 84, 88, 98, 111
Warrior (British infantry fighting vehicle), 176
Warsaw, 85
Water battles, 166
Wessex (fictional country portrayed in British maneuvers), 30
Weygand Line, 91
Weygand, Maxime (French officer), 92
Wheeled armored vehicles (as developed by France), 176
Whippet (British light tanks), 11

XII Corps (German formation), 84
XIV Motorized Corps (German mechanized formation), 84
XIX Motorized Corps (German mechanized formation), 84, 92
XV Motorized Corps (German mechanized formation), 84, 87, 92
XVI Motorized Corps (German mechanized formation), 85, 92
XXXIX Motorized Corps (German mechanized formation), 92
XXXXI Motorized Corps (German mechanized formation), 92

Yahara, Hiromichi (Japanese officer), 155
Yom Kippur War (1973), 167

About the Author

BRUCE I. GUDMUNDSSON is a military historian who studies the way that modern armies adapt to radical change in their operating environments. He divides his time between historical research and assisting present-day military organizations with their own attempts to innovate.